D0547118

THE TALIBAN DON'T WAVE

THE TALIBAN DON'T WAVE

by Robert Semrau

John Wiley & Sons Canada, Ltd.

Copyright © 2012 Robert Semrau

All rights reserved. No part of this work covered by the copyright herein may be reproduced or used in any form or by any means—graphic, electronic or mechanical without the prior written permission of the publisher. Any request for photocopying, recording, taping or information storage and retrieval systems of any part of this book shall be directed in writing to The Canadian Copyright Licensing Agency (Access Copyright). For an Access Copyright license, visit www.accesscopyright.ca or call toll free 1–800–893–5777.

For general information about our other products and services, please contact our Customer Care Department within the United States at (800) 762-2974, outside the United States at (317) 572-3993 or fax (317) 572-4002.

Wiley publishes in a variety of print and electronic formats and by print-on-demand. Some material included with standard print versions of this book may not be included in e-books or in print-on-demand. If this book refers to media such as a CD or DVD that is not included in the version you purchased, you may download this material at http://booksupport.wiley.com. For more information about Wiley products, visit www.wiley.com.

Care has been taken to trace ownership of copyright material contained in this book. The publisher will gladly receive any information that will enable them to rectify any reference or credit line in subsequent editions.

Names have been changed to protect allies and sources, and others in the field whose combat role may extend beyond Afghanistan.

Library and Archives Canada Cataloguing in Publication

Semrau, Robert
    The Taliban don't wave / Robert Semrau.

ISBN 978-1-11826-118-7 (print); 978-1-118-26160-6 (ebk); 978-1-118-26155-2 (ebk); 978-1-118-26147-7 (ebk)

    1. Semrau, Robert. 2. Afghan War, 2001—Personal narratives, Canadian. 3. Afghan War, 2001—Participation, Canadian. 4. Canada—Armed Forces—Afghanistan. 5. Soldiers—Canada—Biography. I. Title.

DS371.413.S44 2012   958.104'7092   C2012-904132-7

Production Credits
Cover design: Adrian So
Cover images: Robert Semrau
Interior design: Mike Chan
Managing Editor: Alison Maclean
Production Editor: Lindsay Humphreys
Composition: Thomson Digital
Printer: Friesens Printing Ltd.

John Wiley & Sons Canada, Ltd.
6045 Freemont Blvd.
Mississauga, Ontario
L5R 4J3

Printed in Canada

2 3 4 5 FP 16 15 14 13 12

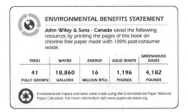

ENVIRONMENTAL BENEFITS STATEMENT
John Wiley & Sons - Canada saved the following resources by printing the pages of this book on chlorine free paper made with 100% post-consumer waste.

TREES	WATER	ENERGY	SOLID WASTE	GREENHOUSE GASES
41	18,860	16	1,196	4,182
FULLY GROWN	GALLONS	MILLION BTUs	POUNDS	POUNDS

Environmental impact estimates were made using the Environmental Paper Network Paper Calculator. For more information visit www.papercalculator.org.

For Amélie, Caméa, and Chloé; and to the men and women, both living and the honoured dead, who served in Afghanistan.

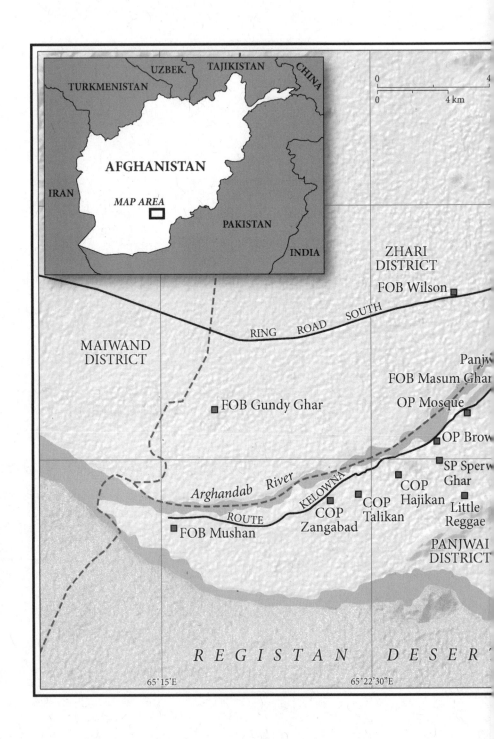

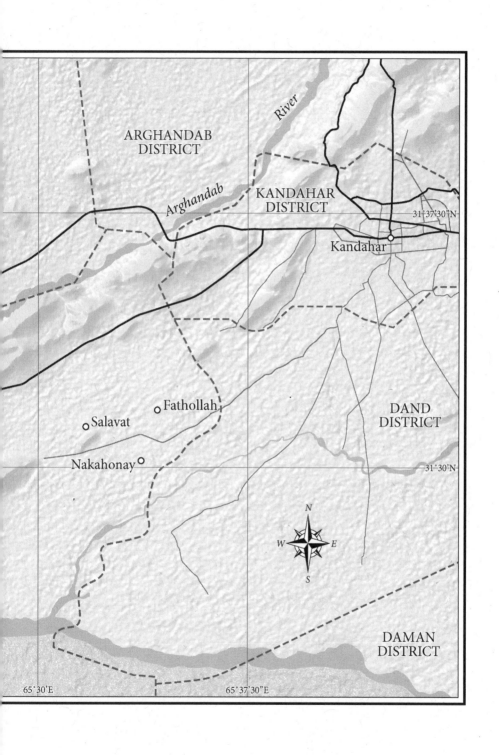

Foreword

With the exception of members of our elite JTF2 special forces, who were inserted earlier, Canadian soldiers deployed to Afghanistan some five months after the attacks of 9/11. This tardy deployment was the result of an embarrassing lack of Canadian strategic airlift, which chronically required us to beg a lift with the US Air Force or charter exorbitantly expensive Russian or Ukrainian resources. During this painful wait for a ride, the 3 PPCLI battle group had to cool its heels at its base in Edmonton.

The mission for the first allied units that arrived in Afghanistan was to take down al Qaeda and to assist the indigenous Afghan forces as they replaced the repressive Islamist Taliban regime, which had taken over the country in 1998 following the withdrawal of the Russian military in 1989 and the ensuing civil war. This mission was achieved within months in 2002.

When a dog chases a school bus, it's really fun—until he catches it. That's when the hard part begins, as he must decide what to do with it. The initially US-led deployment of allied forces to Afghanistan faced the same dilemma in 2002. Their mission had been accomplished, but they had "caught" Afghanistan, one of the poorest and most war-ravaged countries on the face of the earth. High-level international meetings were convened to determine, or at least assist with, Afghanistan's future, and terms like governance, education, healthcare, female rights, poppy eradication, and any number of additional projects related to nation building became part of the new strategy. The allied militaries involved in the operation immediately recognized the inevitable "mission-creep."

While those focusing on nation building got on with their part of the pie, the military was forced to take on an increasingly capable Taliban insurgency. It didn't take a rocket scientist to determine that international military forces wouldn't, and couldn't, stick around forever fighting someone else's war. As a result, part of the military's effort was deflected to numerous Provincial Reconstruction Teams (PRTs), building roads, schools, police stations, and the like. Recognizing the need to create an Afghan army capable of containing the insurgency once the inevitable allied withdrawal took place, the concept of allied mentoring of fledgling Afghan army units was introduced, along with the somewhat humorous acronym OMLT (pronounced *omelette*), standing for Operational Mentor and Liaison Team.

The OMLT teams were small, averaging only four or five members each and usually consisting of an officer, a warrant officer, and two non-commissioned members. Their contribution to the Afghan campaign was kept low-key because the media realized the unpredictable nature of their work and the inherent danger, so they wisely rarely accompanied them into battle. The OMLT teams themselves were limited to advising their Afghan counterparts, no matter how incompetent they might be, and, bearing in mind cultural sensitivities, could not take charge of a failing mission no matter how disastrous the situation. On the positive side, they could request allied resources, including fast air and attack helicopters, artillery and mortars, and unmanned aerial vehicles to support their counterparts' mission, although there was no guarantee of availability.

It is one thing to be an advisor to an Afghan unit in support or, to use the accepted term, "inside the wire," but quite another to accompany a unit regularly tasked to make contact with the Taliban. You would be acutely aware that your life was in the hands of someone who, if he had the necessary skills to lead in combat, wouldn't need you along as an advisor.

In August of 2008, Captain Robert Semrau found himself in charge of such a team attached to a unit of the Afghan army. During one particularly risky patrol, his Afghan unit was ambushed by a superior Taliban force. A NATO attack helicopter gunship was called in to provide support, and bursts of 30mm rounds (the length of a beer can and the diameter of a large carrot) delivered at a rate of over ten rounds a second, 625 per minute, devastated a significant component of the Taliban opposition. When Captain Semrau and his team arrived on the scene, the partial remains of Taliban victims littered the area. At one particular moment Captain Semrau wondered why a string of sausages was hanging from the limb of a tree, until he realized it was someone's intestines. Nearby was a mortally wounded Taliban who was, for all intents and purposes, cut in half with a hole, by some accounts the size of a dinner plate, through his midsection. Blood and what was left of his internal organs were splattered on the ground around him. To add to the man's agony, another round had shattered one of his legs. Afghan soldiers passing the scene commented that "Allah will look after him" and moved on; some were later accused of kicking the victim.

Captain Semrau's description of what happened next takes less than ten seconds to read and, interestingly, that was probably the amount of time he had to decide what to do before catching up to his Afghan counterpart. Witnesses indicated that he fired two rounds into the dying—or dead—Taliban fighter, the act subsequently described by the media as a "mercy killing." Some seventeen months later, it took a court martial seven months to investigate, dissect, and analyze those ten seconds, and to determine that this officer with a sterling reputation as a soldier and a leader should no longer be allowed to serve in the Canadian Forces.

The high-profile court martial of Captain Semrau highlighted, in the eyes of many, including yours truly, a deficiency in the court martial procedures within the Canadian Forces.

Until the late 1980s, in general army officers conducted courts martial for army officers, air force officers tried their own, and the navy did the same, usually with a member of one of the other services included as a jury member, an "honest broker." In order to withstand Charter challenges regarding the independence of military courts, a Court Martial Administrative Office was established. While it was a positive move to preclude such challenges, there was a serious downside. The new pool of eligible personnel for court martial duty was massive. As an example, if two lieutenant colonels were needed for a court martial panel, every commander (equivalent to lieutenant colonel) in the navy and every lieutenant colonel in both the army and the air force was eligible. In order to select members, a random selection process was necessary.

In the case of Captain Robert Semrau, the panel initially consisted of a navy commodore (equivalent to brigadier-general), an army lieutenant-colonel, two air force majors, and an army captain. For reasons known only to himself, the army lieutenant colonel withdrew from the panel as all members were about to depart for Afghanistan for deliberations at the site of the incident.

What follows is in no way a criticism of the individual panel members, but rather of a system that needs to recognize and deal with a serious shortcoming.

No one on Semrau's panel had any background in combat operations— and I'm not just referring to combat itself. I include the study of combat and basic training for land combat. During their deliberations it would have been extremely helpful and dare I say, essential, to have at least one individual who could attempt to explain the context of those ten seconds they were dealing with.

The findings of not guilty of second-degree murder, attempted murder, and negligent performance of duty were well founded. The finding of disgraceful conduct as a catch-all can be understood to appease those who didn't understand the context and wanted some form of punishment; however, release from the Canadian Forces was inappropriate. Many, including friends of mine currently holding senior positions within the Canadian Forces, opined that the release was necessary to deter future incidents and send a message to serving soldiers. I strongly disagree. When a soldier is faced with a similar situation in some far-flung battlefield in the future and has those ten seconds to reach a decision, no regulation nor memory or knowledge of Captain Rob Semrau's court martial will spring to mind. It will be his or her own moral code that will dictate their response—nothing more, nothing less.

By the way, you might wonder where the title *The Taliban Don't Wave* came from. I was going to tell you but changed my mind—keep reading.

Lewis W. MacKenzie, CM, OOnt, MSC and Bar, CD

Major-General (Ret'd)

Preface

The first time I laid eyes on Robert Semrau (not counting the front-page photographs) he was sitting in a military courtroom in Gatineau, Quebec, his shoes shined to a polish, his dress uniform green and crisp. In so many ways, the 36-year-old captain was just a typical soldier in today's Canadian Forces, one of thousands of courageous men and women who have risked their lives on the front lines of Afghanistan. But inside that courtroom, nothing was typical. Every step was unprecedented.

Semrau was on trial for second-degree murder—the first time a Canadian soldier had ever been accused of homicide on the battlefield. According to investigators, the captain was on patrol in October 2008 when he encountered a gravely wounded insurgent lying on a dirt path. (The man, shot in the stomach, was bleeding so profusely that one eyewitness said he was "98 per cent dead.")

Under oath, two eyewitnesses said they were with Semrau when he pulled the trigger. "He felt it was the humane thing to do," one of them testified. "He couldn't live with himself if he left a wounded insurgent, a wounded human, to suffer like that." In the end, though, the jury found Semrau guilty of a lesser charge: disgraceful conduct. They fully believed that he shot the injured man, but with no corpse and no forensic evidence, they couldn't be sure, beyond a reasonable doubt, that the man actually died.

Yet in the eyes of so many Canadians—both in the ranks and outside—Semrau was a hero, not a criminal. His trial sparked a fierce national debate about the ethics of mercy killing in a combat zone, and what happens to the law of war when it comes face to face with the reality of war. Whatever your opinion, the optics were difficult to stomach: if convicted, Semrau faced a mandatory sentence of life behind bars with no chance of parole for ten years. In other words, a brave and articulate soldier who was willing to die for his country—and was forced to make an impossible decision along the way—could be left watching his two young daughters grow up from behind bars.

Before the judge delivered his sentence, he heard powerful testimony and read dozens of emotional letters from some of the soldiers who served with Robert Semrau. One described how the captain saved his life during an enemy mortar attack. Another, Semrau's commanding officer, said he would welcome him back to the battalion "without reservation" if he were allowed to continue serving. One friend and fellow officer said he respects Semrau so much that he would "follow Rob through the gates of hell."

This book—a rare battlefield memoir from a Canadian soldier—helps explain why. It is Semrau's chance to tell the other side of his historic story, the one that began long before his fateful encounter with that wounded, unnamed man.

Michael Friscolanti
Senior Writer, *Maclean's*

List of Abbreviations

'geers combat engineers

2 I/C second-in-command

2 Para elite British Army airborne light infantry unit, the best of the best

421/422/429 different types of authorization to engage anyone who may not be posing an immediate threat

72A Seven two Alpha

72C Seven two Charlie

ack acknowledge

ANA Afghan National Army

ANP Afghan National Police

AO area of operations

Backblast the extremely hot and dangerous propellant that exits out the end of a rocket launcher when it's fired

BFG big f-ing gun

BIP blow in place; blown up in place

boom-stick Canadian M777 artillery gun, or any type of large cannon/rocket launcher

BUB battle update briefing

CF Canadian Forces

CFB Pet Canadian Forces Base Petawawa

comms radio communications

COP combat outpost

CP command post

CSM company sergeant major

DEWS donkey early-warning system

FAM fighting age male

fives and twenties five- and twenty-metre checks for IEDs

FMP field message pad

FOB Forward Operating Base

FOO/FAC forward observation officer/forward air controller

GAFF "give a fuck" factor

go firm halt

GSR gunshot residue

Icom two-way radio, used by the Taliban

IED improvised explosive device

int intelligence

Int O intelligence officer

in the shit in a life-and-death situation, usually in combat

IR infrared

KAF Kandahar Airfield

KIA killed in action

LAV light armoured vehicle

LCMR lightweight counter-mortar radar

LD line of departure

leaguer vehicle camp

LN local national

LO liaison officer

locstat location and status

loggy; loggies logistics personnel

MBITR multiband inter/intra team radio

mikes minutes

MIST method of injury, injury, signs, treatment given

NCO non-commissioned officer

NDS National Directorate of Security (Afghanistan's version of the CIA)

Neil Diamond negligent discharge (accidentally shooting one's weapon)

net radio network

nine-liner a nine-line radio report for wounded personnel

NIS National Investigation Service, a special branch of the CF Military Police

NVG night-vision goggles

OC officer commanding

O-group orders briefing

OMLT Operational Mentor and Liaison Team

op operation

OPSEC operational security

OTR on the run

PKM Russian belt-fed light machine gun

PPCLI Princess Patricia's Canadian Light Infantry

PPE personal protective equipment

PRR personal role radio, used by the OMLT small teams and CF platoons to talk to each other

PRT Provincial Reconstruction Teams

PT physical training

PX post exchange (US army base store)

QRF quick reaction force

R&R rest and relaxation

RAF Royal Air Force

Ranger Ford pickup truck

RCR Royal Canadian Regiment

recce reconnaissance

RG–31/RG mine-protected armoured personnel carrier, usually outfitted with a remote-controlled weapon system on the roof

RPG rocket-propelled grenade

RRB radio re-broadcast

RV rendezvous

sec–for security force

SIGACTS significant actions/activities

sitrep situation report

SOP standard operating procedure

spec ops special operations forces

Spig 9 Russian recoilless rifle

tac tactical

TCCC tactical combat casualty care, an advanced combat first-aid course

terp interpreter

TI time in

TIC "troops in contact" with the enemy

TLA three-letter acronym

trace projected route

UAV unmanned aerial vehicle

UXO unexploded ordnance

VSA vital signs absent; dead

wire protective confines of a base

Prologue

I looked around the room and wondered how in God's name it had all come to this.

I wasn't in combat, fighting in the heat, dust, and confusion of Afghanistan. I wasn't in that God-accursed country, fighting for my life, scared out of my head, just trying to stay alive. I was somewhere much more frightening—a climate-controlled courtroom in Gatineau, Quebec, charged with murder in the second degree, attempted murder, conduct unbecoming an officer, and failure to perform a military duty. And all things being equal, I would rather have been in "the Stan," taking my chances there.

I looked around the courtroom and at the five members of the panel, the men who would be responsible for handing down my fate, and wondered if they had ever been shot at—or mortared, or rocketed, or blown up. I wondered if any of them had ever heard a bullet, travelling at supersonic speed, crack the sound barrier as it passed an inch from their head, then felt a sickening fear in the hollow of their gut. I wondered if they had ever been literally soaked in another man's blood, or held a fellow soldier as he was dying, with no help on the way.

My team of Canadian soldiers belonged to the Operational Mentor and Liaison Team, or OMLT for short. And because of that, we were training the

Afghan National Army soldiers and patrolling and fighting right alongside them. When they got shot at, we got shot at. We shared the same hardships, and when they suffered, so did we. Because of that, we experienced things both in combat and in daily life that were so far outside the range of normal that it was hard to believe.

I thought I was having an okay tour. And then, before I knew what hit me, two military policemen got off a Chinook helicopter at my lonely outpost in the far west of Panjway Province in Afghanistan, and placed me under arrest. Suddenly, I was back home—charged with murder by the country I love, and sitting in an air-conditioned courtroom while the five officers in the panel snatched looks at me, wondering who I was and what, exactly, had happened over there.

I knew the truth. I knew exactly what had happened, and yet . . . I still couldn't believe it.

Chapter 1

If the commercials are true and Disneyland is truly the happiest place on earth, and if everything in life must have an opposite, then the saddest place on earth must be Afghanistan. I once heard it described as the dark side of the moon, but with mines.

I had been in Afghanistan once before, as a member of the British Army's Second Battalion, The Parachute Regiment, so I had a better clue than most of what we were about to get into. I was on an operation in Macedonia when 9/11 happened, and right then and there, we all knew the world had changed. Within a couple of months, my parachute battalion joined the first coalition troops to form ISAF, the International Security Assistance Force. We landed in Afghanistan at Bagram, north of Kabul, on January 7, 2002, and the Royal Marines we were replacing, who were meant to hand over their ammunition to us, got onto our Hercules transport aircraft and took off, leaving us with nothing. No bullets, no grenades, nothing. I told the lads I'd be okay, because I knew how to shoot mind bullets. No one laughed. We then made the long, scary drive down from Bagram to Kabul with no ammo. *Nice.* Chalk up another reason why the Paras hate Marines.

On our tortuously slow, winding route through the hills north of Kabul, we passed several burned-out Russian tanks, and quickly sped through the obvious ambush and choke points. Thankfully nothing happened—that time. That was my first taste of the Stan, and as any sane person could imagine, it tasted awful. Passing through the towns and villages we saw—up close— extreme poverty and utter despair, with almost every single building bombed or burned out to the point where it was uninhabitable. It was brutal to have to see people living in such terrible conditions.

The choking dust coupled with the smell of garbage and raw sewage made your eyes sting and your throat gag. I found out that most of the damage to Kabul was actually done by the Afghans fighting each other in their civil war, *after* they'd kicked the Russians out.

A story that nicely summed up the Stan for me came out of that tour. We'd been there a few months when somebody at the coalition headquarters in Kabul asked a bunch of famous British soccer players to come and play a fun game of footy against the Afghan national team. The day of the match would coincide with Afghanistan's recently scheduled first-ever "Day of Peace." There would be a band, some doves, a few speeches, and then a great game of soccer. So a group of brave footballers (and because I was an ignorant colonial I hadn't heard of any of them) came down to practise a bit and then play a match.

We were posted outside of the stadium in Kabul (where the Taliban used to publicly execute people) on the day of the game to act as a quick reaction force if the Taliban decided to attack. More likely, however, we would act as riot police since there were ten thousand angry spectators locked out of the stadium because only government lackeys and their families were invited to sit inside to watch the game.

Shortly after the opening ceremonies we all knew things were going Pete Tong wrong. If Paras have a gift, it's the ability to sense danger and smell violence in the air. I had just looked at one of my friends and said something along the lines of, "It's going to kick off here, big time!" when I heard a sound like cattle stampeding, and then people screaming. I spun around and looked up at the stadium just in time to see several people get violently pushed over the railing at the top. They seemed to tumble in slow motion as they fell at least three storeys to the hard cement below, where their bodies made a wet smacking noise when they hit the ground. Some Dutch troops who were also on duty casually walked over to the pile of twisted, broken bodies and started commenting on their injuries and debating the order in which to triage them, as though seeing people fall to their deaths was no big deal.

I guess that sort of thing happens all the time in Amsterdam. Being from Moose Jaw, Saskatchewan, this was a new experience for me.

Things quickly began to escalate out of control. The crowd on the outside of the stadium, eager to see the action from the inside, started pushing up against us. I gently started shoving people back with my 7.62mm general-purpose machine gun, when this Afghan cop/thug came up to me. If I was reading his body language right, he was saying, "*You're doing it all wrong.*" He then started swinging his AK-47 by the barrel like a baseball bat, violently cracking people on the head and face with it.

I couldn't believe what I was seeing; this was a policeman, one of the so-called good guys, and he was dropping people left and right with his AK-Louisville Slugger! I ran over to stop him but people in the crowd started shouting and running all over the place, knocking into me and trying to pull my weapon out of my hands. Angry Afghans began climbing up on to a German armoured vehicle, but the wily Krauts (like all good Germans) had a contingency plan. One of their soldiers popped out of the hatch with a fire extinguisher and started hosing down the civvies, spraying them in the face with chemical fire retardant.

A Para friend of mine screamed, "Fuckin' 'ell lads, it's kickin' off! Up your jumpers!" and started delivering vicious kicks to anyone within boot-stomping range. Now the Paras' love of a good riot was *almost* matched by their love of putting *down* a good riot, but this was too much. It was utter madness!

Later that day, I got the story as to how the whole thing started from a friend of mine who was posted inside the stadium. It seems the crowd had seen too many news clips of soccer hooliganism and decided that starting riots (if the rest of the world was anything to go by) was just the sort of thing that one does whilst watching a footy match. So after a brass band played a few notes, the mayor of Kabul gave a flowery speech and then stepped down from his podium to release a bunch of caged pigeons to celebrate the Day of Peace. The poor pigeons, however, having been locked up in this tiny cage for weeks on end, didn't soar for the sky like at the Olympics, but fluttered rather half-heartedly the few feet to the ground and collapsed in sheer exhaustion right in front of their cage.

It was too much for the crowd in the stands. They couldn't get the image of public executions out of their mind. During the Taliban's black reign of terror, the stadium had been transformed into a coliseum. And coliseums were all about *blood*. Now the crowd wanted blood. *Any* blood. *Pigeon* blood!

So like a ten-thousand-strong human wave, they bum-rushed the field and, in their eagerness to take home a memorial pigeon, literally ripped the birds apart in the struggle for possession. My friend told me it was one of the damnedest things he'd ever seen, and he was from east London, so that's saying something. Blood and feathers flew in all directions and people started beating and kicking each other to get a piece, any piece, of the torn-apart pigeons to put on their mantels back home.

By some miracle a small boy managed to capture a live bird and make a break for it. He was halfway across the field when the crowd quickly gave chase and tackled him to the ground. Twenty hands shot in to steal his beloved pigeon, quickly ripping it to shreds as the boy screamed and cried over his murdered pet. My friend saw the young boy later, all bruised and bloodied, crying as he picked up flesh and feathers, as though he'd be able to put the mangled pigeon back together.

Then people began getting shoved over the balcony railing as the crowd in the upper decks fought to get down to the action on the field. That's around the time I saw people falling for three storeys and heard the sickening crunch as their bodies smacked into cement. People were screaming and running in all directions; children were crying because they'd lost their parents; complete strangers were fighting to the death, rolling on the ground, choking and eye-gouging. AK-47s were swinging in parabolic arcs until they made hard contact with soft heads. Crumpled, broken civilians were all over the ground as German soldiers screamed "*Aussteigen!*" in their angry, guttural tones, spraying down civilians in the face with fire-retardant foam. It was total anarchy and chaos.

Sadly, and not surprisingly, it all took place on Afghanistan's first Day of Peace. Needless to say, this didn't bode well for the country.

But that was another time, and on August 25, 2008, as I was reminiscing, the ramp on my Herc came down at Kandahar Airfield (KAF), and there it was again, *the stink of the Stan,* which I had tried so hard to forget. It was a gruesome combination of burning garbage and raw sewage, and it always brought the Stan back to my mind whenever I smelled it anywhere else in third world countries. It hit me square in the face, and for a moment, I was right back in Kabul, smothered in a flood of memories and bad emotions. I looked over at a sergeant I'd never met before, and judging by the look in his eyes, I knew he'd been in the Stan before as well, and that the stink was bringing him back to another time and place, one he'd evidently preferred to have forgotten.

He looked at me, shook his head, and quietly said, "Fuck, I hate this place."

"Tell me about it," I replied and walked down the ramp, into the burning heat, dust, and odours that made your nose sting and your eyes water. I thought to myself, *Ya gotta love it!*

I looked over at my team as they exited the Herc. Warrant Officer Longview, a very switched-on professional, was my second-in-command (2 I/C); Private Fourneau would be our driver; Corporal Hetsa would be our vehicle's gunner and light-machine-gun-toting killer on the ground; and then there was me, their newly minted captain. Most of the guys were from the First Battalion, The Royal Canadian Regiment (1 RCR) from Canadian Forces Base Petawawa, in Ontario. But a few guys, like myself, had come over from 3 RCR (also located at CFB Pet) to make up the numbers. Our Canadian OMLT, consisting of four 4-man teams, would be called 72 Kandak. *Kandak* means *battalion* in Dari, the language of the Afghan National Army (ANA), and the Canadian Forces (CF) had implemented the word in a show of solidarity with them. My four-man team's designation, or call sign, would be 72 Alpha (pronounced *seven two*, not *seventy-two*).

I looked over and made eye contact with my buddy, Rich, who was also in charge of a four-man OMLT team. He smirked and scratched his eyebrow, giving me the finger at the same time. Originally from Cape Breton, he was now a reservist fighting out of Hamilton, Ontario. We'd immediately hit it off when he arrived at CFB Pet and discovered that if I sat in the front seat of his car, I could navigate our way to the Tim Hortons on base and he wouldn't have to drive *off* the base by accident any more. After a series of self-described disastrous life choices, he found himself attached to a regular force unit, about to deploy to Afghanistan to mentor and guide the Afghan National Army during combat operations. His dubious navigational skills aside, he was an incredibly switched-on soldier. All the guys loved him, and we took the piss out of each other constantly.

Rich was what soldiers in the infantry lovingly called a shit magnet. Later on during our tour, almost every time I patrolled next to him and his call sign, *bad things* happened. The enemy was drawn to him; they smelled him from afar and travelled from wonderful places just to kill him and his men. I never liked patrolling with him; I was scared I was going to get caught up in his vortex of death. I labelled him call sign "Bad Karma" because Death seemed to be stalking him.

A logistics (loggy) sergeant had just marched up and was shouting at us to follow her to the tent city, our new home away from home, when a couple of black Hilux Toyotas with tinted windows and cab covers screeched to a halt right next to us, spitting up dust. The window slowly lowered and a full-bearded face glared out the window, spit out some tobacco juice, looked me in the eye, and said in a voice eerily similar to Clint Eastwood's, "You guys OMLT?"

You'd better say "yes," I thought to myself. *He's probably got the drop on ya!*

"Yeah," I said back, not sure who or what the hell I was looking at. He looked like he was in the special forces, the only place you'd be allowed to grow a three-month beard like that. His eyes had big bags under them, like he'd been in the shit (seen serious combat) recently and was just in Kandahar Airfield for a day's R&R (rest and relaxation) before he had to go back to killing the Taliban with his bare hands and tobacco breath.

He snorted and spit another wad of juice into the dirt. "Get in," was all he said, looking straight ahead again as his window rolled back up.

I shouted out to the OMLT boys next to me, "You heard the man—pack your gear in the trucks and let's get outta here!" I moved to the back of the truck with my bags and shouted, "Warrant, police up our men, we're pulling a Jeffersons!"

"What's a *Jeffersons?*"

"We're movin' on up! Better digs! C'mon, let's go." I threw open the back of the truck, pushed in my gear, and helped Fourneau and Hetsa with theirs. We all crammed into the cab. The rest of the boys piled into the other trucks and we sped off into the night.

"Where're we going?" I asked Grizzly Adams. His passenger, an equally bearded man, spoke into a cellphone.

"Yeah, we got 'em; coming to you now." He clicked the phone shut. He leaned over the back of his seat and said, "OMLT don't stay in that shithole! We've got you suites at the vip centre." (He pronounced it "vip," not "v-i-p.") "You'll stay there for two days, listen to the stupid briefings, and then go off to the Panj to win the war for us. We're on our way out, you boys are relieving us; name's Mike," and with that quick explanation, he looked forward again.

"Fair enough," I said, and looked over at Fourneau and shrugged. VIP accommodation sounded a lot better than the surly loggy's tent. The three trucks came to a screeching halt outside a long two-storey block and kicked up enough dust to choke us all out.

"Here we are," Mike said. "Go inside to the first floor; your names are on the doors, the rooms are unlocked, keys are on the desks." He pointed down the street. "Walk down this road for about fifteen minutes, follow the curve, that'll lead you to the American DFAC. It's open from zero-six hundred. Break down your rifles and lock 'em in your army boxes. Just carry your pistols. Then come back for briefings at building Zulu-3 at zero-eight-thirty."

"Cool, but where's Zulu-3?" I asked, having never been to KAF before.

"Can't miss it, you'll walk by it on your way to the DFAC. After your briefings, we'll come and grab you guys and get you squared away for kit."

"Okay, thanks for the pickup and the rooms. Just one more question— what's a DFAC?"

"Whats'a matter?" Mike smirked, "Not up on your TLAs?"

"Apparently not," I said, not really sure what he was talking about.

"TLAs: three-letter acronyms! The army's full of 'em, and you'd better figure 'em out most ricky-tick if you wanna survive here! DFAC stands for dining facility. There's like seven of 'em, but the American one's the best."

"Cool, thanks," I said, wondering if DFAC really qualified as a *three*-letter acronym.

Mike hopped back into the front seat, slammed the door, and shouted, "Fuhgeddaboudit!" The trucks flew off into the night just as quickly as they had arrived, again leaving us to choke on their dust.

"Sir, who were those guys?" Fourneau asked me.

"Mark my words, young man, that'll be us in seven to eight months." Then I thought to myself, *If we're still alive.*

* * *

The next couple of days passed very quickly. One of the boys got his hands on a map of KAF, and that helped us out considerably. KAF was absolutely massive. It harboured at least forty thousand soldiers—more soldiers than my hometown back in Saskatchewan had people. KAF had several runways, thousands of barracks to accommodate all the soldiers, several huge chow halls (apparently also called DFACs), two major hospitals (which I hoped I'd never get to see from the inside), two water purification plants, and a sewage treatment plant that, no matter where you were on the base, always seemed to assault your nose with a delightful bouquet of airborne stench.

To keep morale up, KAF also had the famous boardwalk—a big square in the middle of the base with shops all around it, including a Tim Hortons coffee shop, a Chechen massage parlour (filled with signs that said IF YOU ASK FOR A 'HAPPY ENDING,' YOU WILL BE SUBJECTED TO THE FULL PUNISHMENT UNDER MILITARY LAW!), a Subway restaurant, a Burger King, and some other tastes of home.

There were also a dozen shops run by Afghan locals, selling pretty much anything and everything imaginable. The boardwalk formed a large square with the shops and restaurants on the outside, and a football field and floor-hockey rink in the middle. On the dirt rink, the Canadian team routinely destroyed all comers. Literally every country in NATO had tried to beat them, but as far as I know, it never happened.

But for all its amenities, KAF was by no means an easy place to live; the Taliban mortared and rocketed it almost daily. There were signs all over the place saying KAF HAS BEEN ROCKET-FREE FOR '0' DAYS! And on top of the fear of getting rocketed and killed, the troops stationed there had to face the maddening, perpetual boredom that inevitably sets in when you're trapped in the same place for long periods of time with no respite. You can only watch the same movies, read the same papers and magazines, go to the same PX (post exchange—a US army base store), walk up and down the same board-walk, and jog the same route so many times. Troops who couldn't entertain themselves or come up with a way to alleviate the terrible boredom had a very hard time there. And no one could blame them.

The suicide rate in KAF was rumoured to be astronomical, much higher and out of all proportion to the civilian populations of cities that size back home in North America. I was only there for a few days, and by the time I left, I was happy to be going. There was just something depressing about it, nothing I could put my finger on, but I was happy to *not* be spending an eight-month tour only in KAF. The place had a way of dragging you down. Bad mojo, bad chi—the dark side of the Force was very strong there.

Rich woke me up early our first morning there (we were still nicely jet-lagged), so we grabbed our teams and trudged off to find the American DFAC. It was like all things American in a war zone: absolutely huge! It seemed every NATO country had troops stationed in KAF, and all of them chose the American DFAC as their favourite eatery. The line was out the door and around the block.

We looked around and noticed that almost every EU nation had some troops in KAF, and we saw several African nations represented as well. We finally got inside the building and swiped the meal cards the other OMLT boys had left for us on our desks, and then performed the mandatory hand-washing ritual before we entered the scoff house. I saw a young American soldier standing next to the sinks, looking thoroughly bored. I leaned over to him and asked, "You the hand-washing Nazi?"

He looked at me and yawned. "*Jawohl*. Now move along."

We quickly grabbed some scoff, which was better than anything I'd ever had in Canada, but I figured their food budget was larger than our national defence budget, so they could afford some good growlies. We ate quickly and then marched back to our little neck of the woods in KAF to find Z-3.

We were going to grab a coffee at Tim Hortons, but the line went around the block. I asked Rich if Canadians could butt into the front of the line, but he thought not, since Hortons was, at the time, an American company. Evidently the company's insidious marketing schemes had worked on me, because my sense of national pride was violently assaulted by his uncouth comment, and we angrily debated the ownership of the Tim Hortons coffee and donut empire as we walked through the dust. Armoured vehicles, Jeeps, and tanks were kicking up enough dirt to make us choke, as choppers screamed overhead.

Even at seven-thirty in the morning you could feel the heat building up, and by the time we found building Z-3, another large tent, I was covered in sweat. *As per.*

Being the cool kids in town, we obviously sat in the back row for the briefings. At the appointed time, a captain took the podium and gave us a quick overview of the briefings we'd be subjected to that morning. Then the fire marshal, with a completely straight face, told us we couldn't set up a BBQ pit *just anywhere* outside of KAF. He told us we needed to get a special permit from his office if we wanted to set up a barbecue on the bases we'd be going to. *Wow. Um, okay.* I guessed that somebody must have set up a BBQ next to an ammo bunker and set it on fire, once upon a time.

Then we listened to the mandatory OPSEC (operational security) brief-ing, a modern take on the old "loose lips sink ships" classic.

Then the intelligence officer (Int O) for the battle group took the podium and started speaking in a loud, nasal voice. "This is the map of our current AO [area of operations]. As you can see by the little explosion symbols plastered all over the map, we've had a busy week." He pointed over his shoulder at the PowerPoint presentation on the screen. *A week? All that happened in a week?*

This wasn't a map of the whole country—it was just Kandahar Province, where we'd be fighting. The provincial map had at least three dozen explosion symbols on it.

My throat went dry as it dawned on me that a lot of the explosions happened on Ring Road South, the road we'd be taking from KAF to our bases at Masum Ghar and Sperwhan Ghar, off to the west. There had been at least three explosions on Route Brown, the only road we could take to get to our base at Sperwhan Ghar. Rich looked at me knowingly; obviously he'd caught that too. We weren't laughing anymore.

According to the map, we were about to find ourselves right in the middle of the worst sector for shootings and improvised explosive devices, or IEDs. An IED is basically a homemade bomb; the parts and pieces of the bomb could come from actual explosives like artillery shells, army mines, or homemade fertilizer explosives. The electrical detonators or receivers to make it go BOOM could come from pieces of radios, remote-controlled devices, or whatever else the bomb maker could get his hands on. These explosives were ingeniously made and incredibly well hidden, with their size, style, components, and lethality limited only by the imagination of their creator. IEDs were responsible for the greatest number of coalition casualties.

Then the Int O asked the ultimate question: "How many people here are going outside the wire?" By that he meant how many people were leaving the protective wire of their base to go out into bandit country on a patrol. *Outside the wire*... there it was! Finally. I had wondered when somebody (who had probably never been *outside the wire* in his entire frickin' military career) was going to ask us if we were going outside the wire.

In the Canadian Forces, there were people who really got off on asking that question—at very inappropriate times—and because of them, it was causing a good deal of friction between those who *had* and those who had *not*.

There was another stereotype, a deep-seated belief that had been creeping up and taking hold in the CF; it started right around the time we began deploying soldiers to Afghanistan in 2002. The belief was this: it didn't matter where you had deployed to before in the world, if you hadn't been to Afghanistan yet, you were nothing, and all of your experiences counted for nothing.

That's why guys with a lot of experience, like Warrant Longview, didn't take too well to being asked by some rear-echelon type if they'd been outside the wire before. Guys like Longview had been in the shit on several different continents, but they hadn't been to the Stan before, so obviously, some idiots thought their experience counted for nothing. I got along great with Warrant Longview, but I couldn't help but take the piss out of him because he hadn't been to the Stan yet, and unfortunately for him, I had.

I'd say crap like, "Yeah that's all well and good, Warrant, and maybe that's how you did it against the Russians in Germany, but that's not how it works in Afghanistan." He knew I was only joking, so he graciously refrained from giving me a mouth full of Chiclets.

Back in the briefing tent, it was only the OMLT guys in the back rows who raised their arms to the Int O's question about who would be going outside the wire. The Int O said the next slide was for us, and then went into a detailed point-by-point analysis of the SIGACTS (significant activities) the enemy had attacked us with over the previous month. I hadn't heard about most of these incidents back home—it seemed that a lot more enemy activity was going on than we'd been told about.

It wasn't looking good. They were hitting us at several different places, all at the same time, and with different attack patterns, as though their efforts were being coordinated by a higher headquarters. The Taliban were a lot more organized than we'd been led to believe back home in Canada.

After the briefings were finished, and with the wind thoroughly taken out of our sails, we left the briefing tent and walked back to our rooms. Nobody said too much. I think we were all in a state of mild shock after what we'd just heard. We knew the war wasn't going well, but I don't think anyone realized it was *that* bad. But I didn't have any illusions. We weren't sent to Afghanistan to keep the peace, because there was literally no peace to keep! We were there to *make* the peace, and that meant putting ourselves in harm's way.

* * *

The next morning we ate quickly and then went to the OMLT stores to collect our gear. The store man issued us 9mm bullets and two magazines for our Browning pistols, and I was given twelve mags for my C8 assault rifle (a smaller version of the M-16, with lots of modifications). We also got a laser sight for our C8s, box magazines for the C9 (Minimi) machine gunners, two fragmentation grenades, four smoke grenades, a CamelBak water carrier, a Leatherman tool, a TCCC (tactical combat casualty care) first-aid kit, a one-piece eye monocle night-vision sight with helmet connectors, a compass, an army GPS, and about twenty other odds and sods that you could hook up, connect, or just dangle off your person like a one-man pawn shop. I asked the store man for my issued "stick with protruding nail," but he didn't find that funny.

By the time they were done handing out kit, our total equipment weight—once our mags were bombed up with ammo and we had on our helmet and body armour and some water in our day sack—was close to one hundred pounds. Later in the tour I weighed all of my kit. It totalled ninety-two pounds. Every time I left the wire, I carried ninety-two pounds of kit on my body. I liked to tell the boys that I put the "light" back in "light infantry." They would immediately snarl back, "Actually, you put the 'ugly' back in 'fuck ugly,'" which I promptly amended to *fugly.*

And my kit wasn't even the heaviest, not by a long shot. Our light machine gunners, who carried twenty pounds of ammunition all linked together for their guns, could walk around carrying close to 120 pounds. Try and imagine carrying 120 pounds of equipment in fifty-degree-Celsius heat. Then imagine trying to fight in that, for hours on end. That's what we had to look forward to. But, as crazy as it sounds, we had all joined up as volunteers; we weren't conscripted, so we could only blame ourselves and those great recruiting commercials.

Hetsa had told me his recruiter had actually asked him if he liked going camping. When Hetsa responded "yes," he was told, "Well, son, the infantry's the branch for you!" *Sure, I could see how fighting in Afghanistan was eerily similar to going camping—"extreme sports" camping!*

Something I discovered back home in Canada was that a lot of civilians didn't understand that soldiers *want* to go overseas and do their jobs. It would be like a firefighter who goes through months of rigorous training and count-less exercises, only to stay behind in the fire station when the alarm sounds. You wanted a chance to actually do the job you were trained for.

The next morning, call signs 72 Alpha (72A) and 72 Bravo were slated to hop into some Bison armoured vehicles and drive through Kandahar city on our way to Masum Ghar, our first stop. From Masum, we'd be going to our individual outposts. Another OMLT captain, named John, and his call sign, 72 Bravo, would be travelling on to Forward Operating Base (FOB) Mushan, in the extreme west of Panjway Province. I had found out just a day before we deployed from Canada that my call sign, 72 Alpha, would be going to Sperwhan Ghar.

I wasn't feeling too good about riding in the back of a blacked-out, hermetically sealed Bison armoured vehicle for my ride to Masum Ghar.

The Fear had crept up on me, probably in my sleep. I found myself thinking about that long, slow drive down the IED highway, the only road leading to the west, where I had to go. I kept seeing that PowerPoint presentation, the one with all of the explosion symbols on it.

Rich, always an intuitive guy, must've picked up on my "for those about to die" vibe. That or the fact that I was most often the guy running around trying to keep morale up, and now I'd gone deathly quiet. He walked over to me and looked me in the eyes. "Hey, fucknuts. You okay?"

"Listen Tricky Dick, I'm a *dismounted* warrior, damn it! If I want to coward out and run and hide under a pile of coats, I have that option! I get claustrophobic in a hermetically sealed armoured vehicle that doesn't have quite enough underarmour to protect me from a thousand-pound bomb buried in the middle of the road. And like I've always told ya, I'm allergic to getting blown up!"

Rich cut me off. "Hey, hey, hey. Easy, little camper! Your Uncle Richie's here to tell you somethin'—you're gonna be fine. If you get scared and need a little pick-me-up, you just call your big Uncle Richie, okay?"

Rich leaned back and smiled, then roughly thumped me on the back. "Get a grip of your shit, trooper! You're supposed to be leading your men into combat, not scaring the hell out of them with your doom-and-gloom vibe! You'll be fine. Like you keep telling me, you can't possibly die here, because you've got to pull your thumb out and invent that flux capacitor thingamajig!"

"Thanks, brother," I said, and pretended to punch him in the groin.

He blocked my punch and smirked. "Now get outta here, and don't forget your rifle and pistolé; you *may* need them where you're going. Although the way you shoot, you might as well just carry around a twenty-pound paperweight!"

We said, "Strength and honour," and then clasped forearms like Roman legionnaires. I know we would've made General Maximus Decimus Meridius proud.

Sergeant Donahue, an OMLT hard case, walked over and said, "Remember the unit you came from," meaning I had been in 2 Para in the Brits. "You weren't in the RAF regiment, you're a Sky God! Don't ever forget that!" Then he slapped me roughly on the back. *What the hell was it with people and back slapping today?*

I guess everyone knew, deep down, that this might be it . . . our last piss take together before we met up again at the ramp ceremony, to stand at attention and salute as a friend's coffin passed by. I pushed that morbid thought from my mind. We'd all be okay. My second-in-command's first name was actually Merlin, ergo we nicknamed him "The Wizard." He'd protect us with his level thirty magic!

"Cheers, mucker," I said to Donahue, and returned his back slap. He was an ex-3 Para soldier from the Brit army, so he knew the drill. We'd been to the same places in Northern Ireland, so he knew what I was going through; no airborne warrior liked being cooped up in an armoured vehicle—it was anathema to our nature.

And with that, I walked over to the warrant, Hetsa, and Fourneau. I told them I'd see them in Masum Ghar, as we were being split up for the ride. I then found my Bison vehicle, hopped into the back, and said a silent prayer and reminded myself that *the Lord hates a coward* as the heavy metal door was closed shut, blocking out all the light and air from the outside. I reached into the top pouch of my tactical vest and pulled out my good-luck earplugs, knowing how loud the armoured vehicles could be. Those earplugs had gotten me through some hairy moments before, and I was hoping they could do the trick again, as we rumbled out of KAF and into our little part of the war.

Chapter 2

Our vehicle convoy rambled down the road and through the city of Kandahar, the provincial and political capital of Kandahar Province. At one point a soldier in the top turret shouted down to us in the back, "If you look out your left viewport, you can see the prison where the Taliban recently blew up the front gate and fifty guys escaped." I'd seen the prison on the news, but there was nothing quite like seeing it with your own eyes. One of John's 72 Bravo soldiers held up a phone to the viewport and snapped a picture. *War tourism*, I thought to myself. *Ya gotta love it.*

Thankfully, the ride to Masum Ghar was surprisingly uneventful. That was the problem with so many of our training scenarios back in Canada. In every training scenario back home, the *pretend* enemy who was waiting to get you always threw the kitchen sink at you, in addition to a four-litre jug of two per cent milk *and* your kid's plastic Dora the Explorer plates. It got you so paranoid that you started thinking, every time you left the wire *for real*, that you weren't coming back. How could you? When you got rocketed, mortared, snipered, IEDed, and shouted at by an angry mob every time you left the wire?

We arrived and passed through the front gate's cement barriers and watchtower. I thought about what my major had told me back in Canada. I was to get my team to Masum and, once there, find the outgoing OMLT major and get a briefing from him on the OMLT's SOPs (standard operating procedures) and on my AO. As a bonus I was also hoping to meet my counterpart, a captain from the Princess Patricia's Canadian Light Infantry (PPCLI) out of Edmonton, who would start his left-seat, right-seat handover briefings with me. We called it "left-seat, right-seat" because the guy was right there next to you, giving you the heads-up on everything you were meant to be coming up against. Many times we'd actually be fighting side by side; the outgoing guy and the incoming would be covering each other and shooting back at the enemy during handover patrols. Hopefully by the end of play that day I'd have a much better idea of what we'd be getting into and who we'd be up against, and I could pass the info on to my boys.

I used to give them what I called the *Rob Semrau Guarantee*, which meant that when I knew something, *they* knew it. I'd had officers in the past who were control freaks; they liked to keep the information (that they were expected to pass on to the troops) to themselves, thinking it put them in an elevated position of power, or some bollocks like that. My current OMLT major was a keen practitioner of retaining any and all information—and then at the last minute finally sharing the next day's plan with us.

I was a private once, and I knew what it was like to be treated like a mushroom—kept in the dark and fed on shit. I wasn't going to be that type of officer. My bottom line was to treat people the way I wanted to be treated. I read a book once called *Ethics 101* and that was its entire premise: follow the Golden Rule.

I walked over to the other vehicles and collected the warrant, Fourneau, and Hetsa. "How was the trip, boys?"

Longview looked up and said, "Uneventful, thankfully."

"My thoughts exactly. Warrant, take the guys with you and do some old-school recce [reconnaissance]. Try and find your warrant counterpart; they're supposed to be on the ground here somewhere, waiting for us. For when we get to Sperwhan Ghar, find out the answers to the three most important questions to an infantryman: Where do we eat, how's the food, and where do we sleep? I'll meet you guys for lunch and we can swap notes. Any questions for me? Besides the obvious . . ."

The warrant looked at me with a quizzical look on his face. "And what's the obvious?" he asked. Fourneau and Hetsa stopped what they were doing and looked at me.

"How *do* you stay so damn handsome in a war zone? *Obviously!*" I slapped him on the shoulder and walked off in the direction of some buildings that had a headquarters air about them. A corporal said I could find the OMLT major in the main briefing tent and pointed it out to me. I rounded the twelve-foot-high blast walls and went inside. I stood off to the side while my eyes slowly adjusted to the gloom.

An older officer and a young sergeant seated at a large table in the middle of the tent looked up from the map they were studying and assessed me, hard. I wasn't wearing a beret or helmet so, in military-protocol terms, I wasn't supposed to salute. Instead I snapped my heels together and brought my arms down to my sides, the position of attention *sans* beret, and loudly stated, "Sir, my name is Captain Semrau. I'm the new incoming OMLT captain slated to go to Sperwhan Ghar. My four-man team just got into Masum a few minutes ago. I was told by my major back in Canada to find you here so that you could give me an OMLT SOP briefing as well as an AO briefing for Sperwhan." The officer stood up and walked over to me, extending his hand.

"At ease, Captain. My name's Speers; this is Sergeant Little," he said, turning and pointing to the sergeant at the table.

"Sir," he said, nodding his head.

"Sergeant," I responded, nodding back. I shook the major's hand. "Rob Semrau, sir, just came in on the Bison train."

The major laughed. "No nasty surprises on the trip in?"

"No, sir." I said. "The Taliban don't know I'm here yet, but they'll know soon enough!"

"Nice." He pointed to the chair next to him. "Have a seat and we'll get started."

"Thanks," I said, and sat down on the hard chair. I looked at the map; it was huge, with lots of different areas and symbols marked out on it.

The major started talking, using his best "briefing room" voice. "After we're done here, I'll send you off to find Captain Stephens, the OMLT captain in Sperwhan you're replacing. I've told him to take you up the hill here and point out some features of Masum and its surrounding area, then you guys'll hop into some RGs [mine-protected armoured personnel carriers] and head over to Sperwhan this afternoon. Over the next few days you'll do some patrols with him, all the while conducting your left-seat, right-seat, and he'll be there to answer any questions you may have. For now, I'll do this

AO briefing, then you and your guys can enjoy our fine cuisine in the dining hall." He looked me over to make sure I'd caught all that.

"Sounds good, sir. I don't think I've ever been on the ground before with the outgoing guy, so this'll be a first for me," I said, happily surprised. It was supposed to be that way, but for any number of reasons, it never seemed to happen. *This'll be a first.*

"Yeah, I know what you mean, we've been trying to get this right for a while now but it finally seems to be working with our incoming and outgoing flights. He's a good captain and he's had some great experiences there, so use the time wisely and get as much out of this as you can before he's gone."

"Will do, sir. Do you mind if I take notes so I can pass this on to my men?" I reached into my hip pocket and pulled out my trusty field message pad (FMP). You can't be a good officer without one or, better yet, several.

"Go right ahead. For now," he said, pointing at the map with his pen, "we're obviously here, at Masum Ghar, *Ghar* being Pashto for *mountain.* Don't know if you knew that or not . . ."

"No, I didn't. I've been working more on my Dari . . ."

"Keep practising. Learn a few greetings in Pashto, what the villagers speak, but certainly focus more on Dari, the ANA's language. If you can't talk to the locals, your interpreter [terp] always can. But if your terp gets hit and you can't speak to the ANA, you'll be in a right shit state."

"How are the terps, sir?"

"The usual—some aren't that good, and most are terrible. Okay, Masum Ghar is a sort of political hub for this AO. Whoever your battle group major is going to be in Sperwhan, he'll have to come here to the local *shura* [a meeting of local nationals] once every couple of weeks to discuss their never-ending issues. Obviously we've got our base here with some of the tankers, some artillery boys, lots of engineers, and some Afghan police. Also the QRF [quick reaction force], if you ever need them, will launch out of Masum to come and help you. The OMLT and POMLT [Police Operational Mentor and Liaison Team] here patrol the local area once a day, focusing on the bazaar, or market. We've had a few SIGACTS in the bazaar with some IEDs, a couple of shootings, and Masum itself gets rocketed and mortared almost daily from the surrounding villages and hills. We've done clearance patrols but haven't had much luck in stopping them."

The major then gave me some very elaborate instructions for when I would be operating out of Sperwhan; conditions that had to be met before

I could patrol, and some possible circumstances that could stop me from patrolling. He described several of the key local national (LN) players in my neck of the woods, who could end up either helping me or actively working against me, depending on what kind of mood they were in that day.

He elaborated on the contacts the Canadians had in the past with the Taliban: ambushes, small-arms shootings, rockets, mortars, IEDs. He gave me a very good heads-up on the type of action we could expect in the Sperwhan area. Apparently we weren't going to be bored there. The enemy had been quite busy trying to kill us over the last six months, and I was told my OMLT team could expect the same less-than-cordial reception.

"And here I thought one of the tenets of their religion was being hospitable to strangers in their land?" I asked the major with a smartass smile on my face.

"Yes, indeed—how terribly rude of them. You'll quickly find out the Taliban are what we call *hypocrites*," he said with a big grin. The major sighed. "They'll murder their own people for smoking or drinking alcohol, but they'll produce ten thousand tonnes of heroin a year and then sell it all over the world to poison everyone else!"

The major then pointed to the map and showed me that Sperwhan was actually fairly close to Masum, only about five klicks southwest as the crow flies.

"As you can see," he said, pointing at the map, "one of our problems here is the fact that we've got only one road connecting Sperwhan to Masum—Route Kelowna. If you look at the map, you'll see as you carry on farther west on Route Kelowna, past Sperwhan, that it's also the only road connecting us to our much smaller combat outpost bases, namely Hajikan, Talikan, Zangabad, and Mushan. Only one road in and one road out is going to lend itself nicely to getting IEDed all to hell, which is exactly what's been happening."

"Sir, I thought the ANA were sending engineers to sweep Route Kelowna daily for IEDs?"

"They are. And they're getting ambushed almost daily as well. The Afghan National Army can only send a small team of 'engineers'—and believe me, I use the term very loosely—kitted out with old American equipment that couldn't find an atomic bomb buried under the road. When they're close to finding something, the Taliban usually detonate it and use it as a signal to initiate their ambush."

I'd heard of that before. That technique, not surprisingly, is called an IED-initiated ambush. The Taliban would set up an IED in the middle of the road and then lie in ambush and wait until someone stepped on or drove over it (or they might just detonate it themselves with a command wire or radio-controlled device), and then pop up and shoot the hell out of anyone who was still alive. They would use the shock and fear that often paralyzed soldiers after an IED went off (and the fact that everyone in their kill zone was most likely deaf and concussed from the blast) to mop up any survivors.

"Mark my words," the major continued, "at some point in your tour you'll probably end up going to rescue the ANA engineers after they've been hit."

"Nice," I responded. *Poor bastards.*

"Well, at any rate, you can see why the ANA has become so damn fatalistic. But back to the briefing. . . . In order to get to your base at Sperwhan from Route Kelowna, you've got to travel south on the only road you can take to get there. It's called Route Brown." He pointed to it on the map. "It passes over three water culverts buried under the road, and guess what?"

"They get IED *surprises* planted in them daily?"

"You're a smart man, Semrau. You've been here before?"

"I fought in the Clone Wars before, sir, but only in Kabul where, thankfully, we didn't have to deal with any of this."

"Well, you're in the *real* war now, son. But you'll get used to the daily rhythm of shootings, rockets, mortars, and IEDs. You'll get used to it, or go batshit crazy! Hopefully the former, but the ANA you'll be working with are supposed to be a good crew. You'll be with the First Company of 72 Kandak, 502 Corps. They've just come off two months' rest and refit, so I'm sure they'll be rarin' to go." The major looked at me and smiled.

I wasn't sure if he was being sarcastic or not. *Would they be good to go or not?*

I suppose Yoda's words rang true when he wisely said, "Frivolous, speculation is, when patience will reveal all." I always told Rich any time you could quote Yoda in a war zone, it was a good day.

The major wrapped up his in-depth briefing and told me to call him twenty-four/seven if I ever had any problems. I really liked Major Speers. That was exactly the type of briefing you hope to get when you're new in country, and I thanked him for taking the time.

His final words of advice to me were, "Give 'em hell and make them pay. Watch out for your men and stay safe. And let the ANA die for their country. Don't *you* die for it. Let them go first, let them take the risks. Learn when to mentor, and when to *act.*" *Good advice.* He wished me luck, shook my hand, and told me to go and get some chow.

I left the tent and put on my CF-issued sunglasses to shield my eyes from the terrible glare of the sun. When you left one of the dark buildings and stepped outside, you were temporarily blinded for a few seconds. The CF sunglasses were a great piece of kit, and I took very good care of them. They were ballistic in design, which meant the lenses were fairly soft, so that if you had shrapnel or rocks blow up in your face, the lenses wouldn't shatter outright, but would instead absorb the blast, protecting your eyes.

* * *

I left the HQ and wandered off to find the scoff house. It wasn't hard to locate; I checked my watch and then followed the big stream of soldiers heading uphill. As I followed the herd I thought about the major's briefing. It seemed that no matter who you asked about working with the Afghans, every soldier who had ever served with them invariably told only one of two stories.

One story always seemed to have the Afghans acting like a bunch of steroid-infected, rageaholic Rambos who couldn't wait to close with and kill the enemy, preferably with their bare teeth. Like a bunch of dark-side Jedi, their hatred of the Taliban had made them strong and seemingly bulletproof. That was one version of our soldiers' experience with them—the *semi-positive* version.

Sadly, too many times I'd heard the other version of the Afghan National Army experience—that working with the Afghans was akin to trying to teach university-level courses to small children with severe discipline issues who liked to bring knives to school.

Tales of joint patrols having to be cancelled because the Afghans were smoking joints were rife. Extreme cowardice or ineptitude in the face of the enemy, grand theft, mass desertions, and week-long, unscheduled R&R periods were the norm. Gross corruption in their officer corps and tales of nepotism that would make a Roman emperor blush, again, were all too common.

Some coalition soldiers said the ANA didn't want to fight because they were afraid of dying; others said it was because the Taliban ranks were filled to the brim with the ANA's immediate relatives, and it would undoubtedly make for an awkward family get-together if two cousins had just tried to kill each other ten minutes before Aunt Edna brought out the lamb casserole.

I was told it took a very special person to work well within the OMLT. Besides being a good soldier, you had to be brave to a fault, and you also had to be a diplomat and a professional problem solver, all rolled into one. Supposedly, ninety-five per cent of your workday was dedicated to sorting out the ANA's problems.

But the most important personality requirement of them all, and the only one that everyone seemed to agree upon, was that you had to possess a biblical abundance of patience, something akin to that of Job in the Old Testament.

You could never become agitated or even remotely worked up with the Afghans, and you could certainly never shout at them, or do anything to embarrass them in front of their countrymen. But you were never supposed to do these things to Canadian troops either, so I hoped it wouldn't be too difficult. Real or perceived insults, innuendo, off-colour references, jokes in poor taste, the actual laying of hands on an ANA soldier, highlighting someone's foibles, whatever...the list of things you could do to guarantee they would try and murder you to avenge their honour was endless.

Some former trainers had inadvertently done things that were perceived to be a gross violation against an Afghan soldier's honour, and the soldier would then, often immediately and on the spot, lock and load his weapon and mow down the OMLT trainer and anyone else who was unfortunate enough to be standing next to him. The ANA soldier would then hop over the wire and immediately join the Taliban.

As a result, the mentoring concept would often break down because trainers didn't feel it was safe to bring up any issues that could cause an Afghan commander or soldier to lose face. I learned very quickly to never single anyone out for either praise or name-and-shame, and I also figured out that I should always word my advice in the form of a suggestion or recommendation, and never as an order, purely so that the ANA wouldn't take offence.

Such was the reality of working with the OMLT. It wasn't bad enough that the Taliban were trying to blow you up and kill you, but you had to be worried about getting knifed in the back on your way to the toilet. As my grandmother would've said, "Well, that's just *swell!*"

I found the chow hall and grabbed a plate of scoff, but only after performing the mandatory hand washing. I entered the large tent and let my eyes adjust to the darkness. I found my guys sitting right under one of the a/c units. *Perfect.* I was what the boys affectionately referred to as "a sweaty bastard." My wife once told me I had a special need: that I required tons of water when most normal people didn't need any, and she was right.

"*Malzheit komradden, guten appetit!*" I said in my best Plattdeutsch as I plopped down on the picnic bench next to Hetsa. "So, find anything out?" I asked no one in particular.

Longview looked up and said, "I couldn't find my alternate; seems Captain Stephens left him back at Sperwhan. What about you, sir? Did you find the major?"

"Yeah, I found him. Good guy, gave a great briefing. Really took the time to get it into my thick skull. I think he was a bit concerned when he looked over and caught me drooling, but I explained it away as jet lag." I elbowed Hetsa in the ribs. "You know me—*always* drooling." The boys just shook their heads and kept eating.

"You guys continue to stuff your faces and I'll tell you what he told me, minus his expletives and sexual bigotry." I got out my FMP so I wouldn't forget to brief them on all the salient points, and proceeded to tell them everything the major had told me. This was the *Rob Semrau Guarantee* hard at work. I didn't hold anything back or whitewash over the scary parts.

I read a book once about the SAS, the British Army's Special Air Service. They're special forces soldiers who are widely acknowledged as being the best in the world. In the book, the soldiers often talked about the "Chinese Parliament." The idea behind this was that anyone who's about to put his life on the line for a mission was given the chance to have his say, to give input. Disagreements were common and no one took anything that was said personally. Sometimes the most junior guy on the team would come up with a better way of doing things, or suggest an idea the guy in charge hadn't thought of. Disagreements were expected, but when a final decision was made, everyone had to get in line.

In honour of the Chinese Parliament I would brief the men, and then I would always give them a chance to have their say. I did this every time I briefed them, without exception. If no one came up with a better way of doing things or had any suggestions, then we stuck with my plan, as it was.

I finished my playback of the major's briefing and looked around the table. Hetsa was absently staring at his half-finished plate and Fourneau looked visibly sick to his stomach. I'm sure I would've looked that way too if this was *my* first tour, like it was theirs. Someone once said the OMLT wasn't a good place to stick a guy on his first tour; too much stuff was guaranteed to happen and you should have some experience under your belt first. But I always thought the only way to get any experience was for someone to take a chance on you. Sometimes soldiers rose to the occasion, while other times. . . .

Only the warrant met my eyes, when he said, "Well, it looks like we're in the shit now, but it's nothing we can't handle."

I didn't hesitate, "Absolutely right! This changes nothing," I said, with steel in my voice. "It's what I've told all of you from the beginning. It's just *us*—the four of us. You watch my back, I watch yours, and we will live or die by each other. I promise you this—look at me!"

I paused and waited until all three were looking me straight in the eyes. "No matter what happens, I won't leave you. If that means you're so badly hurt that I can't push, pull, or drag you to safety, then I will die next to you. They will only get to *you* over *me*, because I won't leave you. I've told you this so many times I feel like a damn broken record. What we're about to do, this job, the OMLT gig, that's a special forces' job. Our spec ops [special operations forces] guys are so overtasked they don't have time to do it, but every other coalition force here has their spec ops guys doing the job we're about to do."

I elbowed Hetsa in the ribs again and reached over and squeezed Fourneau's nose. "But the job's now landed on our plate, and the only thing really special about us is the fact that we're too stupid to know when to quit. That's our secret weapon! We're too damn dumb to know when to throw in the towel! We're going to find Timothy [a nickname I had given the Taliban] where he lives and breathes. We're going to kick down the front door to his hovel, scream, 'Booyah!' as we rip him from his piss-soaked bed, and give him the stompin' of his life!"

The boys were smiling. *Mission accomplished.*

"Now, finish your borscht and let's go win this frackin' war so we can be home in time for Christmas!"

* * *

We wandered around until we found the Batcave, the OMLT HQ at Masum Ghar. I led the boys down the stairs and smashed my head on the low ceiling. *Nothing like a good first impression....*

"Welcome to the Batcave," a voice said from one of the underground offices. A young man walked out wearing an untucked brown shirt, faded Canadian-issued desert pants, and a brown baseball cap with a khaki Canadian flag patch on it, and extended his hand toward us.

"I'm Captain Stephens, the outgoing OMLT commander from Sperwhan; you newbies must be 72 Alpha." The casual air about him, with his shirt, ball cap, unbloused combat pants, and the big smile across his face, all worked to make a guy feel a lot more relaxed, especially after everything we'd just heard from the major. I knew from my first impression that I was going to like this guy.

Nobody needs some ramrod-stiff officer type shouting at his soldiers because they have a speck of dust on their beret in the middle of the desert. On Parliament Hill in Ottawa, with the ceremonial guards, certainly, but never in a war zone. I always thought you should try and maintain the fine line between being chilled out and still getting the job done properly. If anything, when you're getting shot at, you need to be fairly calm, not wound up so tight you're going to pop. As a leader, I always felt the men needed to look at you and see a very calm example. Easier said than done when you work on a two-way firing range for a living, and like Warrant Longview would've jokingly said about me, especially difficult when you suffer from increasingly debilitating panic attacks.

"Rob Semrau," I said, shaking his hand, "and this is Warrant Longview, my 2 I/C and the brains behind the operation; Corporal Hetsa, our automated gunner/killer; and Private Fourneau, our wheelman."

Stephens shook everyone's hand and then passed out some bottled water and cans of iced tea. Fourneau and Hetsa went off to the movie room while the outgoing OMLT captain took the warrant and me up to the top of Masum Ghar, where we had an incredible view of the Panjway valley. Warrant Longview and I bombarded him with questions about the enemy and his SOPs, how to be proactive in a hostile environment, the weather . . . At times our little Q&A session seemed to cover the entire spectrum of counter-insurgency ops.

I joked with Stephens and the Wizard and said, "Our use of TLAs in our TTPs will lead to SOPs IOT keep us from becoming VSA or KIA in a TIC." *Oh, how the army loves its TLAs.*

We went on and on, but thankfully the outgoing OMLT captain was a very patient man who always seemed to have a well-thought-out answer to our questions. He had clearly gained a lot of experience in this war, and undoubtedly he had a good, long career ahead of him in the CF. Finally, after we'd exhausted our long list of questions, I thanked him for the excellent briefing, and we walked back down the hill toward the Batcave.

"Grab your guys and your gear and let's get out of here," he said while looking at his watch. "We want to get the hell out of Dodge before 'coward hour.'" That was the designated time for everyone to strap on their body armour and don their helmet; the time of day Timothy was most likely to commence rocketing and mortaring Masum Ghar. "Kit up and I'll meet you and my guys at the RGs in fifteen mikes [minutes]," he said over his shoulder.

"Okay, thanks," I said and made my way to the Batcave, careful this time not to stove my head in again on the low ceiling.

"Mind your head, new guy!" the warrant said behind me.

"Yeah, got it, thanks." We walked into the Batcave, grabbed some water, and found the movie room. Up on a high shelf was a big flat-screen TV showing Mel Gibson's *Braveheart*, always a favourite amongst soldiers. My good friend Marc, a fellow Canadian whom I'd left in the Paras and who subsequently went on to join the Brit special forces, could quote every single line from the movie. It was actually sort of disturbing to hear him do it.

"Pack up your shiz-nit, boys," I said. "We're off to Sper in ten mikes." Fourneau and Hetsa groaned, grudgingly got up, and walked past me, clearly upset to be taken from their movie. "Calling all men of Union!" I said, slapping them on the backs. "Enlist now, and together we'll whip the Secesh!"

We gathered our kit and our two green army boxes, and clambered down to the car park. We found a bunch of soldiers quickly moving around the RGs and making sure their kit was strapped down tightly to the sides of the vehicles.

The RG-31 first entered service in the CF back in 2006. The vehicle was originally thought up and designed by the South Africans, after they'd armoured up a bunch of buses to get their kids to school without getting blown up by IEDs. Someone took the original idea and applied it to the current war and, voila, the RG-31 was born. It was twelve feet high, nineteen feet long, and seven-and-a-half feet wide; and to counter the IED threat, it had almost three feet of ground clearance. The bottom of the vehicle was shaped like a boat, with a V-design meant to funnel an IED blast up and around the vehicle instead of into the passenger seats. So far, by most accounts, it had been doing very well. I went up to a sergeant and asked if these RGs were part of the convoy heading to Sperwhan.

"They *are* the convoy," he said incredulously, looking me over. "We don't have tanks or LAVs [light armoured vehicles] to spare for escort duty! Hurry up and get your boxes strapped to the outside of them; use the bungees and rope already there, and then split yourselves up and get inside. Save the front seats for the *outgoing* OMLT guys." He quickly turned his attention to a young private, whom he started jacking up because his .50-cal (calibre) gun wasn't made ready yet.

I took his comments on the chin and didn't let his tone get to me. He couldn't see my rank, with my flak vest and tac (tactical) vest covering my chest insignia, and besides, I knew everyone there was getting short, meaning their tour was almost up. *Everyone just wants to finish their tour and get home.*

I passed on his instructions to my team, then we each picked an RG we felt would be the lucky one—the one that didn't get blown up on the way to our new base. We paired up and passed each other the green army boxes that held all of our earthly belongings and got them strapped to the truck, no easy feat considering its sides were twelve feet high. I reminded Fourneau to be extra careful with my box since it held all of my fine officer's china and silverware.

At the same time, I silently cursed Don and Jean, my beloved parents, for not letting me go to ninja camp in Japan every summer during grade school. "If you can pay for it, you can go," was their favourite comeback to my ceaseless requests. Because of their penny-pinching, I was forced to start my ninja training in Saskatoon, Saskatchewan, and that was only once I reached university. Far too late! I had needed to start my ninja mind tricks and phasing-between-walls training when I was a young child, before my medulla oblongata had fully formed. *Damn it, I can't even levitate yet!*

We "cleared customs" and slowly made our way through the concrete barriers that formed a serpentine path at the main gate, then quickly passed into the town.

I got my first good look at the Masum Ghar bazaar, the centre point for all of the villagers. As with most villages in Afghanistan, the beef and lamb shanks hung out in the air on hooks, directly in the hot sun, flies buzzing all around them. Children ran through the streets; shop vendors sold their wares under tattered awnings, trying to avoid the worst of the sun and heat but to no avail. Men haggled over prices, shouting at each other as though whoever was the loudest would automatically win the argument. It was business as usual at the busy market.

The male civilians were mostly wearing "man-jammies" by the looks of it; a long, loose-fitting tunic that flowed down to their knees, with sandals covering their feet. The men had on a variety of hats; some wore tight turbans, others wore knitted skullcaps. We could easily identify the women in the market, wearing their long burkas or ghost gowns, most in some shade of blue. They were covered from the tops of their heads to the tips of their toes.

We travelled west down Route Kelowna, passed an Afghan outpost called OP Mosque, then continued toward Sperwhan. I saw a small Afghan base—I guessed it was OP Brown—nestled on top of Route Brown. It looked like it had managed to survive only by the good graces of Timothy looking the other way.

Canadians had nicknamed the Taliban "Timmy" long before we ever arrived, and the name had stuck. "Timmy shot at us yesterday," or "Timmy tried to blow up our tank," and so on. I found the name a little too cutesy for an enemy who could be incredibly cunning and devious. To me, Timmy sounded too much like a freckle-faced, red-headed kid from down the block who drove your dad nuts because he liked to ride his bike over your lawn. No, for me, Timmy wouldn't do. So I went with "Timothy." Like the Vietnam vets had their "Charlie," I would have Timothy to contend with. And after I had spread the name around, I found out later it had really caught on and made its way up to some pretty high-up circles.

We swung south onto the start of Route Brown. This was the road that Major Speers had told me about, the single lane road connecting Sperwhan Ghar with Route Kelowna, coincidentally travelling over three culverts that regularly had some nice IED Kinder Surprises buried in them.

I looked out the window to the front and caught my first glimpse of Strong Point Sperwhan Ghar. It was a base situated around a very high man-made hill, and it clearly had excellent over-watch for kilometres in every direction. I was told later it had originally been built by the British some years back (many villagers and farmers, years later, were still trying to get money over land disputes because the base had been built on their farmland) and it was now occupied solely by Canadians.

We had a full company of mechanized infantry stationed there: a section of engineers and snipers, some intelligence (int) types, loggies (logistics), sigs (signals), at least four 155mm howitzer cannons with some mortars thrown in for fun, and a full-time doctor and medical team. Also, there was an American civilian from Florida and his bomb-sniffing dog. They went out on patrols and were on call twenty-four/seven. All in all, not a bad little outpost stuck in the middle of bandit country. It was currently owned and operated by the PPCLI battle group, but the battle group I would be working with, Task Force 3-08, would be taking over in the next couple of weeks. So far, the base had never been overrun, but the barbarians had definitely turned up at the gates from time to time.

"Sperwhan Ghar," the vehicle commander said. "Welcome to the Suck!"

Chapter 3

We passed through the concrete serpentine barriers and went by a wooden two-storey watchtower next to the barbed-wire emplacements by the gate. I could see two very disinterested Afghan National Army soldiers pulling back the wire to let us through and an equally bored Canadian watching us from the tower.

We slowly climbed up a twenty-metre slope until we were on a long plateau, now facing to the east. I could see several long, low concrete buildings, which I assumed were barracks for the Afghans, and a few sandbag emplacements dug into the hill along the sides of the road, facing back toward the west. That was the general direction most of the attacks had come from. Immediately off to the left, I could see two large Russian howitzer cannons, D-30s, nestled up close to a couple of the concrete buildings.

Our RG convoy again came to a dust-shrouded halt and our vehicles began quickly disgorging passengers. I clicked my voice pressel, or button, on the radio and thanked the RG crew for the lift.

"You can thank us by getting the fuck out! We gotta get goin'!" the commander snapped. *Fair enough.*

I got out and climbed up the side of the vehicle and grabbed my boxes, then carefully handed them down to Fourneau. I found his and passed them down to him; there was no point in both of us risking our necks. Everyone quickly stripped their boxes off the sides of the RGs. Clearly the RG convoy was manned by reverse vampires who had to get back to Masum before dusk. As it said in the American Ranger handbook, that's when the French and Indians liked to attack during colonial times; apparently Timothy had read the manual, took it to heart, and put the fear of God back into these soldiers.

I found the Wizard and Hetsa "the dirty Hungo" lugging their boxes in our general direction as several Afghan soldiers came out of their barracks to check out the newbies. Stephens walked up to us and said, "Welcome to your new home. We've left it in good shape for you, besides a few rocket holes, mortar holes, RPG [rocket-propelled grenade] holes—well, you know."

"Thanks for having us," I said with a smug grin. "It's a real pleasure to be here." I looked around and soaked up my new environs. Immediately to my front there were four more of those barracks-looking buildings, and another five or six farther down the road. The a/c in the RGs had done a good job; I'd forgotten for a few minutes how hot it was outside. My shirt started to get slick with sweat. Lugging two forty-pound boxes didn't help. Thankfully, I'd been on Op Massive, my PT (physical training) regimen for the last twenty years, to get ready for this moment.

"*Ah salaam ah'laikum.*" I said the traditional Muslim greeting to some Afghans who were watching us.

"*Wa ah'laikum salaam,*" several replied, in perfect unison.

Stephens led us past some ANA barracks and over to our building, right across from the OMLT HQ, where he and his boys hung their cowboy hats. We would be in a makeshift storage room until his crew moved out of their much nicer accommodation in a couple of days. Until then, we had a single large silver fan to keep us cool. No windows, no a/c. I had stayed in worse places, and so had the warrant, but judging by the looks on Fourneau's and Hetsa's faces, they were disappointed by our new digs. *It'll be good for 'em. Put some hair on their chests!*

We dumped our kit and then walked over to meet the outgoing OMLT team. I knocked loudly on their door and heard a "C'mon in," so we walked inside and immediately felt the nice cool air from their air conditioners on the walls going full blast.

"Hey guys," Stephens said, "let me introduce you to my band of killers." One guy was shirtless, cleaning his C9 (Minimi light machine gun) over at a table, and another guy who seemed quite a bit older was working on a computer. Stephens's youngest team member was playing an Xbox game in a comfy chair over by the TV. "This is Mike, Chris, and Joe," he said. They came over and we all shook hands.

"RCR in the Stan!" Chris said, "You guys'll have a hard time killing the Taliban, what with your daily show parades and fancy drill sessions on the main square three times a day!" *Ah yes…our reputation for immaculate parades precedes us.*

"Five times a day," I quickly replied. "But the Regimental Sergeant Major said we can cut them back to two, if we work extra hard to clean up your guys' mess and finally win the damn war!" I finished shaking hands and said, "We've heard that the PPCLI has cocked this little sweep-and-clear operation right up, so we're here to put things straight with our boot bands, spit, polish, and sharp drill! By the way, I like the OMLT fish hook on your door—I take it you guys have been used as bait a few times for Timmy?"

"Hmm," Stephens mused, "you could say that. I'll show you later, but I've got a set of orders from a battle group operation that states, 'OMLT will patrol forward with the ANA until they come under contact, then manoeuvre until the battle group can take over.' Nice, eh?" His team wasn't laughing. Clearly this had been the battle group's SOP a couple of times too many for the OMLT's liking.

Seven Two Alpha broke off to mingle with their opposite numbers as my counterpart showed me around the building. They had a pretty good set-up. Encrypted work computers in the corner; an entertainment centre; a bunch of bunk beds in the back, with Hessian sack hanging over them for privacy.

Stephens then took me outside for the full tour of Sperwhan. We walked past several rows of ANA buildings, including their kitchens and ablutions building. Whenever we passed any Afghan soldiers and said *ah salaam ah'laikum*, they would stop whatever they were doing to say hi back.

I looked at Stephens's travelling hobo look and asked, "Hey, what's with you guys with your shirts untucked and not wearing your trouser pants tucked into boot bands? We'd catch major flack if we tried that!"

"Screw that," he said, "We're OMLT. We dress to kill! Do you really think we have to follow the stupid battle group's dress code? To hell with that! Keeping your pants tucked into boot bands isn't going to win this war!"

"Brother," I said solemnly, "right now, you're facing the choir and preaching your sermon to the converted and the perverted. You need to do a one-eighty, and face the heathen in the pews! I'm already a believer, baby!" Finally, someone understood that boot bands weren't Canada's secret weapon that would win the war in eight weeks. I was always so hot anyway, the last thing I needed was to trap heat in my pants. I needed to vent, damn it!

I saw the Canadian artillery howitzers, or "boom-sticks" as I liked to call them, in the southeast corner and hoped I wouldn't need to use them. Then we walked by the showers and ablutions tent, where I was told we could shower once a day, for exactly one minute. The water for the showers was in huge bladders outside the tent, being heated by the sun. Stephens told me the gym was on the far north side, and as far as gyms in war zones went, it supposedly wasn't half bad. Some engineers had a shack attached to the main building, which contained the battle group soldiers' and officers' living quarters, as well as the HQ.

I tried to forget about my sticky armpits and the sweat dripping off my forehead and pointed out another building with a hand-washing station next to it. "I take it that must be the kitchen."

"Yep. Breakfast is zero-six hundred to zero-eight hundred hours, hot food and cereal. Lunch is cold food, sandwiches and subs, stuff like that. Supper is hot again, from sixteen-thirty to eighteen-thirty hours. Hand washing is obligatory."

"Do we have a hand-washing Nazi stationed here?" I asked.

"Yeah, sometimes, when the officers catch the men not using the stations, some numpty gets posted on Nazi duty. Over there you see an old-school hand pump for water. The ANA are allowed to take purified water from here, but they steal it at all times of the day and night, and they use up everyone's share, so every now and then we have to cut them off and force them to use the hand pump. They play the game until we give them our water, and then they do it all over again. It's never-ending."

He then led us into the HQ building and went over to a fridge by the door to grab us some Freezies. I looked inside a room to see how the battle group lived. They had large rooms with double bunk beds, and it seemed comfortable enough. Their weapons were left outside their rooms, along with their body armour and tac vests, which were placed on rows of wooden "t"s that looked like small crucifixes to dry out their gear after patrols.

Stephens continued to the end of the hall and knocked on the briefing-room door. We walked inside, and he looked over at one of the guys and said, "Sir, this is Captain Semrau, the RCR OMLT captain who'll be replacing me. He and his three guys just got in this afternoon." Stephens stepped aside so I could shake hands with the OC, the "officer commanding" Sperwhan Ghar.

"Hello," he said, not bothering to extend his hand, and barely looking up from the papers on the large map table in front of him. He was about my height, around five ten, but of slight frame, with a sort of distracted look about him. Clearly he was too busy to worry about being polite, but I supposed not everybody made it to the lofty height of major in the Canadian Forces because he won the Good Joe of the month award back in basic training.

"Hello sir," I said, extending my hand. He looked at me and then slowly walked over so we could shake hands. *Holy crap, I'm not going to rob you!*

"Hello," was all he could muster, again. An awkward silence filled the briefing room. *Was I supposed to say something? Wasn't it his job to say, "Welcome aboard, blah, blah, blah?"*

I walked over and introduced myself to his company sergeant major (CSM), who kindly asked if we needed anything from a PX back in KAF. He was going on a convoy run and offered to bring us back some gear. I knew that Hetsa, Fourneau, and I all wanted an American-style day sack with a CamelBak water carrier inside of it, so I gave him some money that I'd already collected from the boys and told the CSM thanks a lot.

"No problem, sir. My room's just across the hall; come and get me—day or night—if you need anything or got any questions."

"Great, thanks." I looked at the OC and said, "Goodbye, sir," as I walked past him toward the exit. He didn't respond. As the door closed behind us, Stephens clapped me on the back. "Well, that went well!" he said, smiling away.

"Oh, didn't you know? I'm the guy who wrote that Pulitzer Prize–winning novel entitled *I'm OK, You're an Idiot.* Everywhere I go, Stephens, I make friends and influence people to my way of thinking through the often-neglected consensus approach."

"Apparently," he laughed. "But I wouldn't worry about your *all-important* first meeting with the new OC too much."

"Well, I was a private once upon a time with the Brits, and I was like every other enlisted guy in the army: I developed a pretty good BS detector, and sussed out pretty quick who's going to come and help me when I'm wounded in open ground, and who's going to sit there and watch me bleed out!"

He then explained in detail how the snipers on top of the hill had repeatedly requested the authorization to fire on insurgents who were planting IEDs on Route Brown, but they were apparently denied permission by the major. It was a serious, ongoing issue, with no clear end in sight.

We walked back to our shacks where the warrants were already working on their handover. As the newbs, we had a lot of kit to sign for: the vehicle, all the heavy weapons, the shoulder-fired LAW (light anti-armour weapon) rockets, the ammunition, maps, computers, television . . . the list was nearly endless.

Stephens invited us to go outside the wire with them the next morning for our first handover patrol, and after establishing the times and particulars, I went back to my shack. Although it wasn't much, it was still a lot more comfortable than I was expecting. My first time in Afghanistan, we lived in a bombed-out school with no running water or kitchen, so my new accommodation was a major step up. Even if it didn't have a/c, we still had two hot meals a day and a shower, and a soldier couldn't put a price tag on that kind of luxury.

I opened the door and walked over to Fourneau and Hetsa, who were leaning over something in the open area of our new barracks.

"Look what I scrounged from the snipers, sir," Hetsa said, his face beaming in a toothy grin. He held up a large can of spray paint.

"What've you got there, sailor?" I asked as I came up to the kit they'd put on top of some milk crates. They had their personal weapons spread out next to all of their magazines. It looked like all of their mags had been debombed (the rounds taken out of them). Clearly I had interrupted them before they could spray-paint their kit. All of it. I could see a certain someone in our four-man team, the oldest and by far the saltiest member of our little band of brothers, losing his mother-lovin' mind over this!

"Boys . . . um . . . it looks like you've got some good old-fashioned Christian fun planned here, but . . ."

"What do you mean, sir, by *Christian* fun?" Hetsa interrupted.

"You know, Christian fun . . . the kind of fun where nobody gets hurt or pregnant. But I gotta ask ya—does the good warrant know we're about to spray-paint our kit? I mean, all of it? Because I can see him losing his nut over this! And I take it you've at least found some shade of khaki brown?" I didn't want to ruin their fun, but this was exactly the sort of thing a warrant would lose his mind over. It really did look like fun though. *I wonder. . . .*

"Yeah, it's khaki brown, sir. The snipers gave it to me; they said it won't last too long, it's not permanent or anything. And the warrant was there when we got it. He said it's fine, just don't overdo it."

"You said, '*we're* about to spray-paint' and '*our* kit,' sir. Does that mean you're going to join us?" Fourneau asked with a hopeful gleam in his eye.

"That's some good active listening, Fourneau. Well done, good catch. Why the hell not? I mean, it would be rude not to, right? Coming all this way and everything, and then walking around as though we were in Algonquin Park, dressed in forest green? Sure, I told you before, we live or die by each other, and that means we get in trouble together—as a team! Remember that time in Germany when you got busted for trying to solicit that male prostitute, and I had to speak Sauerkraut and explain to the Five-O that where you come from that's all well and good, and certainly not a chargeable offence?"

"No," Fourneau said, without hesitating for a moment. He didn't seem to get that I was joking.

"Well, I remember!" I said, "But that's neither here nor there. It'll look cool as hell! We'll call it 'combat paint,' and we'll spray-paint everything we've got! Besides, nothing makes a better shit shield than an officer! If someone gives you stick, you just say, 'Our officer told us to do it!' Now hand me the can!" This looked like a lot of fun. Hetsa handed me the can, and yep, there it was—"khaki brown." Although I couldn't see anything written on the can about how long it was supposed to last. I took my issued ballistic sunglasses off their spot on my shirt collar and quickly snapped out the protective lenses.

"Sir, I don't know about that . . ." Fourneau started to protest.

"Everything means just that, Fourneau. Ev-er-y-thing! Call sign Seven Two Alpha doesn't do anything by halves. We half-ass nothing! Like Homer Simpson once said, 'We use our whole ass!' Now go get your sunglasses and take the lenses out so we can spray-paint the frames! We'll be super cool, like the first kids on the block with an Atari 2600!" They both looked at me, either unsure of what an Atari 2600 was, or trying to decide whether I'd just given them an illegal order. They stood their ground, hesitating.

I looked at both of them and said, "Go on, git!"

I laid out my frames on the milk crate and gave them a good spraying down, making sure to get them from every angle. By the time Fourneau and Hetsa came back with theirs, I was already done. Fourneau looked them over and said, "Cool, that really worked!"

I looked at them with pride; my shades had gone from a dark forest green to a *combat cool* light brown. "I know. It looks awesome, eh? You guys crack on, and I'll go and get my kit."

We spent the next twenty minutes spraying down everything we had with combat paint splotches: our weapons and magazines, our sunglasses; I even covered the sight picture on my scope so I wouldn't get any paint on it, and then sprayed down its green rubber protective cover. *Much better.* I took off my black belt and gave it a couple of swipes of combat paint. By the time the warrant walked into our ad hoc spray-painting and chop shop, we'd gotten everything we owned combat-painted up. *Dy-nooo-mite!*

"Oh . . . my . . . *fuck!*" the warrant growled in disbelief. "What have you guys done?!"

"You said you were okay with it, Warrant!" Hetsa quickly protested.

"Yeah, but I also said, 'Don't rip the ass out of it,' and you guys have sprayed down everything you've got!" The warrant had nudged Fourneau and Hetsa aside so he could see the extent of our handiwork, and more importantly to him, assess the damage.

"Well, not quite everything," I interjected. "We haven't done the radios—I didn't think that'd be a good idea, and we haven't done our pistols yet." My smile slowly began to fade. *Crap, maybe we did overdo it. A bit.*

"For the love of God," the warrant shouted. "Don't spray down your pistols! You've done plenty enough!"

"I know, but check it out, Warrant. Seriously, how cool does that look? Check out the shades!" I said as I held them up, trying to impress him with my artistic spray-painting.

"Okay," he started to smile a bit. "I'll admit, that looks pretty cool . . . but seriously, guys . . ."

"Look, Warrant, we can sit here all day and debate semantics, or you can go grab your kit, and we'll help you give it a good ol' dose of combat paint!" I said, hoping he'd be game.

"Aw . . . fine!" The Wizard slowly walked off to his bunk, shaking his head, probably thinking to himself, *I can't leave the kids alone for a minute!*

Someone once said that the army was just like the Boy Scouts . . . except *without* the necessary adult supervision. Sometimes, like that day, the saying rang true. And although it may have seemed childish, moments that could lift up our morale were few and far between, so you had to take them or make them wherever you could. Morale in a war zone wasn't something illusory: it was a tangible, living entity, and you had to take precious care of it.

We finished off with our kit and did a combat re-org, getting everything laid out the way we wanted it. Under our beds, in our tac vests, in our day sacks, everything had to be organized just so. If we got "stood to" at 0100 hours, we had to know where everything was and how it was laid out. When we had finished helping the warrant, we walked over and had supper and relaxed for the rest of the evening, trying to come to grips with the brutal heat and choking dust.

That night, we said good night in the *Waltons* fashion, taking the piss as everyone wished each other a good night, pleasant dreams, and "don't let the bed bugs bite." I told the guys that if I started screaming in my sleep, they should just ignore me. If I continued screaming for more than a few minutes, they should throw a bucket of water on me. "But whatever you do, don't ever touch me to try and wake me up! For your own safety . . ."

I then suggested we start a new tradition. After we'd said our good nights, I would say, "This is who we are," and in unison they would say back, "So say we all." We tried it out and had a laugh, so we decided to make it a 72A tradition from then on. I always said *make war fun*, because I knew how scary this place could be, and how our morale was about to take a massive kicking from the constant grind of patrolling and facing one's own mortality. Because I had three previous tours under my belt, I knew how hard things were going to become, so I made it my personal mission to always try and keep our team's spirits high.

* * *

The next morning, before the patrol, I was sorting out my kit on the picnic table outside of our shack when the boys came out to join me. I looked at the guys' trouser pants tucked into their boot bands and feigned shock.

"What the hell, boys?" I asked, pointing at the warrant's trouser bottoms.

"What?" he asked, not sure where I was going with this.

"Don't you know? Boot bands are Canada's secret weapon. You can't patrol outside the wire with boot bands on! What if you're killed, or worse, captured, while still wearing your boot bands? Haven't you guys ever heard of OPSEC?"

Hetsa, always quick to stick it to the Man, said "Are you saying we don't have to wear our boot bands, sir?"

"That's exactly what I'm saying! We don't wear boot bands anymore, not outside the wire, not in Sperwhan proper. We're OMLT," I said, quoting Stephens. "We dress to kill! Now get 'em off, get 'em off! And if anyone gives you crap, you just tell 'em Captain Samrow said you don't have to play their game anymore!" I didn't have to tell them twice; even the warrant quickly shed his tight boot bands. We had a laugh, and sat back down on the picnic tables, waiting for our cowboy brethren from the PPCLI.

Well, do something productive, I thought to myself. "Let's do a PRR [personal role radio] check. I'll start," I said, all excited. It didn't matter what I said: only the four of us could hear me on the PRR. The warrant and I were the only guys on our team with radios that could communicate with the battle group.

"In today's news," I opened with, "the Human Torch was denied a bank loan." Whenever possible, we liked to quote from one of our favourite movies, *Anchorman*.

Hetsa joined in the fun. "I love Scotch," he said over his PRR. "Scotchy, Scotch, Scotch!"

Fourneau picked up the ball and ran with it, saying, "I have many leather-bound books, and my apartment smells of rich mahogany!"

Warrant Longview finished off with, "I don't know how to put this, but I'm kind of a big deal." We smiled at our cleverness and went back to being bored.

I got up and pointed my rifle toward the hill, the safest direction I could find, and made it ready, then made sure both of my weapons were on safe. As we were supposed to be mentoring the ANA, it wouldn't do for my weapons to accidentally go off. I had put some oil on them, but not too much; you didn't want too much oil that would soak up all the dirt and grime in a desert country. *Tended to jam one's weapon quite nicely.*

I then gave them the time off my watch, so we could synchronize our watches. My watch was based off of Stephens's time. We'd done the same thing the night before in the CP (command post), at my request.

The captain and his crew came out, seemingly very disinterested. I suppose it was all the same old bollocks to them, having done this a hundred times during their tour. We all greeted each other, then Stephens called me into his building and closed the door behind us as the others walked off to find the ANA.

"Look Rob, I'm not trying to jinx us and say the shit's about to go down or anything, but if bullets start whanging down range, I'll be in command of us. All of us. I know you're a captain too, but I'm the guy who's been here and . . ."

"Stephens, I read ya loud and clear. If the shit goes down, then I suggest you give all the reports and returns to higher HQ, and you can treat me and my boys like a crack team of Imperial stormtroopers just waiting to get sent off to the flank to start sniping folk! We'll be 'rifle section number three' and you can order us around. I'm not going to get into a pissing contest over who's in charge during a two-way range. You don't have to worry about me *or* my team . . . you just tell us what to do, and it's as good as done."

"Sounds good, thanks. I just wanted to make sure we're singing from the same song sheet. I'll call the CP and let them know we're heading out." I listened as he called it in, giving our estimated departure time, saying he expected there to be forty ANA and eight Canadians on the patrol, and giving our estimated return-to-base timing. The CP acknowledged and told him good luck.

We quickly found our guys in the open area behind the ANA buildings. Unfortunately, our little patrol was missing one important, *mission critical* asset—the Afghan National Army.

I realized Stephens's team and mine weren't on the same PRR channel so I asked which one they were on so 72A could switch over. I thought to myself, *That could've been bad.*

We waited ten more minutes until Stephens's 2 I/C said, "Here comes their recce element," and pointed over my shoulder toward the ANA buildings.

We turned around to see a lone ANA soldier walk slowly, methodically over toward us. He was wearing an old American, forest-green camouflaged uniform and carrying his AK on his shoulder and holding it by the barrel, as the ANA liked to do. He came to a full stop in the middle of the open area and just stood there, looking at the ground, extremely bored. After another five minutes, some more soldiers bumbled into the rendezvous (RV) point, and finally, their CSM arrived and started shouting at everyone to hurry up. Finally, their officer walked over, and Stephens introduced me to him.

"Captain Rob, this is Captain Ibrahim, the ANA First Company commander."

"*Ah salaam ah'laikum,*" I said, placing my right hand over my heart while saying *hello*, as I'd been taught by the Canadian Forces' Afghanistan cultural advisor (a scholar, I later learned, who hadn't been back to his home country of Afghanistan in the last twenty-odd years).

"*Wa ah'laikum salaam,*" he said back, touching his right hand to his heart as well. He called over a young, long-haired interpreter named Ali and began talking in rapid-fire Dari, the language of the ANA. Ali wore some old American pattern camo pants, a green American-issued helmet, and a maroon PPCLI T-shirt. He also wore a *shemag* around his neck, a type of Afghan scarf that he would use to hide his identity if he thought the Taliban were trying to sniff him out. Working for the coalition forces as an interpreter was a crime the Taliban considered punishable by death through torture.

"The captain says he is sorry for the late . . ." Ali searched for the proper word, "arrival. They thought the patrol was not starting until six-thirty."

"Please tell him that's fine. Are they ready to go now?" Stephens asked.

"Yes, he says they are ready now," Ali told us.

"Okay, Rob, stay with me; Warrant Longview, join Warrant Joe at the front. Mike and Chris, you guys take your opposite numbers. Okay boys, let's get this flying gong show on the road." He pressed his radio pressel and reported to the CP that our patrol was now leaving Sperwhan Ghar, as we slowly started walking to the west and then down the small slope to the lower level. I realized that once we were on the hill going down to the main gate, we were almost on even ground with the village, and anyone to the west of Sperwhan could see us leaving and then report our patrol's size and composition to Timothy. I asked Stephens about it.

"You're totally right," he said. "The moment we come down the slope, they've got eyes on us. I get my terps to carry an Icom-brand radio—I think they're out of Pakistan or something; sort of a cheaper version of a Motorola radio. But anyway, it's the preferred non-encrypted, two-way radio of choice for the Taliban. They use them everywhere in the Stan, and talk in the clear over them, so if you get your terp to listen in, sometimes Timmy shows you his hand and lets you know what he's doing."

"So you've got dickers in the village, watching you all the time?" I asked.

"Sorry, *dickers*?"

"Oh, sorry, 'dickers' is what the Brits call them. I mean 'spotters,' guys whose sole job is to monitor your movements and then report in to their higher HQ."

"I'll say it again, the moment we come off the plateau and start down the hill, they've got us clocked. You'll hear them talking about your patrol over their Icoms, all the time. They refer to the ANA as 'green Christians,' trying to insult them by calling them Christians, and of course we're the 'white Christians,' and terps are the 'little Christians.'"

"Nice. So they talk openly on their Icoms? Not too big on OPSEC?" I asked.

"No, they're lazy as hell. Sometimes they'll speak in code, you can task Ali to try and figure it out; they'll be talking about the weather for ten minutes, storm clouds, when the sky is actually clear. They know we monitor them, so sometimes they'll try and feed us disinformation—'We see them now, our ambush is ready,' crap like that. You shouldn't completely change your patrol plan, but you can't entirely ignore it either; because like I said, they're lazy, and they may actually be telling the truth about their upcoming plans."

"That's good advice," I said, "Thanks. So we stay next to the ANA captain and try and mentor him, and the warrants go with their CSM?"

"Yeah, we always stay next to the ANA captain, because obviously, that's who you're supposed to be mentoring. The warrant will be with the CSM if the ANA actually have a guy up front who knows how to navigate. Otherwise, your warrant and his fire team partner will be your nav [navigation] team, usually right up at the front. Believe me, you'll want an experienced Canadian up front helping them find their way around. Seriously, say you're in a village, or a field with high walls, and they can't see Sperwhan's hill anymore, suddenly they'll get all excited and worked up, thinking they're lost; but really, you're only a hundred metres outside the wire!"

We walked past the watchtower with the Canadian sentries, past a few ANA guards, and followed the road to the front of Sperwhan, winding our way through the concrete barriers. I looked over to my left and saw a small roofed building made entirely from sandbags.

"What's that?" I asked.

"That's where you'll place any UXO [unexploded ordnance] or IEDs that you find on patrol. Put them in there, let the guards at the main gate know, and then tell the CP to get the engineers to come down and BIP [blow in place] them. We've done it a couple of times."

Our column started to string out as the ANA split themselves into two groups, one on either side of Route Brown, heading north toward the culverts. The plan called for us to check out culverts one and two, then make our way east into the villages and have a *shura*, or chit-chat, with the village elders. The villages were supposedly fairly stable, and relatively free of Taliban interference, but you never let your guard down. *Always a first time.*

We marched down Route Brown and checked the culverts as we passed them, but they were clear. The sun was coming up and we could feel the heat under our helmets and the weight of our gear. Sweat began to trickle down my forehead.

The captain told his warrant up front to lead our patrol to the east, into a small village. We slowly meandered our way through the village, which was made up of about ten huts. Some kids were playing near the pathway and stopped to say hi to the ANA soldiers, who gave them some goodies.

"I didn't think we were supposed to give the kids candy," I remarked to Stephens.

"Usually we don't, but if there's only a kid or two, and we're not going to start a riot over the chocolate, then yeah, we can give out a few things. As long as the kids don't start following you and begging for more. Just make sure when you give it out that there's only a kid or two, 'cause they'll fight to the death over it if there's a group of 'em and you don't have enough for everyone." I nodded as I remembered some of the ugly things I'd seen before in Kabul.

He got out his map, checked his GPS, and radioed the CP, giving them our locstat (location and status). I checked my watch: it was almost 0700 hours and the sweat was really starting to pour out of me. I looked over at Fourneau, who looked like he wasn't sweating any more than if he was walking across the street.

"How you doing?" I asked him. "Staying topped up on water?"

"Good, sir. I'm fine. But how are *you* doing?"

Stephens overheard him, finished putting his map away, and came over to see The Incredible Sweating Circus Freak for himself.

"Holy shit! Are you all right?" he asked with a concerned look on his face. I'd seen that look on people's faces before, too many times to count. But I had fooled them all because I was still alive. I guess I just looked worse than I thought.

"Yeah I'm good—I have water-retention issues. I'll be all right. I just gotta drink enough water to supply a small village, that's all."

"Your shirt's soaked already!" he said, looking at my sleeves, which were already dark with sweat. "Okay, um . . . we'll go a bit farther and then try and find some of the elders to have a friendly chat," he quickly suggested.

"Don't change the plan because of me," I said, probably a bit more angrily than I should have. "I'm good, seriously; this is all very normal for me."

Stephens pressed his PRR radio pressel, so team members, but not the battle group CP, could hear him. "Warrant, go fifty metres farther and then come to a halt. I think we're almost at the village centre. We'll stop here and have a Lima November *shura*." He used the phonetic alphabet for *L* and *N*, meaning, in this case, *local nationals.*

We walked on a bit farther until he seemed to recognize a certain gate in front of a large compound. He walked up to it and gave it a good hard knock.

Several elderly males greeted him through Ali and asked us to come inside. Ali and I followed him in and I "watched his six," or covered him, as he discussed some issues with the village elders. I remembered Trevor Greene, the Canadian officer who had removed his helmet as a sign of respect during a *shura* and was attacked and axed in the head by a Taliban who almost killed him. The officer who gunned down the Taliban told us the story during our officer training, and it wasn't something you'd ever forget, so I stayed close to Stephens to cover him.

The elders were all wearing the Afghan male fashion statement: man-jammies—loose, flowing, one-piece shirts that came down to their knees. Stephens joined them as they sat down in the dirt to form a circle. I walked over and stood on the edge of the meeting so I could cover him properly and overhear the conversation.

He greeted all of them and then got right down to business, asking if they had any problems with the Taliban. Had any recent recruiters come through the village, trying to get fighting age males (FAMs) to join their cause? No, they all said collectively with much gusto, they hadn't seen any Taliban in these parts in years, certainly no recruiters. Obviously we thought their claim was highly dubious, but Stephens let it go and changed his angle of questioning.

"Has anyone in the village received any night letters lately?" he asked.

"No, no, there have been no night letters; the Taliban hasn't been in these parts for years," they replied through smiles that were missing a lot of teeth. Clearly that was the party line, and the village elders were doing their absolute best to seem convincing. The night letters were death threats the Taliban posted on people's doors, obviously at night.

It was a psychological operation they conducted: terrifying the poor villagers into thinking on any given night they'd be ripped out of their beds, put up against the nearest wall, and shot to death. "We're watching you. We know you ratted us out to the coalition!" or "We know your son works on the highway project; we're going to kill all of you!" Their intention was to sow terror, and it worked remarkably well. *It would work on me*, I thought to myself.

After talking back and forth for about fifteen minutes, Stephens called the village meeting to an end. He thanked the elders, reminded them to let us know if they needed help or if the Taliban was coming around, and then shook their hands and said goodbye.

We started patrolling back to Route Brown, when our terp, Ali, pointed out a young male who looked like he didn't belong to the village. The captain told the ANA to search him, but they did a terrible job. I pointed this out to Stephens, who said I couldn't search the guy again because I'd cause the ANA to lose face. He was right, of course, but I was worried any number of weapons or IEDs had gotten through the ANA's haphazard search.

Through the interpreter, Stephens asked the young fighting age male if he could conduct a GSR (gunshot residue) test on him, looking for traces of explosives or gunpowder on his beard or hands. He agreed, and the test quickly came back negative.

Unfortunately, Stephens chose to conduct the test right in front of a pen where a cow had been staked out to be impregnated by a randy bull, and we found ourselves blocking the locals' view of the live bovine sex show. Each hut and wall had several villagers perched on it, and they quickly became upset and began shouting at us to "get out of the way," and "down in front," only, of course, in Pashto. I thought it was pretty funny, but Stephens (who was near the end of his tour) experienced a total sense-of-humour failure and quickly stomped off.

I looked over at Ali and started laughing at the ridiculousness of the whole thing. *Good first patrol story,* I thought to myself. *Some guys get shot at; other guys have front-row seats for bovine coupling.*

We caught up to the captain and I changed the subject as I pestered him with questions the whole way back. He was incredibly patient and always took the time to answer them. We made it back to Sperwhan, he asked the ANA for their input on the success of the patrol, and then he thanked them for the good patrol. We split up and dumped our kit at our bed spaces and then gave our weapons a quick brush-down.

Thankfully the patrol had been a milk run (an easy patrol where nothing exciting happened), and it was just what we needed for our first trip outside the wire.

I asked the warrant and Hetsa if they felt there was anything we should know about their side of the patrol. The warrant seconded the captain's assessment that the ANA couldn't navigate to save their lives. I asked him if he and Hetsa were willing to stay up front with our ANA when they arrived and we started going on patrols.

"If they're anything like this group," the warrant said, "I don't see as though we'll have much choice. How was it for you guys, sir?"

I looked over at Fourneau and we both started smiling. "Well, Warrant, it was . . . a real journey of self-discovery. Wouldn't you say, Fourneau?"

"Oh definitely, sir."

Hetsa looked at us and clearly wanted to be let in on the joke. "Why, what happened?"

"You tell it, Fourneau," I said. "It's all too fresh for me. I don't want to relive it again, so soon."

So Fourneau told them they'd just missed the greatest show on earth because they were up front navigating, but he and I had had the best seats in the house.

The warrant cursed his bad luck and commanded, "Next time, call me back, and we'll get some pictures for the OMLT yearbook!"

* * *

With their last patrol ending on such a glorious high note, the PPCLI lads decided that would be enough for them. They'd been patrolling for the last eight months, so we all knew they had done their part, no two ways about it.

Stephens and I talked and mutually decided that from now on, it would be 72 Alpha's show. He offered to come and play guns if things got particularly hairy and we needed backup, but otherwise, 72A would start conducting daily patrols just as soon as enough of our ANA turned up. I was fine with that, and more than eager to get started.

The day after our auspicious first patrol, some of the ANA from the First Company, 72 Kandak, rocked up in their brown Ford Ranger pickup trucks and started off-loading their kit, just chucking it anywhere. I grabbed 72A and we went off to meet them.

I spotted a fairly tall Afghan, sporting the standard black beard, who seemed to be giving directions and barking out orders. Longview had gone off to find Ali to translate for us, and when they came over, I asked Ali to approach the ANA officer and introduce us.

"Captain Rob," I said to the ANA officer and placed my right hand over my heart. "*Ah salaam ah'laikum.*" While on tour around Afghanistan, I had decided to call myself *Captain Rob*, knowing that nobody pronounced my last name correctly anyway, and that *Rob* would be easier for everyone. The officer spoke to Ali and then shook my hand.

"He says his name is Lieutenant Aziz," Ali said, standing beside me. "He asks where his men are supposed to place their equipment."

"In this building right here, for a start. The outgoing ANA are moving out today, so there will soon be enough room for his men." I paused to give Ali time to translate. "Please ask Lieutenant Aziz how many men from the First Company will be arriving." I looked over at the warrant, Hetsa, and Fourneau, who were watching the ANA dump their kit all over the place.

"He says there will be one hundred and fifteen, maybe one hundred and thirty, if they find some of their men who have run away. In the next few days, there will be around fifty turning up. His OC, Captain Shafiq Ullah, will not be here until next week; he is still on leave. Lieutenant Aziz is the executive officer [the ANA used the American system of rank and titles for their companies] so he will be in charge until Captain Shafiq Ullah arrives. Another officer, Lieutenant Azmar, will be here later today."

"Great. Please tell him thank you, it was nice to meet him, and to come by for *chai* [tea] or coffee any time." Ali translated, we shook hands, and we walked off as the ANA began shouting at each other. I looked at the ANA and realized that the outgoing ANA were loading up steel bunk beds into the backs of their trucks, and the incoming ANA had just caught them red-handed. *Nice.* I could foresee massive fisticuffs over who gets the kitchen sink and who gets left with the dirty dishes!

I asked Ali over to my building for a friendly talk. Even in the late afternoon, and in a bit of shade, it was still stupid hot. I excused myself for a moment and walked into Stephens's building, going over to their fridge. I said hi to the boys. The Wizard was at the computer with Warrant Joe, and Fourneau was watching Hetsa and Mike playing an Xbox game. I grabbed two bottles of water and headed back outside to my interpreter.

"The ANA don't seem too keen to go out on patrols," I said, wiping the sweat from my forehead and the dust off my sunglasses.

"The truth is, sir . . ." Ali hesitated for a moment, unsure whether or not he should continue.

I saw the opening I'd been after ever since I'd met him, so I took it. "Ali, no matter what, you and I will always tell each other the truth. We must trust each other. You can tell me things, and I promise I won't repeat them to the ANA. I have to know what's going on here. I have to know the truth, or I can't do my job properly. In war, not being able to trust each other could get us all killed." I looked at Ali with a very serious expression, hoping he'd get my point.

"I understand, sir. Yes, I will always tell you the truth. It is like this, sir. I have worked with these ANA before and I know many of them are very tired. Lieutenant Azmar, the other officer who will be arriving, has been fighting since he was a small child; first against the Russians, now against the Taliban. They have seen many sad things. They have seen their friends killed very badly. Many of their families have been murdered by the Taliban. They *were* angry and mad, but after so many years of fighting, they are tired. They are worn...through?"

"Worn out."

"Yes, sir, they are worn out. And they are scared when they have to work with new Canadians. You have come here, and you want to find the enemy and kill him. But that puts everyone at risk. You, your men, and the ANA who are with you."

"That's the job, and my men and I accept those risks!" I said, not feeling too sympathetic. It was our mission statement, and I felt it was the only way we'd ever win this war. The Taliban didn't *want* to negotiate. They didn't want peace. They wanted the Afghan national government's unconditional surrender, and then they wanted to set up their daily beheading schedule at the soccer stadium again.

"Yes, sir, that *is* the job. But many of them do not want to do it anymore. They just want to live. They do not want to take risks, they do not want to die. They have a good wage, very good for Afghanistan, and they just want to do the bare..."

"Minimum."

"Yes, and survive. That is all. They are afraid that you are new here, you will not understand what they have been through, and you will get some of them killed, and then you get to go home. But they are still here." Ali looked at me apologetically, as though he had said too much.

I thought for a long moment and then said, "Yeah, I think I get what you're saying, Ali." *That made sense, from an Afghan perspective, I suppose.* "Well, if they ever ask you, you can tell them I said this: 'Captain Rob will never ask *them* to do something that *he* will not do. When they go to find the enemy and fight, he will be right there beside them, the whole time, taking the same risks they are.' I want peace for this country, Ali. I don't want to come back here again. I want you and your family to live in a country where you can do what you want, say what you want, and *be* what you want to be. That is what all of us are here for, to help your country get to that point. But we have to find and stop the Taliban first, or there will never be peace here. It will be civil war, all over again, with no end in sight. And Ali . . . I want to live *too*! I have a beautiful wife and an incredible baby girl who I want to see again."

No one ever accused me of being the world's brightest guy, but I could see what he meant. They'd been at this a lot longer than me, and when I left, they'd still be here. That is, of course, *if* they were still alive.

No benefits were paid to their families if they were killed. They didn't get any compensation for limbs lost in the line of duty. No insurance was ever paid out; in fact, their families wouldn't even get any help with the funeral costs.

I thanked Ali for the talk and sat in the hot shade, thinking to myself, *How am I supposed to mentor soldiers who don't want to fight anymore?*

Chapter 4

The next morning everyone continued their handovers, eager to wrap the long process up. The warrants kept signing over paperwork, while Hetsa and Fourneau met with their opposite numbers to figure out what their jobs entailed in Sperwhan. I went with Stephens to the major's battle update briefing (BUB) and met all of the outgoing officers. We listened as the major and his int sergeant briefed us on the last twenty-four hours of activity in our area of operations.

Later that morning, Stephens and I talked over a large map on the wall of his OMLT shack. He showed me where they'd been almost slaughtered in a three-sided Taliban ambush west of the base. Several ANA were immediately wounded, so everyone had to pull back, and they were chased all the way back to Sperwhan. Then they got engaged by the ANA quick reaction force, which arrived in trucks and confused the Canadians and ANA with the Taliban. The ANA QRF fired on them, but luckily, no one got hurt.

It was a harrowing story, and to hear it first-hand from the commander on the ground brought chills to my spine. They were incredibly fortunate, and they knew it. Ever since that day, their ANA had refused to patrol to the west, past the 29 Easting on the map. The "29 Easting" (a line on the map labeled "29") started to take on a mythical importance to the ANA; it was like their maps were labelled, "There be dragons!" Forever after that ambush, the ANA refused to cross that line on the map, for fear of suffering a repeat performance.

I was sharing the story with Warrant Longview over lunch when a runner from the CP sprinted up to us and wanted to know if we were the new OMLT team on the ground.

I said we were, and he quickly informed us that snipers had just seen someone plant an IED in the middle of Route Brown, only a few minutes ago.

I wondered aloud why Timothy hadn't had the top part of his head shaved off by the snipers and then I answered my own question. *Let me guess…they weren't allowed?*

"They requested permission to fire, sir, but by the time the major was found and started asking the snipers questions over the net, Timmy had finished and packed up. Can you come with me, sir, to the CP? The OC Major Bane wants to brief you."

"Crom's bones, man," I snapped, "There's no time for that! We're men of action, and enough time has been wasted as is! Isn't it obvious what we've got to do? Cordon off Route Brown to stop any civvies from blowing themselves up, and then go and kill or capture Timothy! We'll go and mobilize our ANA and get out there, ASAP. Tell Major Bane to push us the engineers and then sit back and enjoy the show!"

I turned and started jogging back to our shack, hoping the warrant was following me. Longview jogged up and slapped me on the back and said, "Well said, sir. We can sit around here and talk to death, or we can go kick some ass!"

"Roger that, Warrant. This isn't the time for committee—groupthink—this is the time for unilateral, decisive action! Get the boys kitted up and I'll meet you at our wank pits. I'm going to get Ali so we can assemble the Justice League." With that, I ran up to Ali's door, knocked rapidly on it, and told him to grab his helmet and body armour and follow me, quickly. He grabbed his kit and we jogged over to Lieutenant Aziz's building, right next to ours. He was outside, watching the rest of my team as they ran past him and into our building, his dark beard probably hiding a confused look on his weathered face.

"Lieutenant Aziz, I know you said you would be ready to go on patrol tomorrow, but we need some of your men right now. They think the Taliban have just planted an IED on the main road, not far from here, and we have to go now before any villagers get hurt by the bomb." Ali was translating as I was still speaking. *Damn, he's good at that.*

Aziz seemed to think it over quite seriously and then said, "I will come with you and bring fifteen of my soldiers."

"That's great, thank you. We need to leave in the next five minutes. Can you and your men be ready?"

"Yes, of course."

"Okay, I'll meet you right here. Ali, go back to your room and get your helmet and vest on and then wait for me here. Oh, and say your prayers!" I turned and ran the fifteen feet to my building. Stephens popped his head out of his shack.

"What's going on?" he asked.

"IED on Route Brown, we're going to cordon it off."

"Good luck," and with that, he turned to close the door.

"Thanks." *It's our show now, and by the mighty Ganesha's trunk, Timothy ain't gonna know what hit 'im!* I ran inside to my bed in the back corner and grabbed my kit. I had it all laid out, for just this sort of emergency, and was kitted up in under thirty seconds. "Dress me, Hetsa!" I said, turning around so he could clip up my tac vest.

"All right boys, here's the plan. Basically, Lieutenant Aziz is coming with fifteen ANA; it's not enough, but it'll have to do. Remember, the snipers have been right every time, so we trust their judgement [*Unlike certain other people*, I thought to myself]. We know Timothy's out there, so stay switched on and watch each other's six. We'll *didi mau* close to the IED, get the snipers to guide us near it, then get Aziz to put his men in some semblance of a cordon, hopefully around the IED, not on it! The battle group will then push out some LAVs and the engineers to us. Questions?" I looked into their eyes, but they were good to go.

"Negative, sir. Let's do it," Longview said.

Hetsa shouted, "Dress me, sir!" and raised his arms and spun around so I could get his clips. I snapped them in and my Para training took over as I slapped him on the shoulder and shouted, "Four, okay! All right, PRR check." I clicked the team pressel and said, "Red five, standing by!"

Longview said, "Red six, standing by," a big grin on his face. Men like him were called from on high to be soldiers.

"Red seven, standing by," Fourneau said, looking a bit grim.

Hetsa, however, was all smiles, "Gold leader, standing by!"

"Ya had to ruin it, didn't ya?" I asked. I didn't want to tell him that at the end of *Star Wars* Episode IV, Gold Leader was killed in action. "Okay, let's get this flying gong show on the road." I led us outside, and the second I cleared the door I chambered a round, making my rifle ready to fire as I whispered, "Sing for me, baby!" and then slung it around my back so I could make my 9mm gat of justice ready to fire. We walked over and saw Lieutenant Aziz getting into his kit while Lieutenant Azmar (the newly arrived third-in-command officer) simultaneously helped him and shouted at some nearby ANA. I nodded at Aziz to let him know the Canadians were ready as we walked past him toward the open area. I radioed the CP, whose call sign was "two" on the battle group network, or "net" for short. "Two, this is Seven Two Alpha, radio check, over."

"Two, reading you loud and clear, over."

"Seven Two Alpha, roger, our call sign is figures zero four Canadians, figures one six Alpha November Alpha; we are heading to the main gate now, over." I grabbed Ali by the shoulder, looked him in the eye, and said, "Stay right next to me, the whole time. Don't wander off. If anything happens, get into cover and stay down, okay?"

"Yes, sir," he said, coming up alongside me. I knew he'd seen a lot of combat with Stephens's OMLT team and was good to go. *Or was he tired and sick of it all too?*

The command post cut in and said, "Two, roger, Seven Two Alpha is four times Canadians, one six times Alpha November Alpha, over."

"Seven Two Alpha, roger, out to you." I knew the snipers would be monitoring the battle group net so I radioed them, as well. "Six Six, this is Seven Two Alpha, has there been any recent activity at the IED, and where is it located? Over."

"Six Six, negative, no activity; it is located in the *middle* of Route Brown, between culverts one and two, over."

"Seven Two Alpha, roger, pretty ballsy of 'em! How many FAMs planted the device, and what was the nature of the device? Over." Aziz was corralling his men, and our two groups started walking quickly past the sandbag emplacements toward the sloping hill to our west. Some ANA were sent back to their buildings by the ANA sergeant major to get missing kit like their helmets, while others ran out to join us.

I spoke out loud so the group would hear me. "Remember that once we crest this hill going down, they've got eyes on. They'll know that we know that they know we're coming! Fourneau, say that five times fast!" I said, hoping to cheer him up. Judging by the dour look on his face, I thought that Phobos, the ancient Greek god of fear, was probably creeping around in the shadows of his mind, ready to pounce.

The sniper spoke confidently over the net. "Six Six, three times FAM, headed west, lost sight of them, no weapons seen. They planted what looked like a large howitzer shell in the middle of the road, over."

"Alpha, roger that, three times FAM planted howitzer-type IED between culverts one and two and then headed west. Any civilians in vicinity of device? Over."

"Six Six, negative, no civilian activity, no activity *period* near the device, over."

"Alpha, roger, keep us advised, over."

"Six Six, done and done, over."

"Alpha, cheers big ears, out to you. Two, this is Seven Two Alpha, over."

"Two, send over."

"Alpha, departing the wire at the front gate now, figures five mikes to reach the suspect device, over." I turned to my men. "Warrant, you and the dirty Hungo head off with those guys on the right; Fourneau 'the Fornicator' and I will stay on the left with the good lieutenant." They quickly jogged over to join the ANA speed marching down the ditch. In their eagerness they marched past the ANA in the lead, so now they were the first troops to cover the ground. *Not good. What did I say about letting the ANA go first?* I spoke over the PRR net. "Warrant, that ditch hasn't been cleared, let the ANA go first, just point them in the right direction, then fall in behind them."

The warrant responded, "Roger, sir," and although he didn't sound impressed with me, he slipped to the side and signalled the ANA to pass him and Hetsa as Aziz led our ten-man group into the ditch on the left of Route Brown. I stepped out of line and scanned through my three-times magnification rifle scope. I could see down the ditch only to my front, not to the west, because there were too many high walls and trees. *Nothing in front of us.* No activity of any kind. *Timothy could easily pop over the walls to our left and give us an old-school pasting before we'd even know what happened. Keep an eye on it and crack on.*

I quickly spoke to Ali, who looked like a child soldier now that he was wearing his armoured vest and helmet. I asked him to tell Lieutenant Aziz what was going on. Then I remembered that Fourneau could hear only my side of the conversations I had with the battle group CP, so I quickly explained to him what was being said over their net. *Knowledge Dispels Fear* was the motto of the RAF instructors who taught me how to jump from planes, and they were right. If I was in Fourneau's shoes, I would've wanted my officer to keep me in the loop.

We marched quickly toward the first of the culverts. I pressed my PRR button and said, "Easy Warrant, I think you're coming up to it. See if there's a pathway going off to the east towards the ville that you could task a couple of ANA to block."

"Roger, sir," he responded, looking to his right.

"Six Six, this is Seven Two Alpha, are we almost there? Over."

"Six Six, roger. Your first ANA are just coming up to it ... now, over." *If the Taliban know we're on to them, they'll probably blow it any second now.*

"Seven Two Alpha, roger. Any activity to the west? Over."

"Six, negative, you're all clear, over."

"Seven Two Alpha, this is Two-niner, over." Major Bane's voice cut in.

"Seven Two Alpha, send over."

"Two-niner, we are sending you a QRF platoon with LAVs and engineers. Cordon off the device and stand by, over."

"Seven Two Alpha, roger, over."

"Two-niner, out."

Well that was some good news. The LAVs would act as a strong deterrent to anyone wanting to have a go at us, and the 'geers would take care of the IED.

But the major cut into my transmission with call sign Six Six. I had to let the snipers know that I had heard their last transmission. "Six Six, this is Seven Two Alpha, I ack [acknowledge] your last, over."

"Six, roger out."

I spoke over the PRR and briefed Fourneau and Hetsa on the major's update, then asked Ali to tell Lieutenant Aziz about the plan. I looked at Aziz—he didn't really seem to know what was going on. Surely he'd done hundreds of cordons before. *That's all we ever did in Northern Ireland. In this place? I bet he's done a thousand!*

"Ali, please ask Lieutenant Aziz where he would like to place his men to form the cordon." Ali quickly translated.

"He does not know what you mean, sir."

Okay ... "Well, I recommend he places his men all around the device. Someone at the twelve o'clock position, someone at three o'clock, six, nine . . . you know. We need to put up a protective cordon around it and make sure no one goes in toward it. We need to block the roads. Please explain that to him." Fourneau and I looked at each other, not really sure what to make of it all.

Ali then asked me, "He would like to know, where do *you* think they should go?"

"Well, uh, like I said, I would recommend that he places his guys at the twelve, three, six, and nine o'clock positions, but I recommend that . . ."

The sniper quickly spoke over the net. "Alpha, Six, be advised, you've got . . ." I looked at the road.

"Hey, you! Stop! DON'T GO NEAR IT!" I shouted at one of the ANA who had casually walked right up to the spot where the IED was buried. I guessed he was eager to shed mortality's oppressive yoke. "Ali, tell him to get the hell away from it!" I radioed the warrant, "Wizard, muckle on to that idiot before he gets us all killed!" I couldn't believe what I was seeing. I owed the snipers a courtesy call for their timely heads-up. "Six, Alpha, thanks, over."

"Six, can't take the children anywhere, be careful, out."

Warrant Longview called the soldier toward him, but remained ducked in the ditch so that if Timothy decided to blow the IED, the blast would hope-fully pass over his head. Lieutenant Aziz ripped into his curious soldier from twenty metres away and gave him a healthy verbal ass-kicking, right in front of everyone. Then he looked at the sloppy, haphazard arrangement of his men and began barking orders until they began fanning out. This wasn't quite how it looked in the IED manual, but so far, we didn't have any curious civilians to deal with (only dangerously curious ANA), so I hoped our luck would hold.

"Sir, the two ANA on our side of the ditch seem to have found something." Fourneau pointed at two ANA about ten metres north of us. I told Ali to let Aziz know and said, "Let's go," to Fourneau as I started walking toward the curious soldiers.

Some trees about twenty metres away had been blocking our view to the west and northwest, but as we came even with them, I could make out a large, two-storey compound about two hundred metres away to the northwest, and what I saw there made my heart start pounding. I didn't want to waste time asking Longview and the snipers, so I radioed the snipers only, knowing the Wizard would hear me over his radio. *Ah, this is not good . . .*

"Six Six, Seven Two Alpha—do you see a kite flying from the top of a two-storey compound, approximately figures two zero zero metres, at five eight zero zero mils [on the compass] from my position? Over." I looked through my scope toward the compound, knowing the warrant would be doing the same thing. "Fourneau, follow my rifle barrel and check out that compound, two hundred metres away to our northwest. Do you see a kite, and a FAM wearing a white *shemag* over his head and face?"

This was going from bad to worse. People in Afghanistan, at least in the villages away from Kabul, didn't fly kites. The Taliban still considered it one of their deadly sins, and if they got word that someone was flying a kite, they'd come and pay him a visit. And wearing a *shemag* over his face? *Dodgy as hell.*

"Yeah, sir, a white kite . . . can't see who's holding it." (The sniper started talking loudly into the radio earpiece in my left ear as I tried to listen to Fourneau with my uncovered right ear. "Seven Two Alpha, Six Six, roger, white kite and single FAM on rooftop wearing a *shemag*, no weapons seen, will observe and advise, over.") Fourneau was still talking—". . . and a FAM with a *shemag*, ducking behind the top of the wall on the compound. No weapons yet."

I spoke to Fourneau. "Okay, thanks. Keep your eye on them, all right?"

"Six, Alpha, roger, that's what we've got too. Keep us posted. Out."

I knew the CP would be tracking the new information. I called Ali closer to me and asked, "Ali, young guys wearing *shemags*—is that normal for around here, covering their faces like that?"

Ali looked very grave. "No, sir, that is not normal. That is not good." He quickly turned and started speaking with Lieutenant Aziz, who looked equally disturbed by what Ali had just told him. Aziz started speaking quickly over his American radio to Lieutenant Azmar, back at Sper (Sperwhan).

Longview's voice came over the PRR. "Sir, Warrant, yeah, we got 'em too. We'll keep eyes on 'em from over here."

"Thanks, Warrant. You ready to set the new 72A sniping record?"

"Do you really need to ask? Born ready!"

"Sir, it looks like they found a wire," Fourneau said, bringing my attention back to the ANA on our side of the ditch. Fourneau and I quickly walked up to the two soldiers and saw one of them holding a thin black string in his hand. He dropped the string and they walked a few paces down the trench, toward the west.

I quickly realized it wasn't an electrical wire that could carry a signal to the IED howitzer shell to make it detonate, so whoever planted the device must've attached the string to a rudimentary pull switch, and they would likely detonate it by giving it a big tug. I called over Aziz, who walked up, clocked what I was talking about, nodded a few times, and then (before I could say or do anything to stop him) quickly pulled out his combat knife and deftly cut the string. *GEEEWWWW!*

I involuntarily flinched, knowing that we were still danger close to the IED, but more importantly, I also knew that many IEDs had an anti-handling device that would detonate the explosives the moment some jackass cut the cord attached to it! Again, this wasn't quite how we were supposed to deal with these sorts of things (those actions were the sole domain of trained coalition engineers), but I secretly thanked Aziz for doing what he did when, after a few seconds, nothing happened. Complete silence.

I followed the string to the west, from where it seemed to originate. The Taliban hadn't even tried to bury it, and in their haste to plant the bomb, they left the string lying out in the open, resting on the dirt trail. The string ran through the middle of a steep V-shaped ditch, between two high grape-field walls. I followed the string toward a high wall that ran perpendicular to us, fifty metres away, where it seemed to run up to a man-sized hole in the wall. The two ANA soldiers facing the wall shouted something in Pashto toward the wall, and then time slowed down, stroboscopic style, as we all began turning around to see what he was shouting about.

CRACK CRACK!

We all flinched and spun around, bringing our weapons to bear as the ANA soldier cracked off two rounds. *Are we in contact? Why was he shooting? Who was he shooting at?* I followed the direction of the soldier's barrel and saw what looked like a wisp of cloth as it disappeared out of sight behind the wall. Fourneau and I found the nearest cover, out of the firing line of the trench, as I shouted at Ali, "Get behind me," because he hadn't budged, he was still out in the open. He slammed into the wall next to me.

"Ali, ask them what they were shooting at." We weren't receiving any incoming fire, *yet.*

They had a quick talk and Ali said, "He says they saw two FAMs standing in the hole in the wall, holding the string. They ordered them to come and talk to us, but they turned and ran away. They were not wearing shoes, so he shot at them."

"What's not wearing *shoes* have to do with it?" I had to hurry. When shots were fired, you had to let everyone know what was going on, ASAP. Rightly so, folk tended to get a wee bit interested.

"Sometimes the Taliban do not wear shoes, because shoes are expensive, so if they do not wear shoes, it is because they are going to run away. It is a . . . suspicious thing, sir. So that is how the ANA knew they were Taliban," Ali explained.

"Okay, Ali, tell them good job and to get into cover."

Shots being fired—incoming or outgoing—were an attention-seeker's dream, because suddenly the spotlight was all on *you,* but I couldn't send up the proper radio contact report, because technically, we weren't *in* contact—the ANA had only fired warning shots. *Technically.*

I had enough TI (time in) to know that if I said *contact* on the radio, the whole coalition world would suddenly get very interested. Then one of our soldiers who was fighting farther down the road, who really *was* in a full-blown contact, would watch impotently as his desperately needed assets (like unmanned aerial vehicles—UAVs) got rerouted to me. And so far, no one had shot back at us. *How do I play this out on the radio?*

I took a deep breath, so I wouldn't sound panicky, and calmly said, "Charlie Charlie," over the radio, using the call sign for every friendly in the area to listen in. "Seven Two Alpha, two times FAMs holding IED initiating wire have fled to the west. The ANA have fired warning shots, *only* warning shots, we are NOT in contact at this time, I say again, we are NOT in contact at this time. Six Six, do you see any FAMs fleeing to the west? Over."

"Six, negative, the grape-field walls are obstructing our view, will continue to observe, over."

"Alpha, roger, any activity in the compound? Over."

"Six, roger, now figures three FAMs on the compound roof, one wearing a *shemag*, over."

"Alpha, roger, out."

Just then, the two ANA nearest me, the shooter and his surprised friend, got their blood up and decided to charge down the "V" trench, following the string to the hole in the wall where Nice-Shootin' Rasputin had just tried to perforate the triggermen.

My "Sergeant Rock combat antenna" went off big time and began screaming a warning klaxon in my head. *This isn't right, they're setting us up. They wanted us to find the wire, that's why it's black and not buried, they wanted us to see the three scrotes, they turned and burned, hoping we'd give chase!*

Am I getting gun-shy in my old age, or am I right? I looked at the end of the trench, at the hole in the wall, and saw a head peeking up over the berm at us. Someone was still there, waiting. But waiting for what?

Waiting for us, dickhead! To give chase, and then once we're all running down the trench toward him, he can swing a PKM (Russian light machine gun) over the wall and perforate us!

My brain raced. If he opened up on us, we couldn't escape over the walls—they were too high. He'd have us in perfect enfilade, firing bursts down the entire length of us, and we'd be helpless. The only place we could run would be either toward him, but he'd still be over fifty metres away, or back the way we came, and he'd shoot us all in the back.

They launched the kite as a signal, to tell the three guys at the wall that we're coming and to get into position, to let themselves be seen. Admiral Ackbar's accented voice shouted in my head, *It's a trap!*

Oh, no… "Stop, Stop! Ali, tell them to stop!"

Ali shouted at them and they came to a screeching halt, looking back at him to explain.

"Ali, tell them to get out of the ditch and over to the sides. Someone is still there, waiting on them to give chase. Tell Lieutenant Aziz that I've seen a guy on the other side of the wall, waiting for us. Why would someone be waiting there? Why didn't they bury the string? When do they ever make it that easy for us, unless they *want* us to find it and give chase!" Ali quickly translated for the ANA soldiers and Aziz.

Aziz quickly spoke to Ali, who said, "He agrees with you, and thinks that you are right. Thank you for stopping his men; surely it is an ambush. We will wait here, for now."

"Tell him thank you, and I think he's doing the right thing—we should wait here for a few minutes. The LAVs will be here soon; they can cover us as we take a different route toward the wall."

I pressed the PRR pressel, "Warrant, Red five. We just found a Taliban come-on, but we didn't buy what they were selling." I explained over our team net what had just happened and the warrant said he wasn't sure if I was right.

"You forget, Warrant, the Force is unusually strong with this one! I'll tells ya what. If the 'geers come and dig out the howitzer shell, and it's a dud, or a smoke shell, I'm totally right, and you owe me fifty bucks! The Taliban aren't going to set up a come-on by using a real IED—they wouldn't waste it. No, it'll be smoke or inert. Stand by to eat some crow hair pie! Fifty bucks!"

"We'll see. Here come the cavalry," he said. I looked toward Sper to see four LAVs and a Bison armoured vehicle racing our way.

"Seven Two Alpha, Two. Four times LAVs and engineer Bison on Route Brown now, coming to you, over."

"Alpha, seen, over."

"Two, roger, out."

I walked out of the ditch and up onto the road where they could see me, crossed my arms in front of my face, signalling a stop so we could talk face to face. I really didn't have much time on the LAVs; I had only been in the armoured behemoth two or three times since my phase four officer training. *Was that the right signal? Or was I telling him to speed up? Maybe I'll just step over to the side a bit....*

As effing always, they raced right up to me and then came to a grinding halt, burying me head-to-toe in a tidal wave of dust. *Assholes!*

One of the platoon commanders I'd met the day before at Major Bane's BUB, a guy called Reggie, hopped out of the LAV turret and clambered down toward me. I saw an engineer sergeant walking toward us from the Bison at the rear of the convoy. "Hey Rob, whaddya got?" he asked, noting the new coating of dust I'd just received, as he tried (unsuccessfully) *not* to smile.

Everyone's got a limit, and I had reached mine. "First off, tell your driver if he ever does that again, I'll kick his fucking teeth in!" I wasn't laughing. The old leave-'em-covered-in-dust PPCLI routine was getting a bit old.

"Sorry about that. So, what's going on?"

I waited a few seconds until the sergeant joined us and then suggested we move behind the LAV so that it could serve as a shield between us and the suspected IED. We shifted behind the steel cover and I briefed them on the last ten minutes of my life. Suddenly artillery fired over our heads, making all of us violently flinch. I looked over Reggie's shoulder at Sperwhan, but couldn't see the guns. It sounded like a freight train going "mach chicken" only five hundred metres over our heads to the north. Clearly, someone was about to get the good news.

"TIC [troops in contact] near FOB Wilson," Reggie said, with the same bored look most of the outgoing guys carried on their faces. "Some of our guys just got ambushed. Choppers are en route. They're in the shit, big time."

"Well, our light fandango is nothing compared to that," I said, and then pointed out where I thought we still had a dicker/shooter watching us from behind the wall to the west. Then I briefed them on the string and pointed out where the snipers thought the IED was buried.

"Holy shit, who cut it?!" the engineer angrily asked, holding up the severed string.

"Take a SWAG [scientific wild-ass guess], Sergeant. I know better than that. My friends over here," I nodded toward the Afghans, "not so much."

"Well . . . um . . . see that they don't do it again!" was all he could muster.

"How do you say 'no promises' in Pashto? Well, do your thing, we'll plug our ears and cover you . . . from over here. Break a femur!" I said, slapping him on the back. I had nothing but respect for IED/UXO bomb-disposal guys. They were batshit crazy, no two ways about it. I'd only ever de-mined a culvert once as an assault pioneer in Kabul, and I never wanted to do it again. Longest hour of my entire life!

I looked over at Fourneau and shouted, "Anything going on?"

"Negative, sir," he shouted back. "No movement by the wall or at the compound. But the kite has been lowered."

"Figures. Thanks, Fourneau. Stay frosty!"

The engineer sergeant went back to his Bison and started collecting his gear. Warrant Longview and Hetsa walked over to our group, and the Wizard gave me a big smile.

"Fifty bucks, eh? You sure you can afford it, what with your new baby and all?" he asked.

"You know me, Warrant, I'm like Fred Flintstone—bet . . . bet . . . bet, *BET, BET, BET!*" I said as I shook him by the shoulders.

We had a good laugh as the tension of the last few minutes slowly bled out of our systems. I asked Hetsa to go keep Fourneau company as he covered our western flank.

"Thank God they stopped," I told the warrant and Reg, meaning the ANA, who had been about to give chase down ambush alley.

Before they could say anything, we heard a Ranger truck horn blaring angrily behind the Bison at the back of the convoy. Reg, the Wizard, and I peeked around the LAV to see what was going on. I grabbed Lieutenant Aziz and Ali and started to walk past the row of LAVs toward six or seven ANA Ranger trucks, with the lead vehicle's horn blaring away. *How terribly rude.*

Aziz walked up to the lead truck and gave the driver a blast of crap. The driver quickly pulled his hand away from the horn, but beyond that, seemed fairly unrepentant.

Aziz spoke with Ali, who then turned to me saying, "He says they must get by. They have to be in Masum Ghar before night. They must pass. We must move out of the way to let them pass."

"I take it these are the outgoing guys?" I asked Ali, as the ANA driver shot me a stinkeye from hell.

"Yes, sir, they are Captain Stephens's ANA, and they really want to leave."

"Yeah, I gathered that. Please ask them to stop honking, and to sit there for a minute. I'll be right back."

The engineer was standing next to us at his Bison, getting his kit all laid out, ready to do his job. "Hey, Sarge," I said. "I know you just got here, and I don't want to rush you, but how long do ya figure?"

"Shit, sir, no way of knowing that. Screw 'em, they'll just have to wait like everybody else!"

"Okay." I looked over at the ANA convoy. It would soon be last light, so they really did have to get going soon. *What to do…*

I realized that we couldn't move the Canadian vehicles into the ditch so that the ANA could pass; if they rolled over, everyone inside would be crushed. Besides, there was a reason the Canadians were on the road. They had an elevated position so they could engage the enemy from farther out and hopefully kill him long before he could get close enough to kill us. And if they moved, the ANA in the trucks would drive right over top of the IED.

This would make a good training scenario for back home.

Reggie walked over and said, "Hey, just tell them to hold it. Just *order them* to sit still and wait!"

I looked around to make sure he was saying *order them* to me, and not to Aziz. *Nope, he meant me.* I leaned over and whispered to Ali, "Don't translate this for Lieutenant Aziz." Ali quickly nodded, smart enough to know this wasn't a conversation we wanted Aziz privy to.

"Reggie," I sighed, "I can't order them to do jack shit. OMLT doesn't give them orders."

"Why not?" He asked incredulously, "Since *when*? Stephens *always* told them what to do—all the time! It was like they were *his* company. Just order them to…"

"We *advise* them, Reggie, we don't *order* them to do anything. If we always took over and told them what to do, we'd be here for the next hundred years. Besides, it's their country, not *ours*. They're going to do whatever they want."

"Yeah, but just tell them this is a Canadian operation, so this is a little piece of Canada and they have to do what they're told." Reg was starting to get a bit choked up by my apparently negative attitude.

I had always been told back in Canada that a huge part of the OMLT job was having to explain to the battle group types what the ANA could and couldn't do, and more importantly, that the OMLT wasn't meant to be bossing them around. Their own officer corps and NCOs (non-commissioned officers) did that. We *advised*. We *mentored*. Period.

I ignored Reggie and asked Ali to please tell the outgoing ANA to sit tight for a minute, as I walked back to join the Wizard next to the lead LAV.

"What was that all about?" the Wizard asked, as Apache helicopter gunships screamed over Route Kelowna on their way to the firefight in the north.

"Holy . . ." I said, looking at the choppers going balls out to get into the fight, probably trying to save our fellow Canadians. "We're in the war now, aren't we?"

"No doubt. What did those guys want?" he asked, nodding toward the Afghans.

The warrant's voice was drowned out as the seven ANA Ford Rangers zoomed into the ditch and blew past us, kicking up dust, not overly concerned with ruining the poor engineer's concentration as he tried to defuse a bomb! *Dickheads!*

Reg shot me a look that said *I told you so*, but I wasn't about to start ordering the ANA around, and I was surprised by Reggie's accusation that Stephens had been doing just that with his ANA. I told the warrant what Reggie had said about the outgoing OMLT captain.

"I was going to tell you, sir, when I had the chance, but I wanted it to be just you and me."

"Is it true?" I asked, not wanting to believe it. We weren't *supposed* to be in command of the ANA! *I thought everyone knew that!*

"I've been reading Warrant Joe's handover notes, you know, Captain Stephens's 2 I/C, and he said stuff like, 'If your captain thinks he's on his company commander's course while he's over here, get a grip of him quick, because we're not supposed to be ordering the ANA around.' So yeah, I guess it's true." The warrant seemed as disappointed as me. But maybe Stephens had had no choice. If he didn't direct them, either there would have been no patrols, or there would have been the risk of friendly fire.

After the dust had settled from the ANA flying past us in the ditch, the engineer began his methodical task of locating the IED. We all watched in silence and wished him good luck. *Ballsy!*

We kept our eyes on the compound and the wall, but Timothy seemed to have packed up shop and lit out. *Seemed to.* You could never let your guard down or get complacent. One of the Paras' favourite sayings was "complacency kills." We would relax and let our guard down only when we were back in our shacks on the base.

Everyone in 72A knew that when we were outside the wire, we stayed switched on at all times. It was hard, and in the terrible heat one's mind tended to wander, but you just got back on track and watched your arcs of fire (where you're told to watch—between one o'clock and eleven o'clock, for example), ready to engage; always trying to find potential choke points, ambush points, places where IEDs might be hidden. The list was endless. No wonder everyone was tired after a patrol. It was mentally exhausting. And the ever-present fear of a gruesome death lurking around every corner probably didn't help much either.

After about forty minutes of waiting, the engineer spoke over the radio to say he had found the IED, but that it was too dangerous to move, so he was going to BIP the device right there. He spent the next ten minutes rigging up his C4 explosives to the shell, and then told everyone to get behind cover. We all got into the ditch or behind some walls, everyone in the LAVs battened their hatches, and the CP was advised that there was going to be a controlled explosion. After they acknowledged, the engineer strung out his detonation cord from the IED, joined us in the ditch, and then gave a countdown.

"Moment of truth, Warrant. Get your fifty bucks ready to hand over!" I put my right finger into my ear. Before we left the FOB, I had put a good-luck earplug into my left ear, knowing I wouldn't have time to put it in when the fun and games started. Then I cranked the volume to high on my earpiece, so I could still hear the radio traffic. I made that my SOP from then on.

"Bite me," the warrant haughtily snapped back.

"Hey, Sergeant," I said. "What type of IED was it, anyway?"

"Howitzer shell, but I'm a little busy right now, sir!"

BANG! Rocks and dust flew outward from the explosion in all directions.

We peeked over the top of the ditch to see grey smoke billowing out of the hole where the howitzer shell, the *smoke*-howitzer shell, had been. *C'mon, big money!*

"Huh," I said, in my best smug voice. "I wonder what that amazing grey, *smoke-like* substance wafting lazily out of the shell could be? Oh what, pray tell, could it *possibly* be?"

"How many times has that smart mouth of yours got you into trouble?" the warrant asked with absolutely zero trace of a smile on his salty face.

"Too many times to count. Now pay up, Marky Mark!" But I wasn't really going to take his money. I remembered what Lieutenant Winters said in *Band of Brothers*: "Don't ever put yourself in a position where you can *take* from the men." I agreed with that sentiment.

"I'll get you when we're back in Sper; unlike you, I'm not a compulsive gambling alcoholic, so I don't carry copious amounts of money around with me on a patrol."

"Hey, you never know when we'll be OTR [on the run] for our lives, a battalion of Taliban hot on our heels, and the only thing that's going to save us is my hundred Yankee dollars for a taxi ride into KAF!"

"Mr. Engineer," I said, speaking to the sergeant before the warrant could get out of earshot. "Well done. But for the record, would you say that was a smoke shell, or an artillery shell?" The warrant started walking away. I shouted after him, "Hey, Warrant, you gotta hear this!"

"It was definitely a smoke shell, sir."

"Thanks for that. But good job out there, and I'm sorry about those ANA pricks; nothing like helping a guy concentrate, eh?"

"Sad as it is, I've had worse. Yeah, let's mount up. See you back there."

"Yep, first beer's on me. Well, *near*-beer, of the decidedly non-alcoholic type."

I walked over to Lieutenant Aziz and said, "Now that they've blown up the IED, and since we still have the LAVs to provide us with covering fire, if we follow this wall here," I showed him the point on my highly detailed satellite map, "I think we could sneak up on the Taliban behind the wall. What do you think?"

"No, I do not think so," he said through Ali, who looked a bit embarrassed.

"Okay . . ." *Mentor, Rob, mentor.* "Can I ask why not?"

"I think they would have left by now, so we might as well leave."

"Well, that may be the case, but we could at least go and see where they were setting up, to see what they could see."

"No, that would be too dangerous. Many times, they plant IEDs at their trigger places," Ali said for the good lieutenant, "and they *hope* we will come and see where they were."

"I see. So, that's it then . . . we might as well head back?"

"Yes, let us go back now," Aziz said, and started to walk back down the ditch toward Sperwhan, speaking into his radio.

I was a bit frustrated, but I didn't want to get into an argument with him in front of his men, and certainly not on our first patrol. Especially since he could've made a lot of excuses for not coming out to play guns. *So I guess I should be grateful, really.* I thought to myself, *WWDCD, Rob? What would Don Cheadle do?*

I looked over at the big hole in the middle of the road. Even though it was only a smoke shell, if Timothy had detonated it when a driver—or worse, when someone on foot—passed over it, it still could've ripped their legs off.

I talked over the PRR. "All right boys, put your out-of-office messages on, shut down your computers, kill the office lights—we're heading home." I knew the warrant was still watching his arcs, but this was Fourneau and Hetsa's first real patrol, first IED, first shooting, first BIP, first come-on—hell, it was their first tour! So I said over the PRR, "Stay switched on boys, this is the most dangerous time, when we head back in to the ranch." I didn't want to play the part of Captain Obvious, but this was one of the most dangerous times on a patrol: when we could see the barn, and all we thought about was getting back to our stable.

I spoke over the battle group net. "Two, this is Seven Two Alpha, we've closed the book on this one, our call sign is coming back to Sperwhan Ghar now, over."

"Two, roger, good work, see you when you're back, over."

"Alpha, roger out." *Not a bad day out,* I thought to myself. We stopped an IED from hurting anyone, we didn't get suckered in by their come-on, and we let them know we'd respond quickly to try and kill/capture them. All in all, not a bad day's work.

The LAVs did eighteen-point turns and then flew past us on their way back in, again kicking up a hellacious amount of dust. *What is it with these guys? Hasn't that one gotten old by now?*

Our two columns joined up just before the gate, then we marched single file through the barricade. I waited until we were past the ANA and Canadians at the watchtower and behind the blast wall for cover before I radioed the CP that call sign 72A was complete, back in Sperwhan Ghar, and had nothing further to report.

We marched up the hill, and I thanked Lieutenant Aziz for coming to help and for his excellent work on the ground. He swelled a bit when Ali finished translating. I had been told that stroking ANA egos was a big part of the job. Unpleasant, but necessary. I told him I would like to come over to his HQ tonight to plan tomorrow's patrol and he said to turn up after supper. We shook hands and parted ways.

As we walked over to our building and began clearing our weapons, I called the boys in for a huddle. "Really good job, guys; nicely done. Good teamwork, good communication. High-fives all around!" I said as we slapped hands in the air. I'd told them at the start of the tour that I was going to bring the high-five back to Afghanistan, and thereby speed up our ultimate victory. I asked the team if they had any points for me to add to the patrol report that, as the officer, it was my job to write.

Hetsa reminded the warrant and me not to stand around too much together, for fear of one RPG killing both of us, and then he and Fourneau would have no comms (communications) with higher headquarters. I thought it was a valid point. Sometimes though, I explained, it was necessary to have a face to face.

"Like when you're betting money on smoke shells or not?" Fourneau cheekily asked.

"Exactly," I said back. He was right, so there was no getting away from it. The warrant shot him a look that could easily kill, but I let it pass. I was happy we were all okay and had done some good. They had no other points, so we took off our gear to let it dry out on the little wooden crucifixes, and as per, my kit was absolutely soaked. They all looked at me as I stripped off my vest, to see my shirt drenched all the way down to the sleeves.

"Fear will do that to a man," I smirked. "That, and hyperhidrosis! I'm going over to say hi to the PPCLI muppets and tell 'em how awesome we are!"

I knocked on their door but didn't hear a "C'mon in." *Odd.* But I had to go in to write my patrol report on the encrypted computer and send it to Masum. So I let myself in, and saw all of Stephens's team in the middle of the room, drinking Coke and iced tea, and just sitting at the table in soft chairs, staring into space.

I was a bit giddy because I still had some adrenalin monkeys riding on my back. I was happy to be alive after my first patrol, instead of dead, like in so many of the training scenarios, so I said, "We made it," with a big grin on my face. "We're all alive." But my smile quickly faded as I realized something was terribly wrong. No one laughed; no one had even looked up.

"Some of our friends *didn't* make it," Stephens quietly said, not with a reproachful tone, but with a heartfelt sadness to his words. "We know three were killed for sure and a bunch more wounded. We're on comms lockdown, so no calls home, no e-mails. You'll have to tell your guys."

I felt sick to my stomach, especially after what I'd just said. "Guys, I'm sorry—we hadn't heard. I'm really sorry. I'll come back later to write my report." I quietly walked out the way I'd come in, cursing myself for being such an ass. What the hell did I think was going on to the north, with chopper gunships and artillery firing over our heads? When I was making that comment—*we're in the war now*—my fellow soldiers had probably already been killed.

I walked into my building where the boys were still on a high, but one look at my face and their mood became sombre. I let them know as gently as possible, and we all slumped down on our beds, not really saying anything.

A *good* leader would've known what to say, but I was numb. Our country was at war: we had already lost soldiers and, sadly, I knew we would lose more. But when you're there, in that place, and you got the news that someone was killed, whether you knew them personally or not, it still hurt. You felt terrible for the soldier's family, you felt bad for his or her friends. We had such a small military, where so many people knew each other by name, that these weren't faceless soldiers. Warrant Longview probably knew all of them.

And as strange as it may sound, I felt bad for my country. Everyone back home was so supportive, constantly encouraging us, and backing us all the way, so I knew these soldiers' deaths would deal the whole country a devastating blow.

And no matter how hard you tried, you couldn't help but wonder: *When is it going to be my turn? Am I going to die here? Like that?*

I looked at the guys, sitting on their beds, probably with the same thoughts running through their heads. I wanted them to know something.

"Guys," I quietly said, and waited until they were looking at me. "After something like this, I'm supposed to set up chairs in a circle and give everyone a chance to talk about their feelings, but I'm not going to do that. All of you guys know that if you want to talk—about anything—I'm available, any time. But I will say this: we will honour their memory the best way that we can, and that's by going outside the wire tomorrow. That's how we'll honour them: by carrying on with the mission."

Their deaths brought it all home to us. And the feeling was a little too real.

Chapter 5

At the next morning's BUB, Major Bane told us that Corporal Seggie, Private Horn, and Corporal Grenon, all from 2 PPCLI, had been killed the day before, during a patrol. In the ensuing firefight, five other Canadians were also wounded.

Major Bane then apologized to the sniper sergeant because the major had forgotten to get the different types of authorization (called 421, 422, and 429) from the lieutenant colonel the other day, and that's why he couldn't let the snipers kill the IED planters yesterday. The lieutenant colonel in charge of the battle group had to make the call about killing or not killing suspected Taliban in situations like we experienced yesterday. He could keep the 421/422/429 authorization in his own back pocket, or he could give it to his majors, who in turn could give the shoot/don't shoot authorization down to their platoon commanders, snipers, whomever. Or like Major Bane was doing, he could keep the authorization all to himself and make everyone ask for it. But the major, as part of his duties, had to request it daily from his lieutenant colonel. And since the major forgot, he wasn't allowed to let the snipers shoot until he got the permission from higher up. His little *oopsy-pie* could've cost all of us our lives—especially when the ANA soldiers liked to walk right up to the IEDs.

Then, as though reading my mind, he said, "Oops. My bad," smiled, and quickly changed the subject.

The voice of my inner drill sergeant (which sounded remarkably like my nemesis from 2 Para, Sergeant MacVitty) shouted his less-than-kind opinion of the good major inside my head. Sometimes, when something terribly idiotic or stressful happened in my life, the sergeant's cruel voice would make a guest appearance.

The major then explained some more things, and finally the sniper sergeant couldn't take it anymore and said, "And what about the IED on the haystack now, sir?" The way he pronounced *sir*, it sounded more like *cur. Wait a minute... what IED?*

"Well, Captain Simran and his ANA can get out there and cordon it off," the major flippantly replied, mispronouncing my name. *What the hell?*

I rudely interrupted to explain that no one had told me anything about an IED, and I had no idea what they were talking about. Major Bane then patiently explained that an IED had been planted in the haystack at around 0500 hours, just this morning, and someone would now have to go and cordon it off and wait for the Canadian engineers. I said I was very curious as to why I was just finding out about this now, and equally curious as to why our snipers hadn't shaved off the top three inches of Timothy's head when he tried to plant the IED. A painfully awkward silence followed my question. No one spoke, someone nervously coughed, and Warrant Longview saved me from losing my temper and flat out demanding an answer by letting himself into the briefing room and whispering into my ear, "I just heard. Fuck me! But now there are kids playing on the IED. We gotta go."

I stood up and told the group of officers and senior NCOs that children were now playing on the IED. I said we would finish this talk later, but right now, I had to go. I didn't wait for approval or further discussion.

"Holy crap, sir!" the warrant said as we jogged back to our building.

"Tell me about it. *Unbelievable!* Okay, same drill as yesterday. Assemble the Avengers, and I'll go muckle onto the Justice League."

Again, just like yesterday, I found Ali, together we found Aziz, and he graciously agreed, again, to go and cordon off an IED, which again (in my opinion) should never have been planted in the first place. I ran into my bed space, shouted, "Dress me, Hetsa," and spun around so he could help with my tac vest.

I spoke quickly to my group of like-minded individuals, "It's Groundhog Day boys, but not the funny movie variety. Same drill; snipers will have eyes on; they'll talk us near it; we'll cordon and watch for wires and come-ons; and more importantly, make good and sure the ANA standing next to you don't go up to the device for a look-see! Questions?" The boys were professionals; they had none and knew the drill, so we left our building on the double. I knocked on Stephens's door to tell his guys we were going out again for the same drill as yesterday. They all said "Give 'em hell!" and wished us luck.

Just then a sniper from the top of the hill sprinted down to us and quickly handed me a small map he'd made on a piece of paper. It was a great sketch. It had the culverts, the haystack just off to the right of culvert one, and the ever-present, critical "north-pointer" arrow. Angrily he started to cast blame for it all, but I wasn't going to get into that now, and certainly not with him. Officer issues are meant to travel *up* the chain of command, not *down*. He told me that I would have to hurry, there were now six kids playing on the haystack. I thanked him and he took off again, sprinting back up the hill. I handed Longview the map, telling him to make sure the dirty Hungo and the Fornicator got to see it too.

We found Aziz and Ali, who had remembered to wear his armour and helmet, and we took off at a quick march, heading down the slope, toward the main gate. I told Ali to tell Aziz everything that I knew about the situation so far. Aziz had only two questions: "Why are your snipers not killing them?" and "Why are they just watching the Taliban as they plant IEDs?"

"I don't know," was all I could come back with, "but I'm going to find out." As we marched, I gave the command post our patrol composition and ETA to the site. Aziz had roped about thirty men into today's rescue op. I looked at the sketch again: the IED was almost perfectly in line with the smoke IED from yesterday. Someone had said Timothy was a creature of habit, and that could be both good *and* bad for us.

"Where you off to today, sir?" one of the young guys on the gate asked as we stormed past him.

"Another IED, same spot as yesterday. Same ol', same ol'."

"I hear that! Stay safe."

Just as we were about to exit the concrete barriers, Major Bane's voice came over the radio. He ordered my call sign to "go firm," so I called the patrol to a quick halt and we found some cover around the barriers. I wasn't sure why he stopped us, but I gave him the benefit of the doubt; surely he understood we were now in a life-and-death race to save the children. *They must've seen something . . . .*

"Seven Two Alpha, this is Two-niner. We think we've got eyes on the trig-german, about fifty metres to the west of the device, wait . . ." *West? Didn't he mean east? But more importantly, does he really think I'm going to be able to catch this FAM? Does he have a blocking force set up behind the triggerman, one I haven't been told about?*

"Two, we think we've got him spotted; suspicious FAM to the *east*. You will divert your group from the haystack and capture him, over." *What? Had he lost his freaking mind?*

"Seven Two Alpha, how do you suggest I capture a FAM wearing only man-jammies when I'm carrying almost a hundred pounds of gear, in fifty-degree heat? Every second we waste talking, the kids who are *playing* on an IED-infested haystack get closer to being killed, over!"

I couldn't believe it—some guy in an air-conditioned office was telling me what to do out on the ground, and he *actually* thought somehow I could capture the FAM? We didn't have enough men, we had no element of surprise, we had no one waiting behind him to capture him, and we were debating this as kids were playing on an IED haystack! *Absolutely insane!*

Major Bane's voice came back over the net, "Two, uh . . . you will . . . use the element of surprise and flank him, and then you will . . ." His voice trailed off.

"Seven Two Alpha, we have NO element of surprise! The second we crested that slope down Sper to the west, every Taliban and his dog knew we were coming! They have dickers, correction, spotters, all of the time, just watching us. That's what they do! There is no element of surprise, and I can't catch a guy wearing pajamas who's got a fifty-metre head start on me! I'm not that fast! There are children, *children*, playing on a haystack with a big, fuck-off IED *right in the middle of it*! I'm the commander on the ground, it's my call, and I'm going after the children! Seven Two Alpha, out!"

Over my PRR, I angrily ordered, "MOVE OUT, double time! Get to those kids and get them off that haystack! NOW!"

The warrant and Hetsa were already up in front of the ANA, and with that order, they cut loose and took off at a dead sprint. It was one of the bravest things I would see during the entire war. They knew, as I did, that they were covering the ground first, and the Taliban easily could've planted IEDs to try and kill anyone attempting to save the children. The children were being used as live bait. We all knew that, but the lecture I gave them both the day before about "letting the Afghans go first to clear the route" was thrown to the wind because now there were children's lives at stake, and they cared more about the children than they cared about themselves.

No officer could've been more proud of his men. I would have put them both in for medals later on, but little did I know that my time in Afghanistan would be cut short. And afterwards, well, who would take any medal recommendations I made seriously? It was a terrible injustice to these men.

We all knew (well, everyone on the *ground* knew) that it was now a race to see if we would get the children off of the haystack in time, or if the Taliban knew the jig was up and would decide to kill the kids just out of pure spite—a common situation in Afghanistan.

Our column strung out as the faster ones amongst us overtook the slower in the ditch, everyone racing toward the haystack. I could see it now, with the kids still on it, and I was terrified we wouldn't get there in time. I was sprinting with everything I had; I knew I would never forgive myself if anything happened to those kids.

Longview and Hetsa began shouting as they sprinted, and made sweeping motions with their arms in the air, getting the kids' attention, and then terrifying them as the Canadians ran at them, shouting and hollering. The kids leaped off the haystack and ran into the village. *Better scared than ripped to shreds!*

"They're off the haystack!" Longview said breathlessly into the PRR.

"Thank God, Warrant. Good work! You boys got some damn wheels on ya! Start to get a cordon set up; I'm right behind you." I pressed the battle group pressel. "Two, Seven Two Alpha, we've secured the IED, the children are safe. We're setting up a cordon now, over." I looked to the east to see if I could catch a glimpse of the alleged triggerman. High walls and village huts completely obscured my view of the spot where he was *supposed* to be hiding. How could he be the triggerman if he couldn't see his IED? How would he know when to detonate it? *With remote viewing?* The CP acknowledged my transmission, but that was it; they failed to mention if the Canadian engineers were en route to the IED. *Strange.*

The ANA began to filter in and Lieutenant Aziz put up a loose cordon, but somehow managed to cover both ends of the roads and major pathways leading up to the haystack. It was a marked, noticeable improvement from yesterday's cordon. *Baby steps.*

I radioed the snipers to ask if they had eyes on anyone suspicious: FAMs, people a little too interested, whatever. They came back with a negative and told me they'd continue to observe. I got out my FMP and, using a cheat sheet, I quickly wrote up the IED contact report and sent it over the net to the CP.

I advised Aziz that he should get his men to pull back from the IED, with cover from a blast and access to the paths and roads, and once everyone was in as good a position as they'd ever get, I suggested that we head east to see if we could find the FAMs. He agreed, so the lieutenant, around fifteen ANA, Fourneau, and I marched off between the village walls to try to find them. And there they were—two teenagers, bearded and in man-jammies, hanging out on a rooftop, watching our every move.

But were they really *the* triggermen or just bored kids? I asked Aziz if we could give them a GSR test and he thought it was a good idea, so he shouted at the kids to come down off the roof. They were casually searched but the ANA found nothing, certainly no incriminating detonators. I gave them both the GSR test. Both tests came back negative, but Aziz still felt they might be the triggermen, so he took them into his custody and sent them back to Sperwhan with a few of his soldiers acting as guards. I didn't recall this scenario coming up with Captain Stephens, so I wasn't sure how the Canadians would take to ANA bringing suspects in to *their* base. I felt a courtesy radio call to the CP couldn't hurt.

I called it in and said the ANA had taken a few detainees suspected of involvement with the IED, but they were Afghan detainees and the Canadian OMLT team had nothing to do with them. I suddenly realized I'd said the D-word—*detainees*—and the CP immediately came back with, "Detainees, or persons of interest?" I sheepishly responded, "Persons of interest; not, I say again, NOT detainees." Our radio traffic was monitored in KAF, and I'm sure the moment I said the D-word, alarm bells went off all the way to my nation's capital.

Canada did not take detainees. There had recently been a political uproar about whether or not Canadian soldiers had handed suspected Taliban detainees over to the Afghan government, who then allegedly tortured them for information. So we were no longer allowed to say "detainees." We now only took "person(s) of interest."

We rejoined the ANA and the rest of 72A by the haystack, got behind some cover, and hunkered down in the hot sun to wait. And wait. And wait some more.

I was sweating terribly, but at least this time, I wasn't alone. Our little jaunt had taken the wind out of almost everyone's sails. But the heat problem was greatly compounded by the fact that Ramadan, the month of religious fasting for Muslims between dawn and dusk, had begun. The ANA, in accordance with their religious beliefs, were not eating or drinking anything between first and last light. None of them were allowed to drink any water, even in the incredible heat. We felt truly sorry for them, and only snuck a sip of water when we were sure none of them would see us.

They knew that we were Canadians and therefore (in their minds) good Christians one and all, but that our faith didn't require us to fast during this period. But I had said before to my team that in a show of solidarity we would always do our best not to drink or eat in front of them, out of respect for their faith. I asked Ali if the Taliban were observing Ramadan. He said they believed that because they were waging jihad (holy war ordained by God) against the infidel, God did not require them to observe the traditional fasting or abstaining from liquids between dawn and dusk.

Everyone tried to find some shade, but we were exposed, with only a few walls and one tree providing anything that could help block the sun's burning rays. The warrant and Hetsa covered the north end; Fourneau and I were on the south. I radioed the command post to ask when the engineers were coming and was told that the engineers and QRF out of Masum were tasked out, and wouldn't be available to us.

I wanted to ask "Since when?" and "Doing what, exactly?" I could only guess what was happening. It was now close to eleven and the sun was blistering hot.

I knew guys were going to dehydrate quickly in this heat, so I told Longview and Hetsa to come and join us at the base of a large tree. It was the only shade around for two hundred metres. I set us up so we would cover all of the cardinal points, then we sat down and waited for the Canadian engineers to finish up their task and come and help us out. But nothing happened. It was now 1200 hours and we'd been waiting almost an hour and a half. We had told all of our jokes; we'd taken the piss out of each other, as one does; Fourneau and I debated whether or not the three *Star Wars* prequel movies rightfully belonged within the sacred halls of official canon or were merely blasphemous aberrations; but now the waiting was just getting stupid.

I asked over the net about our chances of someone, *anyone*, turning up any time soon, and the sergeant manning the radio in the CP, apparently without any malicious intent, asked me right back if we could requisition the ANA engineers to come and take care of it. *What ANA engineers?* Did he mean the guys who sweep Route Kelowna? *Are they even remotely capable of taking care of something like this?* But at this point, it was worth a shot; the heat had grown almost unbearable and we were sweating the water out faster than we could get it in.

I asked Lieutenant Aziz if he could call in the ANA engineers. He put in the request through his HQ, waited about fifteen minutes, and was then told they were on their way. *Gods of war, may your hammer be mighty! About freakin' time!*

I had never (in all of the time I had spent in two different armies) seen or experienced what was about to happen next. It began when the ANA engineers actually turned up. *Hey, that's great!* But they were four hundred metres away, and they began very slowly and methodically minesweeping the road. *Oh, that's bad.* Lieutenant Aziz, who I would quickly realize was not the most patient man in the ANA forces, lost his temper and began shouting at them to "Come over here! The IED is right here!" *Hey that's great! You tell 'em, Aziz. Let's get this cake and ass party over with!*

But they rudely ignored him, and continued slowly sweeping Route Brown. *Oh, that's bad; he's not going to like that!* But in all fairness to the engineers, that was probably what they were trained to do. There could have been secondary devices: you can't just rock up to an IED all willy-nilly. But you didn't have to be a cultural expert to understand that Aziz had just lost a serious amount of face and felt incredibly slighted by the fact his engineers had just blanked him completely, and carried on methodically with their minesweeping.

So now he totally lost it, and angrily marched over to the IED haystack. *Crap*, I thought to myself, *he's not really going to climb onto it, is he? That's suicidal!* He leaped on top of the haystack like a man possessed and I shouted, "Take cover!" as we peeked over the wall to watch him as he fired up his best Stompin' Tom impression. *Geeewwww!*

He was angrily smashing his feet up and down, on top of an IED, and shouting like an old man who just missed his bus. *It's an IED barn-stormin' hoedown!*

I radioed the snipers to let them know, just in case they were wondering, that *yes*, that was my ANA lieutenant jumping up and down on the haystack, and *no*, I would not be joining him any time soon! They laughed and told me to keep my head down.

Now my Dari wasn't that good, but I had always been a keen student of non-verbal cues and subconscious body language, so I think I got the gist of it. As he flailed his arms and violently cursed, I think it went a little something like, "*It's over here, you sons of braying donkeys! I'm standing on it! Quit dicking around and get over here and do your damn job!*" or words to that effect; only, of course, in Dari. Ali kindly translated for me, and I was pretty close. "Yeah, I gathered he's upset, yeah." We had all taken cover behind the nearest mud wall, rightfully afraid his lack of patience would quickly be the hideous, exploding death of him, and equally afraid his severed head would soon form a flying meat torpedo at over two hundred kilometres an hour!

They say God loves fools and children, but hates the poor, bloody infantry, so I thought for sure Aziz's number was up. But the higher power decided it wasn't his time, and mercifully chose to ignore his apparent death wish. To be fair to Aziz, it was really, *really* hot, and all of our tempers were a bit frayed, *but still!* To date, that was one of the craziest things I'd ever seen. I didn't know it then, but I would soon see worse.

The IED never went off. The engineers casually walked over toward Aziz as he continued his IED hoedown, contested who was stupider, and then Aziz sullenly stomped back over to us, unfazed and unrepentant. The engineers shook their heads, and a young guy with them (who was either the most qualified or, more likely, the bravest) walked over to the haystack, gave it a few passes with his antiquated mine detector, casually brushed the hay aside, and found the IED. We sunk a little lower behind our cover, afraid, as we had been with Aziz, that parts of the engineer's exploding body would make deadly projectiles. I couldn't help but sneak a peek; it was like watching someone's house burn to the ground. You hated yourself for watching, but could easily justify it by saying you had to walk the dog anyway, so there you were.

The engineer calmly tied a long piece of 5 / 50 parachute cord around the end of the IED, walked ten feet away, and gave it a healthy tug. *GEEEWWWW!*

Not on my how-I-wanted-to-die-in-Afghanistan list: by an engineer's lifeless head turning into a meat bowling ball and ripping off mine. But I guess the Force was strong with him because he managed to survive.

He then strolled over to me, as I gently shook my head in reproach, unable to help myself. I knew enough to know that was not *really* how it was supposed to be done, but he was still alive, so what did he care? He stuck his hand out toward me, palm up, and asked for something.

Ali translated and told me he wanted to borrow my Leatherman tool to cut something. Before I knew what I was doing, I reached around my back to my belt, pulled out the tool, and handed it over to him, thinking he needed it to cut off his string. It was good string, and I was sure that stuff wasn't too easy to come by at the Masum bazaar. Besides, it was closed on Fridays.

He marched back to the IED with a sense of divine purpose in his stride, walked right up to it, located the red and yellow detonating wires sticking out the top of the device, and then deftly snipped them—with *my* Leatherman tool! *Gaahaaaa!*

"What the fuck?" the warrant shouted. We all looked at each other, in a state of total shock.

What in the hell was going on today? Were we in Bizarro Land? Had the world gone mad? Did the normal rules of IED physics and common sense no longer apply? The young engineer picked up the heavy IED—it was a forty-pound, brand-new pressure cooker—and removed its lid. Two things were clearly evident: it had a remote-controlled detonator on top of it, and Timothy's local RadioShack had let him down by selling faulty electronics. The detonator had failed to trigger the device.

The engineer, bless his socks, obviously thought I would like a closer look at the device, which he thought he had rendered inert *(was it?)*, so he manhandled the IED over to me and loudly dropped it at my feet with a dull, sickening thud. *GAAHAAAA!*

I knew it was some sort of weird, tribal acceptance thing, or more like an Afghan man test, so I tried my best not to flinch, quickly looked it over (without moving my feet an inch or even touching it), asked Fourneau to get a picture for the OMLT yearbook, and then calmly said, "Great, well done. Now get it the hell away from me!" Ali translated and the engineer smiled, handed me back my Leatherman tool, picked up the IED, and roughly slung it over his shoulder like a sack of wool.

Even though it was pretty clear he had been trying to slip the surly bonds of earth, I still had to admire his sand. I asked Ali to tell him that the next time I saw him, I would give him a Leatherman tool: with the caveat that he didn't use it to snip anymore detonating wires! The engineer smiled and asked me to promise. I gave him my word and then he strolled away with the IED. I felt bad for the ANA. They wanted to do the job, but they had none of the necessary tools. *Imagine trying to be an engineer without a tool like a Leatherman?* When he was twenty feet away I began to breathe normally again and asked Aziz if he'd like to head back in.

We'd spent nearly five hours in the brutal heat and everyone was done in. We formed up into our standard two columns, and I told Ali to gently ask the still ill-tempered Aziz if he would have done anything on the cordon differently. He wasn't sure what I meant, since we had found the device, saved the children, rendered the IED inert—a job well done, as far as he was concerned. I told him that Allah must love him very much, because he could've been blown up from jumping up and down on top of the IED.

"*Inshallah* [*if Allah wills it*]. If Allah wanted me to die, I would have died," he said and shrugged.

"I know," I politely countered. "But you took a helluva chance, climbing on top of it like that." *Clearly, I'm not getting through to this guy…*

"*Inshallah,*" he said and shrugged again, still not sure what I was getting at. I felt my blood rising, and even though I'm a pretty even-tempered guy, his laissez-faire attitude was starting to get to me. I wanted to grab him by his ears and shout in his face, "*You put all of us at risk with your little temper tantrum, you stupid idiot!*" but stopped myself, thinking that probably wouldn't be well received. The warrant could see I was losing my patience, so he walked over to me and gently put his hand on my shoulder.

"Let it go, sir. It's done now; we'll know better for next time," he calmly said, out of earshot of the ANA.

"Numbnuts doesn't even get that the rest of us were danger close and could've been killed too!" I angrily whispered back.

"Next time we'll give him a thousand-metre standoff, now that we know he's suicidal," the warrant laughed.

I laughed with him and started to cool down. "There won't be a next time. I quit! I've seen enough crazy crap in the last two days to last me a lifetime. I'm tapping out, Warrant!"

Like a patient father he said, "As your life coach, I strongly suggest you breathe in deeply and feel the nice, burning-warm air sting your lungs. Then say *woo-saaaa* five times, and take a nice, long sip of burning-hot water, to heat you up from the *inside*. You'll feel better in no time—you'll see!"

I radioed the CP, wanting to say, "Thanks for nothing!" but instead, took it on the chin and reported our locstat, saying we were done and coming back in. I gave Aziz his space and joked with Fourneau on the way back in.

The ANA engineers took the pressure cooker IED to the UXO/IED sandbag hut next to the watchtower, and I radioed the CP to tell them the ANA had dropped off a TNT gift for them. I thanked Aziz for coming out to play, and told him how impressed I was with his team's fortitude. To be able to do all of that on zero water intake, in that terrible heat, was truly impressive. He seemed to appreciate my comments, and we parted ways, agreeing to meet after supper to discuss tomorrow's patrol.

We cleared our weapons by taking the loaded rounds out of the chambers of the barrels, and I asked Fourneau to get a picture of me. There wasn't a spot on me that wasn't soaked through with sweat. I entered our building and changed my clothes and scrubbed my pits down with baby wet wipes, what we used to call in The Parachute Regiment a "3 Para shower." I asked if anyone had anything to add to my report, but no one had any comments. We walked over to the OMLT building and immediately raided the fridge for cold drinks and Freezies.

We had all lost pounds of water, and our faces looked drawn and thin. I thought about the ANA as I chugged down water, apple juice, and iced tea and felt incredibly sorry for them, knowing they weren't allowed to drink anything until sundown. *Hardcore.*

I wrote my report, but omitted the argument between myself and Major Bane, and Stompin'Tom's big debut. I sent the warrant to find out what Aziz had done with the suspects. The Wizard came back to say that he was quietly questioning them in his HQ, and "that he would not require our assistance." I was sure it wasn't because anything untoward was happening, but rather that he didn't want us to find out that he had no clue how to properly question "persons of interest."

One by one, my teammates borrowed the satellite phone from the outgoing crew and went off to call home. It would be our first communication with our loved ones back home in over a week. I kept working on the report, and when I was finished I asked the warrant to join me; I wanted him with me when I confronted Major Bane regarding his apparent live-and-let-live policy regarding Timothy. I desperately needed some good answers as to *why* the Taliban IED planters weren't being slaughtered by our world-class snipers. Then I asked Hetsa to find the sniper sergeant and ask him to please join the warrant and me in the briefing room at the HQ. *There will be a reckoning.*

As we walked toward the HQ I asked the Wizard how things were back home and he said everything was fine. I was happy to hear it, and looked forward to calling my wife, Amélie, that night. Hopefully I'd be able to say the same.

We entered the HQ building and grabbed some Freezies before making our grand entrance. *Nothing like a little liquid-sugar courage.*

We entered the briefing room, and I politely asked the major if he, his CSM, my 2 I/C, and the sniper sergeant could discuss some ongoing issues. He seemed to fidget and looked visibly distressed as he thought about it for ten seconds, and then finally agreed. He asked a corporal to go and grab his CSM and then to not disturb us. The sniper sergeant arrived and joined the Wizard and me on one side of the table, and the major and his CSM sat down on the other. The line in the proverbial sand had been drawn between the shoot/don't shoot factions at Strong Point Sperwhan Ghar, although I wasn't sure which side Bane's CSM was on.

The major began by saying, "So, what seems to be the problem, Captain Semroo?" *Would it kill people to get my name right?!*

"Well, sir, first off, thanks for taking the time to discuss some things that have been troubling me lately."

"And what exactly has been *troubling* you lately?"

"Sir, I get it. I'm the new guy. We've only just arrived, I get that. But in the short time I've been here, it seems obvious to me that the snipers have been asking for permission to kill IED planters, and they're constantly being denied permission."

"And what if they're wrong?" the major interrupted.

"They *haven't* been wrong. Not once. They've said they've got someone planting an IED and they've been denied permission to shoot—by you." *And there it was!* We all stared at each other across the table.

"Okay, Captain. How can you tell me, with one hundred per cent certainty, that they're right?" *Holy crap, was he for real?*

"Because they have a very good, proven track record, sir. They haven't been wrong, not once, and with all due respect, sir, we're fighting a war, so there's no such thing as 'one hundred per cent certainty.'"

The major snapped, "You can spare us your lectures on war, Captain." He was pissed, but I knew I had to strike while the iron was still hot. *All right Rob, time to put on your barracks-room lawyer suspenders!*

"Sir, if you're looking for one hundred per cent certainty, let's look at the burden of proof. The first strike against the planters is we know the guys working in the middle of Route Brown at three in the morning aren't employed by the local city council to do road repairs. Second strike against them: they're not wearing the red lights that every farmer has been told to have on when they work in their fields at night, for fear of being killed by us if they *don't!* And, of course, they're not working in a field, but in the middle of Route Brown. Strike three: they're carrying what looks like howitzer shells and digging in the middle of the road at three in the morning, right between the same culverts where ten other times in a row, they've buried IEDs. They're not pirates searching for buried treasure in the middle of Route Brown!"

The major tried to interrupt me but I was in the zone and really rolling. "The fourth strike against them is whenever we launch parachute flares or fire illumination rounds to light them up, they run, take cover, and hide until the round burns out in the sky. Then they go back to work, burying howitzeresque shells in the middle of the road. Very suspicious. Fifth strike: they're stringing det-cord wire, from said device, over to the side of the road, and then burying the wire. Sixth strike against them is they're stringing the wire to a trigger point fifty metres away, where they'll have eyes on the device. Seventh strike is they're sitting there, and waiting. For hours on end. Waiting for us, or some ANA patrol to bumble along so they can kill them. Eighth and final strike against them, with which I am *now* intimately familiar, is they will turn and burn; they will run away from you, even when armed men are calling to them to come over and talk, when you've found their magic string."

The major wasn't buying it, but the CSM seemed to be agreeing with me.

"So, in my opinion, since we're all smart people at this table, I would think that as a team of professional soldiers dedicated to killing or capturing the enemy so that one day we can all go home again, we could all agree that two or three men, without red lights on, dressed in loose, flowing man-jammies that won't restrict them in their Ben Johnson wind sprints, who peek out from behind cover to make sure the coast is clear, then come out of cover, and begin to dig frantically in the same place where multiple—*multiple*—IEDs have been planted in the past, then bury a fucking howitzer shell in the hole they just dug, then take cover and hide when illumination rounds light up their handiwork, and later bury the wire and string it out to a point fifty metres away where they've got eyes on, and then wait for someone to turn up, are in all likelihood fucking Taliban planting IEDs on Route Brown!"

The major looked at me coldly, but I wasn't finished. "I would respectfully suggest, sir, that when you take those individual pieces of evidence and connect them together as a whole, we would *hopefully* all draw the same conclusions: namely that we've got IED bomb-planters working on Route

Brown to try and kill us, and not city road workers doing pothole repairs, again, at three in the morning."

After a good minute's silence, the major quietly asked, "And *what if* they're wrong?"

I was rapidly losing my patience with his obstinacy. "I mean no disrespect, sir, when I say, if we're going to play the *what if* game, then we probably have no right being here. But the snipers haven't been wrong, sir, not once."

The major continued, "And *if* they're wrong, then what? An investigation? The last thing I want, Semrow, is an NIS investigation into an illegal shooting . . . ."

There it is. Finally! You don't want to give your snipers permission to shoot, because you're afraid of being investigated by the Canadian Forces National Investigation Service (a military police investigative branch). I thought to myself, *Brutal . . . what the hell am I supposed to say to that?*

Longview seemed shocked by the major's admission, the sniper sergeant was furious, the CSM lowered his eyes to the table, and I sighed loudly as I said, "Sir, every time you *don't* give the snipers permission to shoot, the long and the short of it is, you put *my* team, the ANA, the engineers, the QRF . . . you put *all* of us at risk. Ask Warrant Longview, sir; yesterday and today were freaking gong shows, and the ANA are going to get us all killed if we have to keep going out and cordoning off IEDs when the Taliban should have been shot the second they marched out from cover carrying howitzer cannon shells and began burying them in the middle of the—"

"Thank you, Captain; that will be all. You're dismissed," the major snapped.

"Sir, please, I just—"

"You're DISMISSED!" He shouted across the table.

I stood up, stared at the major for a few seconds, and then turned and left the briefing room, the warrant and sergeant falling into step beside me.

We walked about ten feet. I hesitated, mid-stride, and was about to turn around when the warrant wisely said, "Keep walking, sir," and gripped me firmly by the elbow. It wasn't a suggestion, and he had a damn strong grip!

We walked outside into the searing heat. I put on my sunglasses, and let out a long, drawn-out sigh.

"Well, sir," the sergeant said with empathy in his eyes, "it was a good try and you were right, but there's no getting through to him. We're all super frustrated. We thought this was going to be a good go, the best tour we'd ever get, but it's been—"

I don't normally cut people off, but it was too much for me just then, and I couldn't bear to listen. "I hear ya, Sergeant. Thanks for backing us up today. I'm sorry for what you guys have had to deal with, I really am. But we tried, and at the end of the day, that's all a man can do: his best to get through to people and make 'em see the light. No joy, but not for lack of effort on our part. Thanks again." We shook hands and he slowly began the long walk back up to the top of the hill.

Longview and I walked over to the house of international pancakes and army scoff and grabbed a couple of free coffees. The warrant said they were his treat, but I didn't feel like laughing. I stared into my mug of joe and thought about what had just happened.

I knew Major Bane wasn't evil. *Gutless?* For sure. He was so worried about making the wrong call, and then being investigated by the CFNIS, that he wouldn't accept the responsibility that came with his job. That responsibility forced him at times to take certain risks and make tough calls. No one would want to be in the position of, "Sir, we're waiting; do we kill him or not?" But Bane just couldn't seem to trust anyone to do their job properly and present him with enough evidence. I thought that for a guy like him, *no* amount of evidence would have ever been enough. For him, it seemed that putting other soldiers at extreme risk was not as troubling as making the wrong call and shooting someone who didn't have it coming. Although it should've been obvious to everyone present that "they" certainly had it coming!

And since when did we have to talk about evidence? All that talk of evidence would've made someone think we were lawyers discussing a police action and not soldiers talking tactics. But that was the reality of the current war, where every battle group lieutenant colonel had a JAG (Judge Advocate General) lawyer standing next to him, watching the same real-time video feed from a UAV, and advising him whether or not to give the shoot order. I'd even heard that sometimes the lawyers were more aggressive than the lieutenant colonels!

But the snipers weren't psychopaths. They weren't going to shoot some-one just to be the first kids on their block with a confirmed kill. They used the burden-of-proof method like I'd mentioned, and after enough evidence came in, it was up to the major to make the call, or a more trusting officer would have given the snipers the permission to shoot or not shoot before-hand. That was entirely up to the major in charge. But Bane refused to let the snipers do their job, every time. And when he refused, he put guys like me and my team, who would then be tasked to go out there and cordon off the IED, at terrible risk. *I suppose the prison warden in* Cool Hand Luke *had gotten it right when he said, "Some men, you just can't reach."*

The warrant let me ponder for a while the deep mysteries of trying to fight a war in the age of political correctness, and then he quietly said he wasn't happy with me. I asked why, and he said, "Sir, you keep coming on strong like that, and you're going to get replaced, and we don't want that to happen. We've only just got you to the point now where we can read your simple mind and manipulate you nicely, but what if we get someone smarter who won't do as he's told?" He slapped me roughly on the back, spilling my coffee.

I half-smiled and said "You're a wise man, Wizard, and one day, I'm sure you'll have a seat on the Jedi Council. Of course, you're also much *uglier* than me, but certainly wiser."

"When you've got the TI I've had, sir, you'll be ugly too!" We laughed and walked back to our shack, not really saying much after that.

It was one of those laugh or cry situations. *That's that, then.* No further discussion. Timothy will keep laughing at us as he plants his IEDs with impunity, knowing that no one will ever be allowed to put a high-powered round through his brainpan. And one day, sooner or later, he'll get lucky.

Chapter 6

Ali came up to us, looking very concerned, and told us the ANA had just received a delegation of elders from the village who wanted their two teenagers back. The ANA said, "Um . . . no," and told the elders to leave. I took Ali over to see Lieutenant Aziz, who said he was almost done with them; they weren't guilty, they were just a couple of scared kids. I looked them over: they were fine, just like how we'd found them. I said I thought if he had no evidence or anything to suggest they were Taliban, then it would be for the best if he let them go. He agreed and said he would in a few minutes. I excused myself to go and track down a sat phone. My ninja sixth sense told me there was no point in writing my report just yet, the gods of war still had a few surprises in store for us. *Might as well try and call the missus.*

I walked into Stephens's shack, found the phone, and walked over to the sandbag gun emplacement by the western edge of the base to call home. Back in Kabul in 2002, I got to call home twice. Once, Amélie was on the Internet (before the days of high speed), so I only got the answering machine. It was still great to hear her voice, but understandably, not quite as much fun as talking to her. The second time, she was on the phone with her mom, so again, I got to leave a message.

This time, however, she picked up on the first ring, and we immediately began telling each other how much we missed and loved each other. She wanted to know right away if it was safe where I was, and I lied through my buckteeth, telling her we were doing great and nothing ever happened in our sector, that all was quiet on our front, and there was nothing to worry about, nothing at all.

I felt terrible for being less than completely honest, but I would rather live with myself than know I caused her sleepless nights, afraid for my life. I remembered the words of the great twentieth-century existentialist Homer J. Simpson, who said, "It takes two to lie. One to lie, and one to listen." I would confess later, when I was back home again and could look her in the eye to better explain myself. But she was far too switched on to be fooled by my pathetic efforts to string her along. She knew what was really going on, but she graciously let me get away with it.

I asked about our newborn daughter, Caméa, and Amélie said she was doing great, she was really growing. Cam was only three months old when I deployed, and I missed her and my wife terribly. I was so happy to hear Amélie's voice and to be able to laugh and tell her . . .

SNAP SNAP! . . . CRACK! CRACK! CRACK! Incoming enemy rounds passed feet and then mere inches over my head as the Taliban opened up on Sperwhan Ghar. *Crap, did Amélie hear that?*

"What was that?" she asked, a familiar tone of suspicion in her voice. It was the same tone I got when she wanted to know what I'd been looking up on the Internet.

"Absolutely nothing! Hey, I'm really sorry, *chou,* but something's come up and I gotta go, right now. I'll call you back as soon as I can." I started to run toward my building, trying to crouch, sprint, and lie to my wife all at the same time as rounds cracked over my head. "Love you, gotta go, bye!" I hung up the phone and ran into our shack. "Stand to boys, the base is being attacked. First man dressed get over to the other shack, use the field phone and call the CP, let 'em know we've got incoming SA [small-arms] fire and we're being attacked. Go go go!"

I think I set my personal best for getting kitted up, and ran over to the other building. The boys were playing vids and working on the computers, not hearing the sounds of incoming fire overtop of their video game—or more accurately, they probably just didn't care. This was crazy exciting for us newbs, but nothing new for them. "Base is under attack," I said and quickly grabbed the field phone. The sergeant on the other end told me that I had to hurry; my ANA were already scrambling out the front gate to go and get some. *Crap, that was quick!*

I asked Stephens and his boys if they wanted to come out and play guns but they were short-timers and knew it, and they weren't about to get pasted on their last day in Sper over some pissant drive-by shooting. I honestly couldn't blame them, not one bit. They'd done their time and now it was our turn.

"Wish us luck," I said, jogging out the door. I met the boys and told them what the command post had just told me. "We've gotta hurry." I made my rifle and the gat of justice ready to sing, and started jogging toward the main gate, listening to the radio traffic over the net.

Fourneau looked sick. "We'll be fine," I said. "Just stay right behind me." As we began to run down the slope we were now exposed to Timothy in the village to the west, where the incoming fire was originating. I remembered a trick from Northern Ireland, one we used when leaving the main gate. It was called "Hard Target," and it meant running zigzag out the gate so that snipers couldn't get a bead on you. I started zigzagging down the slope, trying to make myself a "Van Damme" (Hard Target) and shouted at the others to do the same. I ran as fast as I could down the small hill, eager to get behind the cover of the ten-foot-high blast walls as incoming rounds smacked into the rocks around our feet. Thankfully we all made it into cover and then quickly ran up to the front gate.

I shouted at the Canadian in the watchtower, "What've you got?" I heard a whoosh sound and looked up in the sky as the pretty, grey contour trail of an incoming RPG warhead passed over our heads. The rocket detonated harmlessly into the side of Sperwhan's hill. *Full of sound and fury, signifying nothing....*

"Fuck all! I can't see shit!" he shouted back. I could tell *The Fear* had gotten a hold of him, and was giving his sphincter a good squeeze.

I shouted back, "Get as low as you can, you'll be *fine!*" The warrant looked at me and laughed at my flippancy. I thought for a moment about taking my three trained killers with me and running out after the Afghans, but then dismissed it as an exceedingly bad idea. *Either the Taliban will outnumber us and kill us, the ANA will shoot us out of pure confusion, or the Canadians will assume anyone running outside the wire with guns is fair game!*

I thought again for a moment and asked, "Hey, buddy? Did you see any Afghan soldiers go running out the gate?"

"No, no I don't think so. I'm tellin' ya man, I haven't seen fuck all!"

"Wait a minute, didn't you just call the CP to tell them the ANA were running out the gate to go and stick it to Timothy?"

"No. I told them the ANA had brought some civilians down to the gate, but that was it. I don't know what the hell you're talking about!" *Nice.*

"Okay, so where are they?" I asked, looking around for any ANA and civilian persons of interest, but not seeing anyone matching the description.

"Can't you see them?" he shouted. "Look around, they were there a minute ago! I'm not coming down to find them for you! Shit!" Evidently his pucker factor was going full bore. *Poor bastard, all freaked out!*

"Okay," I shouted back sarcastically, "sorry for bothering you!" I looked over at the warrant and . . .

CRACK! CRACK! CRACK! CRACK!

Time slowed down as I looked at the sandbar just over top of the warrant's and Hetsa's heads. Bullets kicked a long line of dust up in the soft sand, about ten inches over their heads, and although they couldn't see what was happening, surely they could hear it. Amazingly, neither of them so much as flinched. But the noise of supersonic bullets breaking the sound barrier right over their heads should have made them duck just a little bit! I was on the other side of the road, and *I* flinched! I was terribly jealous of their sang-froid.

"Congratulations!" I shouted and smartly walked over to the Wizard and the dirty Hungo, outstretching my hand in fellowship. "First time being shot at?" I asked Hetsa.

"Why, yes! Yes, it is!" he said, shaking my hand in the spirit of camaraderie. His incoming-rounds cherry had finally been popped.

"How about you, Warrant? First time?" I asked, smiling a toothy grin and stretching out my hand.

"Go fuck yourself!" he snarled.

"Okay, no need to be rude about it." I walked back over to Fourneau and put my hand on his shoulder. "First time, young man?"

"Yes, sir." He didn't seem to be enjoying the moment like the rest of us.

"Well congratulations, you're a new man after this! It's a soldier's rite of passage. Like the gunny in *Full Metal Jacket* once said, 'You'll be born again, hard!' Well done!" We shook hands, but it had the same feeling you'd get from squeezing a dead fish.

"Hey guys," I said excitedly, "I just thought of something—we have now officially qualified for our Bronze Combat Badge!" Everyone snickered at my sarcastic comment. The rumour going around the army sewing circle was that Americans were giving Canadians attached to them a hard time, asking the Canadians, "Where's yer combat infantryman's badge?" Because every American who had been in combat (and every army in the world defined *combat* quite differently) wore a special badge to show he'd been in the shit. But Canadians didn't have that.

So someone in the Canadian HQ felt left out, and started floating around the idea of having bronze, silver, and gold combat badges. The three separate badges would be awarded based on the nature of the combat you had survived. Bronze was supposed to be for getting shot at by small-arms fire, rockets, artillery, etc., but *not* actually shooting back, so technically, we all qualified! *Yippee!* Although, we'd all seen pictures of the proposed badges and agreed they were truly hideous, so we weren't exactly sure who would want to wear them anyway.

Just then Lieutenant Aziz decided to make a guest appearance from around the far side of the watchtower, where undoubtedly he and his persons of interest had taken cover as the rounds started coming in. I was about to ask Ali to translate something for me, but *damn it, I forgot Ali!* In my haste to join the ANA outside the wire, I forgot to bring the only guy who could actually talk with them! I heard the voice of an old teacher of mine called Cort say in his gruff voice, "One mistake is all it takes to get a man killed, most of the time." *You idiot, Rob, you can't make mistakes like that and expect to live very long in this place!*

Rounds continued to crack over our heads and into the hill as Lieutenant Aziz hauled the two teenagers over to us and began asking some pointed questions, and even though my Dari was failing me, my psychology degree from the University of Saskatchewan (no honours, *barely* graduated) didn't let me down.

But for some reason (that I could never quite figure out), whenever I saw the Afghans arguing amongst themselves, it always sounded in my head like the authentic, realistic dialogue from the movie *Lawrence of Arabia*, where white, Anglo-Saxon, Protestant males (who had never even travelled to the Middle East) made up fight dialogue that was about as authentic as deep-fried chicken balls were to real Chinese cuisine.

Aziz opened with, "You say you are *not* Taliban, but the moment I tell the village elders 'No, you cannot have them back in time for supper,' our base gets attacked! Explain that, you leprous worms!"

"We are not Taliban, *habibi*, we are simple farmers!"

"You lie like a donkey with a moustache! If you are not Taliban, then who is shooting at us?"

"We do not know, *habibi*. We are simple farmers!"

"Go then, back to your village, and tell your cowardly neighbours to stop shooting at us!"

"We will go now, thank you, but we cannot guarantee the shooting will stop, for we do not know who is doing it, so how can we . . ."

"Go, you sons of pregnant jackals, before I lose my patience and change my mind!" Or words to that effect. . . .

So with a flourish, Lieutenant Aziz pushed them out the front gate to go and mediate at the Sperwhan Village Peace Accords of 2008. And they must've been very skilled diplomats, because miracle of miracles, within five minutes the firing stopped completely. *Huh!* As my Grandma Lockhart would've said, "Will wonders never cease?"

As the sun began to set, we had a good laugh over the madness of it all and walked back up to our building. I thanked Aziz again, and radioed the CP to let them know that we were back in our shack, call sign 72A complete, and told them they had been the victims of the whispers game, where you whisper a simple message to a child and see how many variations of the message you get by the time it reaches the kid at the end of the line. The CP sergeant told us to stand by for further ops. None of us liked the ominous sound of that.

I told the boys that from now on, I was instituting a new 72A SOP. After every patrol, the first thing we'd all do when we got back to our building was top up our water and dust off our weapons, because we never knew when we'd get the call to go back out again. I also reminded them of the cautionary movie *Blackhawk Down*, where the American Rangers didn't bother taking their night-vision goggles (NVGs) out on a day op, believing they'd be back long before nightfall. Unfortunately for them, they could've really used their NVGs before the fighting ended days later. For every patrol from now on, we'd always carry our small NVG monocle that could quickly be attached to our helmet, just in case we got caught outside the wire after nightfall. "These team SOPs are non-negotiable, starting now. And another thing—don't let me forget Ali again! Unless any of us just became fluent in Dari through the powers of reverse osmosis, I'm guessing we might need him one day."

The lads went and grabbed bottles of water and began refilling their CamelBaks, an amazing piece of kit. It had a long hose attached to a three-litre water bladder in our day sacks. We slowly began stripping off our armour and tac vests, but I kept my radio earpiece on, waiting for the word from on high. The rest of the boys took off their gear, still drenched with sweat from the morning, and were about to lie down on their beds when the command post transmitted our orders: "Seven Two Alpha, you will collect as many ANA as you deem necessary, and make your way outside the wire, approximately twenty-five metres northwest to a position designated by the snipers as the location of a dead Taliban insurgent carrying an RPG launcher on his back. He was shot off the back of a motorcycle trying to flee during this last engagement. You will recover the RPG launcher, over."

I was about to say, "You can't order us to do jack shit! We're the OMLT, we don't work for you!" but I realized we had to maintain good relations with the outgoing guys, and we were meant to be fighting the same enemy. It wasn't their fault they had a complete spastic for a boss! Besides, I was getting into the war rhythm and figured, *what's one more op?*

I replied over the net, "Seven Two Alpha, I ack your last. Sure, *why* not? Over, *ksscchh!*" I made the static radio noise from the old seventies cop shows.

"All right ladies," I said to my team, "you heard the man, and you *know* the drill! Assholes *and* elbows!" I pointed at Hetsa and snarled, "Hudson, come here. COME HERE!"

"Good one, sir," he said. Every true infantryman loved the movie *Aliens* and its obvious star, Private Hudson.

"Rebomb your water, grab some chocky bars and get 'em downrange, quick," I said to the team. "We're going back outside the wire, and we want to get it done before Timothy knows we're rooting around in his backyard." I wondered if in the short time I'd been in the Stan, for this round anyway, I wasn't becoming a bit of a war junkie, a guy who enjoyed the highs of adrenalin you got when you were getting kitted up, you had a mission, or rounds were cracking over your head. If it wasn't so terrifying, it would've been exhilarating.

"Sorry, sir, what are we doing?" Fourneau asked, visibly perplexed.

"Right, sorry, I forgot you *don't* have the implanted comms chip in your brain, so you can't hear the transmissions from the mother ship, like me. Okay, here's what's going on," and I quickly briefed up the boys on what we'd just been ordered to do by the CP.

"Shouldn't the QRF be taking this one, sir?" Fourneau asked, and then immediately regretted it as the angry father (the warrant) shot him a look that would kill a yak at fifty yards.

"Technically, yes, but they—" I started to say, but the warrant quickly cut me off.

"Fourneau, get your kit on, and get ready, we're going out again. Top up your water and eat something, quick." The warrant shook his head and I imagined they'd have a private chat when I left the room to go and ask Lieutenant Aziz if he wanted to come and join us for some more excitement outside the wire. *No rest for the wicked, and the righteous don't need any!*

I knocked on Ali's door. He was a good sport, and together we went and found Lieutenant Aziz. He was surprised to see me at his door for the third time today, and quickly said it wouldn't be possible, as the sun was about to set and the Afghans would finally be allowed to drink water and eat something. I said I understood completely, but the corpse was a mere twenty metres away from the gate, and it would be one less RPG launcher on the mean streets of Sperwhan Ghar. We'd need twenty guys, max. We'd go find the body, strip the RPG off of it, and be back no later than 1830 hours.

"Fifteen men, and I don't come with you," he said, raising the bet with his men like they were poker chips.

"Okay, but who will be in charge of your men?" I asked, re-raising him.

"Sergeant Major Khan," he said, "and you must be back by 1830 hours." *He's all in!*

"We will, thank you very much. How soon can they be ready to go?"

"Five minutes," he said and brushed past me to go and prep his men.

I told Ali to say thanks to the back of Aziz's departing head, and we walked over to my shack. I asked Ali how he was doing and he said fine, "but a little tired." In the few short days I'd been working with him, I'd realized he had a great attitude. He was observing Ramadan as well, so he hadn't had anything to eat or drink all day, but you would never have known it. The Afghans' resolve and ability to maintain their fast, while still conducting operations in plus-fifty-degree Celsius heat, was truly astonishing. I know I would've dehydrated at the start of the morning and died of heatstroke if I hadn't been able to keep topped up on water.

Aziz quickly scrambled his men, who never once complained or shot us dirty looks. They were needed and so they went, and that was enough for them. I apologized through Ali as my team of Canadians joined us, and promised them we'd be back as soon as possible. I radioed in our composition to the CP as we began marching down the slope toward the main gate, for the third time today. *Hopefully this'll be a milk run*, I thought to myself. Fourneau called my name so I turned around.

"Sir, you're not going to believe this, but I think we all just walked over an unexploded RPG warhead, and that Afghan there is kicking it like it's a rock down the street!"

GEEEWWWW!!

"Stop stop stop!" I shouted. "NOBODY MOVE!" I trusted Fourneau completely. He was smart so I gave him the benefit of the doubt. The warrant doubled back to join me and the Afghan sergeant major as I walked past Fourneau and looked back up the hill to where an ANA soldier was about to boot an unexploded RPG warhead, just like Fourneau had said.

"Ali, get that man to STOP what he's doing, and back the hell away from it!" Ali shouted at the man who, looking like he just aged twenty years, slowly crept back from the rocket warhead.

"Everyone, very slowly and carefully, do your fives and twenties! Make sure you're not standing next to any more rockets or mortars that haven't exploded!" As Ali translated, I looked around my personal space and performed my five- and twenty-metre check, like I'd been taught by the Brits and then relearned in the CF. Look five metres around you, and when that's clear and you're happy, look twenty metres around you. But they never said anything in the training about Afghans kicking pieces of UXO.

I radioed the CP and advised them we had a UXO that the Canadian engineers would have to come and deal with, *rapido*. CP said the 'geers would be notified.

"Hungo," I spoke into the PRR. "On me," I said, meaning *come and see me*.

He quickly jogged over. I breathed in deeply and paused, then quietly said, "I've got a sinking suspicion the CP has once again run afoul of *das kinderspiel* 'whispers.' To that end, being very careful where you step, be a good chap and make your way down to the front gate and find the Canadian who sent up the report of the *alleged* dead Taliban with the RPG on his back. I'm guessing he actually sent up a report to the command post about there being a UXO on the western slope. I'd go, but I'm afraid the Afghans are going to start an impromptu game of soccer. There's a good lad, cheers." With that, Hetsa carefully began making his way to the front gate.

The warrant called out to him, "If you see something green and shaped like a cone, whatever you do, don't kick it!"

"Yes," I smiled, "that's some good advice. But I'm not going to lie to you, Warrant. I'm a bit embarrassed that three-quarters of our platoon nonchalantly bumbled over an RPG warhead, and none of us noticed it sticking out of the dirt!"

"I know," the warrant said, not laughing anymore. "All we would've heard was a huge BOOM behind us, and we'd turn around to find two Afghans missing, and ten unconscious and bleeding out!"

"Yes, almost a 'bad day in Kentucky!'" *Un-fucking-lucky!* The sun was under the horizon now; it was becoming dark very quickly, and the Afghans were getting bored. A dangerous combination: bored Afghans and unexploded ordnance. A nasty feeling started bouncing around in my mind as Hetsa jogged over to us.

"You were right, sir. The guy at the front gate was totally pissed when I asked him. He said he told the CP there was an unexploded RPG warhead and he could see it, so he went over and marked it with an illumination stick." I looked over at the UXO, but I couldn't see an illum stick. Someone had probably kicked that one too!

Hetsa continued, "He also didn't say jack about any dead Taliban and a motorcycle or an RPG launcher. The only thing he told them was about the unexploded RPG warhead, on the western slope, inside the actual base."

"Let this be a lesson to all of us," I said in my officer voice. "The best, most active listeners in the world do *not* get the CP radio-shift duties!" I looked over at the Afghans. *Poor bastards*, I thought, *they haven't had anything to eat or drink all day.* I called Ali and Sergeant Major Khan over to me, and politely thanked the CSM for bringing his men out, but there had been a miscommunication between the front gate and the CP. We were called to find the warhead, *not* an RPG launcher attached to a corpse rapidly undergoing rigor mortis.

"Thanks a lot for your help, but we'll take it from here; you guys can go back and have supper now. Thanks again." Before I'd even finished translating, the ANA were on their way back up the hill. I thanked Ali for all of his hard work and cut him loose, too. I didn't have to tell him twice.

The Canadians quickly formed a four-man cordon around the UXO, so that no one would be overwhelmed by the same deadly curiosity that had been infecting the ANA these last few days. After the last Afghan passed, we walked down the hill, got behind the cover of the blast walls, and hunkered down.

"Honestly guys," I asked no one in particular, "someone please tell me, what the Sam Fuck is going on around here?" Although everyone laughed, you could tell no one found the joke particularly funny. I thought about it for a second, and realized that it wasn't maliciousness on anyone's part; that was just how war played out sometimes. There was a reason the term *fog of war* had been around for centuries. Some things didn't change, and as technology increased, the problem only got worse.

The CP spoke over my radio again, and told us we'd have to wait out. An American chopper was scheduled to land at Sperwhan, so the engineers weren't allowed to BIP the UXO. So we waited. And *waited*. To keep team morale up I would act as the chair over nonsensical debates, like whether or not the actor Haley Joel Osment would successfully transition from child prodigy to serious adult thespian. The debate was fairly even: some of us cited precedent for such a thing, others felt it wouldn't happen for him. But I had faith.

The Black Hawk chopper arrived, landed, and took off again, and still we sat there with our backs to the hill, with no end in sight. Another hour passed, and finally the Canadian engineers arrived and took over our protective cordon. We thanked them profusely and marched back to our shack, where we dumped kit, topped up our water, and then went off for "Hollywood" showers, in which, as a special treat, you kept the water running and didn't shut it off after you'd lathered up. I figured we deserved it.

Later that night, as I typed up numerous reports, I heard a rap on the door. I got up, eager to get away from the screen blindness I was suffering from, and answered it. If I thought that day couldn't have gotten any more surreal, I underestimated fate's sense of humour.

Next to Ali stood Mr. Snippy-snip, the young ANA engineer, standing in his best clubbing outfit, with hair neatly slicked back and shoes polished, looking surprisingly smart. He said something in rapid-fire Dari.

Ali smiled. "He says 'You promised.'" And with that, the engineer stuck out his hand, palm up.

"So I did! Tell him to wait one." I laughed and went back to my bed space to take my Leatherman tool off my combat-painted belt. I smiled and handed it to him and said, "Be careful," and "May Allah watch over you." I was going to add, "*because you are certainly not long for this earth*," but I didn't want to jinx him. He thanked me, and walked away into the night.

The next morning I approached the battle group store man and told him exactly how I came to be missing one times issued "Leatherman tool, the." He just laughed, walked to the back, grabbed a new one, and handed it over to me.

"Lost in combat, sir."

Chapter 7

We said goodbye to the fighting cowboys of the PPCLI as they packed up and began to depart Sperwhan. I took Stephens aside and thanked him again for his briefings and dedication to making sure we would be okay. I hoped I would do half as good a job as he had, with *my* handover. Some RGs arrived from Masum to pick them up; we walked them over, they wished us luck and then took off. And as per, completely blanketed us in dust, just for old times' sake.

"Seriously, what the hell is the matter with those clowns?" I demanded.

"It's just their way, sir—don't take it personally," Longview replied, as he wiped himself down from the coating he'd received. I took the boys over to meet Captain Shafiq Ullah, the ANA First Company OC, who had arrived late the night before. I happened to be awake—I couldn't sleep in the heat—so I had grabbed Ali and the ANA captain and we talked for a bit. He seemed a decent-enough guy, but like all Afghans, he was wary of the new OMLT team—afraid we would be trolling for a fight and would ultimately get him and his ANA killed. I didn't go into our activities of the last few days for fear of making him think I was another Captain Rich (call sign "Bad Karma") . . . I didn't want him to think trouble was attracted to me, although after the last few days, I was starting to wonder about that myself.

We moved across the street into our new digs, the actual OMLT HQ, and were happy to finally be hanging out in an air-conditioned building. Back in the store room, we couldn't sleep at night due to the extreme heat: we'd toss and turn because we were so uncomfortable from sweating buckets in our sleep. We'd only been on the ground a week and we were already going into sleep debt.

"Am I wetting the bed again? Or is *that* really sweat?" I asked after peeling myself off the cot and looking down at the sweat silhouette I had left on the sheet. I would wake up each morning and literally down a litre and a half of water. *Damn night terrors!*

After the IED haystack, the base attack, and the UXO warhead on the slope, the next couple of patrols had been milk runs, comparatively speaking. On one patrol we got lost in a marijuana field. We patrolled through it, thinking it couldn't be any bigger than an acre. But it was as long as a football field. The stalks were eight feet high, we couldn't see each other, and I realized I was allergic to pot. My eyes were watering like crazy! As a joke, I began calling to Fourneau saying, "I can't see you; where are you?" and "I can hear them, Fourneau! They're all around me!" I remembered a movie that had terrified me as a kid, *Children of the Corn*, and I still cursed Roddy Striker's parents for letting us watch it at his birthday party. I thought about the heroes running through the tall stalks of corn as demented children gave chase.

Even though we were armed to the friggin' teeth and could easily have handled a bunch of knife-wielding patricidal brats from Iowa, if the Taliban had attacked us at that moment, it would've all been over. I could just see the ANA firing madly in all directions, mowing us down. Being lost in a pot field, although undoubtedly the dream of many Canadians from the BC interior, was a little bit creepy and surreal when it happened to you in Afghanistan.

The warrant had to find his way out, and then shout at us to call us over to him. It was all very embarrassing, and we redefined amateur hour that afternoon.

When we got back to our shacks I radioed the CP to say we were back, and I was told "Comms Lockdown." My heart sank. Another Canadian soldier had been killed. I told the guys and a dull feeling passed over all of us. I experienced a lot of the same feelings I'd had the first time we were told "Comms Lockdown," but now I was feeling angrier than I had before. It was hard to describe. We found out later that night that Sergeant Shipway from 2 PPCLI had been killed in action by an IED in Panjway province. Seven others had been wounded as well. I reminded the guys that if they wanted to talk, I was there for them. We cleaned our kit in silence and got ready for the morning patrol.

On that patrol, I was running down the length of a narrow grape-field wall, trying to get some definition on what was going on up ahead of us, when the wall collapsed under the combined weight of my gear and heavy musculature. At least, that was the reason I told the team. They said the wall collapsed because I was fat. Either way, I walked with a nice limp for the next two days—the fall had really jammed my knee. The warrant told me to have the doc check it, but I knew he would put me on a sick chit for the next week, and I had patrols to lead. *I just got here—how would it look if I was already injured?* My high school football coach's words came back to me: "Rub a little dirt on it, an' get back in the game!" I continued patrolling, but I was a pitiful sight (more so than usual), limping up and down the road.

We had done a couple of patrols to the north and east, and I noticed that something odd kept happening: whenever we approached a village or a field where there were donkeys milling about, they would immediately begin braying loudly, alerting everyone within earshot of our presence. I started calling them DEWS, for "donkey early-warning system." Clearly the Taliban had trained the animals to act like guard dogs and alert them when we were sneaking around. It became a running joke on the tour. Whenever someone heard a donkey braying he'd shout, "DEWS! They're on to us; we've been compromised! RUN! RUN!"

* * *

We did a patrol the next morning and it turned out to be one of those fore-shadowing moments. Fourneau and I were with Lieutenant Mujahedeen (whose real name was Azmar, but when we found out he'd fought the Soviets as a teenager, he quickly became "Mujahedeen"), when the lieutenant hopped over a small wall into a farmer's compound. Longview, Hetsa, and several ANA had gone the long way around as Mujahedeen and I walked up to the front gate and realized it was secured with a thick lock. With zero hesitation, he asked me to shoot off the lock. Now, that may work in movies and bad TV shows, but the only thing in real life that worked well on a thick lock was a shotgun slug round. Pistol rounds and rifle bullets didn't always cut it.

And to top it off, I didn't think the farmer wanted me to shoot his lock. *Not exactly "hearts and minds."*

But it didn't look like we had a choice. I was just about to get everyone out of the way and do it when Ali told me to stop because the farmer was going into his house to find the key to let us out. Longview and Hetsa damn near pissed their pants—they couldn't stop laughing at the thought of a farmer rummaging through his house, trying desperately to find an old key to let the infidels out of his compound.

After about five minutes he stomped out of his hut, let us out, and basically said, "And don't ever come back!" or words to that effect in Pashto. But the warrant and Hetsa got a good yuk out of it, seemingly at my expense, although I couldn't really have cared less. I guess shooting a lock would remain on my war to-do list.

Our OMLT company's second-in-command, a captain named Sean, radioed to inform us our OMLT OC, Major Hobbles, had arrived and was setting up in Masum. But more importantly, Major Obermann, the OC of Mike Company from 3 RCR, had finally arrived at Sperwhan, so I invited him into our OMLT HQ to give him an update on the situation so far. I explained in some detail the things I'd been up against, and didn't pull any punches regarding Major Bane. Comments like "one hundred per cent certainty" before he'd give his snipers permission to fire didn't sit well with Major Obermann. He thanked me for the briefing and said, "Stand by for change." I couldn't wait!

Major Bane called a BUB the morning Major Obermann was scheduled to take over. All of the outgoing officers were present with the sniper sergeant and the two OMLT teams (the new incoming OMLT artillery team was made up of Captain Brannon, his warrant, and his two young guys I quickly nicknamed "Ginge and Swede." They had turned up the night before, and were now living in our old accommodations). Major Bane, in a surprisingly gracious gesture, thanked everyone for their hard work, and then handed the briefing over to Major Obermann. The new incoming battle group commander discussed a few handover issues, and then said, "I've been hearing a lot of talk about having to be one hundred per cent certain. Well, gentlemen, that ends today at high noon when I take over. As of 1200 hours today, fifty-one per cent is good enough."

It was great to see Bane finally get his in front of all of his men. The sniper sergeant looked like he had tears of joy in his eyes. Shortly thereafter,

Bane and most of his crew were gone. I think after that official handover, he basically stayed in his room until it was time for him to leave. I didn't waste a single tear over him.

We did our standard patrol in the morning and then showered and ate lunch. I was finishing my patrol report when I heard two friends of mine with Mike Company, Captains Declan and John, begin speaking quickly over the radio. They had turned up with their platoons the night before and were now out on the ground on a handover patrol with Reg. They had just given chase to some bomb makers and my ears had perked up when they trapped the men in a grape-drying hut, just outside Sperwhan's front gate. *Good on 'em*, I thought to myself.

Then I heard them request, "OMLT and ANA personnel to breach the grape hut."

I wasn't sure why they were requesting us; maybe there were angry farmers who didn't want them to enter. Maybe the Canadians needed the ANA to be diplomats. Either way, 72A had seen the Bat-Signal in the sky, and we were always game for some good action outside the wire. I jumped out of my seat and shouted, "X-Men! To me!" as I ran over to put on my gear.

The warrant came in from the picnic table and asked, "What's going on, sir?"

"Rohan calls for aid! And Gondor shall answer! Get kitted up, we're outside the wire in five." That was all he needed to hear. He ran over to Fourneau's bed space, rudely shoved him awake, and started getting kitted up. Hetsa had been reading on the couch, so he was well ahead of any of us. Hetsa and I always competed on who could get all of their gear on first, because the loser had to help the winner with his clips. He was good at it, and we were about even so far. As I got dressed I briefed the guys on the mission.

I grabbed the radio mic and told the battle group CP that OMLT had heard the request and were en route. "Dress me, Hetsa!" I said, all smug because I'd beaten him. "Fourneau, get out there and fire up the Millennium Falcon!"

I jogged outside, found Ali, and then asked Captain Shafiq Ullah if he could spare some men for a quick compound raid. He said no, because it was almost last light, when his soldiers could finally eat.

I said I understood completely. "Just give me twenty guys, and I'll have them back in time for tea and medals." The rest of 72A jogged past me, heading over to the RG.

"Fifteen guys, and be back in ten minutes," he said, haggling over his men.

"Fifteen guys, back in fifteen minutes, done! Thanks." I turned and jogged over to the RG. I hopped up the back step and swung inside, and as was my custom, promptly smashed the top of my helmeted head into the ceiling.

"Aw, damn it!" I screamed, "Every freakin' time!" The shockwave sent a shiver all the way down my spine to my toes. Everyone laughed. I was glad my one-man clown act was keeping team morale high. I radioed the CP to let them know 72A was about to roll.

"Fourneau, give me full power and put shields on double front. Weapons, report!"

"We're good to go, sir. Weapons fully charged and ready!" Hetsa responded. He used the joystick on his remote control console to swivel the .50-cal heavy machine gun on the RG's roof back and forth for good measure.

"Well done, Mr. Starbuck. Warrant, how's our six o'clock, any sign of the ANA?"

"Some guys are hopping into Rangers now, sir. One's pulling up behind us."

"Roger that. Good hustle, men; well done. We've got two, possibly three IED makers hiding in a grape hut. It's almost ANA supper time, so we gotta get back here in fourteen minutes, or Shafiq Ullah will never let his soldiers go to war with us again. So let's make it quick and dirty! We're going in hard, we'll point the ANA at the right hut, and then cut them loose and see what happens!"

"Sir, we've got three Rangers on our six," Longview said.

"That's all we're gonna get. All right, punch it Chewie!" I shouted. "We're going in full throttle; that oughta keep those fighters off our back!"

"Yee-haw!" Hetsa shouted. Fourneau punched the gas and we went flying down the slope, sliding sideways on the turn until he regained control, and screaming up to the front gate, pinning the brakes before we could crash into the barriers. He slalomed the cement barriers like a professional Formula One driver, and we went blazing out the front gate.

"Mr. Fornicator, we've only got thirteen minutes left; give me full power!" I shouted.

"I'm trying, sir, I'm giving it—"

"Damn your eyes, man! What have I told you? Honk the frackin' horn!"

"Sir, we're—"

"Just do it!"

Fourneau began blaring our powerful tugboat horn, alerting all and sundry that 72A was en route to save the day. *If only we had external speakers to play* Ride of the Valkyries. *That would shit up Timothy good and proper!*

I spoke over the vehicle PRR in my *Starship Troopers* voice: "All right, listen up! We are going in with the first wave—means more bugs for us to kill! You smash the entire area, you kill anything that has more than two legs, Do you get me?!"

Hetsa immediately shouted back "We get you, sir!"

I laughed but then shouted, "Stop, stop!" as a Canadian ran into the middle of the road to try and get us to slow down. But the RG didn't exactly stop on a dime. We skidded and swerved and kicked up enough dust to choke out a village before Fourneau managed to regain control. He let out a deep breath and I said, "Okay, I guess we're here. Warrant, on me! Fourneau, get the HMCS *Tippy Canoe* back on a southern bearing. Ion Control, swing the 'heavy' around to cover us as we storm the grape hut. Stand by to fire over my shoulder!"

"Aye aye, sir!" Hetsa said, grinning away. I marched to the back of the RG, careful not to stove my head in again, and followed the warrant outside. The heat hit us full in the face as I looked around for the Canadians. I saw two platoons' worth of soldiers milling around outside the obvious grape hut. The warrant and I jogged over to three platoon commanders, Declan, John, and Reg.

I used my best New York cop accent and said, "Captain Semrau, OMLT, fifty-third precinct. Whatcha got?"

"First off," Declan said, "thanks for coming out. But holy shit, where's the fire?"

"Hey, we're OMLT! We've been runnin' and gunnin' through the streets of Baghdad before *you* left your dad's *bag*! So this is the hut?" I asked, pointing at the one surrounded by a loose cordon. I saw the Florida dog handler and his big German shepherd hiding behind a mud wall near the hut. *I guess that's how they'd tracked the bomb makers.*

"Yeah, that's it. If you can get your ANA to do a hard entry, we'll provide the outer cordon."

"Well, we don't do nothin' *soft*! But for the record, someone please tell me, why is the OMLT taking care of this?" My fellow officers all looked at the ground or off into the distance.

"That's what I thought. All right, let's move 'em out, Warrant!" We quickly walked over to the ANA and, through Ali, briefed them on the plan.

We used cover until we were just outside the hut, then the Afghans jogged up to the door. *Holy,* I thought to myself, *they're looking sharp!*

The warrant and I slotted ourselves into the column and then stood behind a wall, just outside the door by ourselves as the rest of the ANA marched on either side of the hut, passed it, and then walked over to a wall, about twenty metres away. Clearly, something monumental had been lost in translation.

"No . . . no . . . it's here. Where are you going; what are . . . ?" I asked helplessly as I watched my crack team of Afghan door-kickers march past the door they were *meant* to kick in. "Aw, sonofabitch," I said. "Well, looks like it's up to us, Warrant."

"We didn't get all dressed up for nothing, sir. Let's do it!" We both knew what the other guy was thinking. The ANA were about to get seriously perforated if there were any actual bomb makers hiding in the grape hut. There were a thousand missing bricks so the heat could dry and shrivel up the grapes, and any one of those missing bricks in the wall would've made a great firing port. If someone was inside, *and* upset with us, any second now they were going to unload on my mentally challenged Afghans, who were casually marching in front of them.

There's a time to mentor and a time to act! Cry havoc!

I told Ali to stay hidden behind the wall, and then I broke cover and ran up to the door, slamming into the wall next to it. I looked and saw a large lock on it, just like on the farmer's gate the other day. *Damn history*, I thought to myself, *always repeating!*

"Crap, it's locked, Warrant!"

Then I was startled to hear Clint Eastwood's voice come out of Warrant Longview's mouth. He had become the man with no name, as his gravelly voice said, "I got the *key* right here!"

Oh, I thought to myself, *a farmer's turned up with a key again?* I turned around just in time to see the salty warrant racking the pump on a shotgun, loudly chambering a round. "Oh, *that* key," I said, feeling like a total dickhead. *Wait a minute, where the hell did he get a shotgun?*

"Step aside, Hoss," he growled.

"All right Tex, do your thing," I said, stepping to the side so he could shoot the lock off, like a man's man. "We're shooting the lock!" I shouted to the battle group soldiers on the periphery, so they wouldn't think it was incoming fire. Many of them were brand new and you could tell some were visibly on edge. *I suppose rockin' up in the* Tippy Canoe *and honking our horn the whole way down the road may not have eased their combat stress.*

I swung my Petzl head-flashlight from the back of my helmet to the front and switched it on to white light. I hadn't received a tac light yet for my rifle, so like a total numpty, this was the best I could do. I knew the shotgun blast would kick up a hellacious amount of dust. Just then I felt something bump into my back. I spun around to see Ali stacked up behind me, like he was door breacher number three.

"Ali, you crazy son of a bitch, what the hell are you doing? Get back behind that wall, it's too dangerous—"

"But, sir, I must go with you, I—"

Boom!

The warrant's shotgun blasted the lock into a hundred pieces, then he grabbed the door and violently wrenched on it and ripped it right off its hinges, making a hole for me to enter the hut. I ran in with the warrant right behind me, and took two steps to the left as he went to the right. We swung our rifles back and forth, scanning for the bomb makers, as my cheesy head-lamp cut through the dust and gloom. We ran through the building, quickly getting to the end of it. Besides some tumbleweeds trapped in the back left corner, it was completely empty. I shouted, "Clear!" and then radioed the battle group so all the Canucks would know it was a goose chase.

"My goodness, Warrant," I said in a sarcastic tone, "you don't actually think the Taliban have invented a man-portable cloaking device, do you? Have they found a way to teleport? If so, this heralds a frightening new chapter in the war!"

"Mistakes happen, sir," he said.

"Roger, understood, and I'm not saying my shite smells of red roses, but they had a UAV, Warrant! The proverbial eye in the sky! You know, that thingamabob flying around at ten thousand feet that will relay to the troops on the ground the exact location of the enemy, in real time? That thing we never seem to get for our patrols, but ironically, the very thing we need the most! And somehow they still managed to lose the bomb makers!" The warrant, with all of his experience, knew it was just my adrenalin talking, so he let me vent out loud.

"Better?" he asked, and smiled.

"Much, thanks."

"You're welcome. Now switch off your night light, you look like an idiot."

"Right, thanks. Okay, I've seen just about enough. Let's hat up and light out for Swift Current!" I marched out of the building, told the dog handler it was all clear, and walked past my fellow officers, who stared at me in disbelief. "Okay," I shouted to the Afghans as my arm circled in the air. "LET'S MOUNT UP!" As I approached the Canadians I saw Reg shaking his head at me, as if to say, *What the hell were you doing?*

The Canadians watched us as we marched past; the ANA quickly fell in line behind me, eager to get back in time for supper. I sneered and shouted so everyone could hear me, "Seven Two Alpha: cold as ice, *hard* as fuck!"

As per my orders to Fourneau before I led the away team, he had the *Tippy Canoe* turned around and facing back toward Sper. I hopped inside, smacked my head, screamed my usual expletive, and took my seat in the front, putting my headset on over my helmet.

"How'd it go, sir?" the Fornicator asked.

"Same ol', same ol'. Complete cake and ass party! Back to Uncle Owen and Aunt Beru's farm. All ahead full!"

Fourneau gunned the throttle, shooting dust everywhere, as we flew like a land speeder over the Tatooine desert back to Sperwhan.

"Sound the battle horn a few times, for good measure," I said.

Fourneau did as I asked, and I found out later from my friend Declan that we had made quite an impression on the Canadians who were gathered outside the empty grape hut. I suppose an RG going mach chicken down Route Brown, honking its super loud horn the whole way, then spraying dust as two Canadians dismounted and marched over to the hut, while the Afghans marched *past* the objective and joined the outer cordon to watch the Wizard shoot the lock off, while he, Ali the interpreter, and I ran in to clear the hut, probably scared the hell out of anyone who didn't hear my warning. Then, just as the Canadians were asking what was going on, we quickly marched away and mounted up. The RG blared its horn the whole way back as the Afghans tried to pass us in their Ford Rangers to get to supper first. The whole thing had taken less than fifteen minutes. The Canadians, many of them on their first tour, thought something serious had to be going down because why else would the OMLT and ANA take off in such a terrible rush?

Good times.

Back at the CP, Major Obermann and I had a good laugh when I told him the warrant's classic "I got the key right here!" line. I was proud of Longview; that was the stuff of legend! Real *Boy's Own* material. When I was done, Obermann's 2 I/C, a captain I had never met before, called me into the briefing room for a private word.

"Rob," he said, very gravely, "I wish you had let the Afghans go in first."
*Was he for real? Was he there, on the ground? Did he even know what had happened
and why I had to go in first?*

I looked him in the eye and didn't hesitate. "Yeah, well, like my life coach
always says, 'Shit in one hand and wish in the other, then tell me which hand
fills up first!'"

"You're supposed to be mentoring them Rob, not putting yourself and
your warrant at risk, so—"

"Okay," I cut him off, "just so you know, this isn't my first combat
rodeo. In fact, this is my *fourth* combat tour, so don't ever tell me what to
do—or judge my actions—when I'm on the ground and you're sitting nice
and safe in an air-conditioned office! Secondly, I know damn well when to
act, and when to *mentor*, and that was most definitely the time to act. By the
time I would've got them turned around and stacked up, *if* there actually
had been any bombers in there—and I can't remember, so please remind
me, *were* there any bomb makers in the hut?" I paused to let that one sink
in. *You asked for our help, remember?*

He didn't say anything, so I kept rolling. "By the time I would've gotten
them in place, they all would've been killed, so thanks anyway, but how
about next time you just say 'good job,' like you should've done in the first
place, and leave it at that!"

"Okay, I see your point, but . . ." The captain's voice trailed off. We
just looked at each other. I was soaked in sweat, covered in dust, and filthy,
whereas his uniform was immaculate, and his hair actually had *gel* in it!

"Yeah, thanks." I walked out of the office and back to our shack. The warrant had already gotten some steaks from the cooks and was sizzling them
up on the BBQ next to our building.

"Whoa, whoa, Warrant!" I smirked. "Did you get the required BBQ chit
from KAF before you fired that thing up? 'Cause we gots rules, ya know? *Et
les règles sont très claires!*"

"After today, they can poke their rules," he said as he flipped a big T-bone.
"Now shut your blowhole and hand me a paper plate."

Chapter 8

Captain Shafiq Ullah, the officer commanding the ANA First Company, who so far had been Mr. No-show, finally made a guest appearance on a patrol. Then miracle of miracles, he began patrolling with us almost *once* every few weeks. We had been going out six days a week: on our standard patrol in the morning, and then sometimes again later the same day as a QRF for the battle group. Our only day off was Friday, the Muslim weekly holy day. Besides the odd admin day, we went outside the wire constantly, and it was beginning to wear on us. Guys joked less, got impatient quicker, were constantly tired, and if we could have slept three days straight, we would've still felt exhausted. The terrible heat, constant dust, and lingering fear of death could really start to wear you down. One morning, when I looked in the mirror to shave, I actually flinched when I didn't recognize the guy looking back at me.

Every now and then we'd get woken up at around two or three in the morning to take our place on the berm when the enemy was up to no good right outside our front door. One night in particular, Lieutenants Aziz and Mujahedeen woke me up because they saw movement in the fields to the south. I looked through my night-vision scope and could see some farmers working in their fields.

"What do you think?" I asked them, knowing damn well what *I* thought.

They both looked at me and casually said, "Kill them."

"But they have red lights on, like we told the farmers to do."

"Hmm . . . yes. But kill them. They are planting IEDs."

"What, in the middle of the field?"

"That is not a field—that is a road."

Now, I knew that was BS. There was no road right there. We had just patrolled that way the other day so I knew I was in the right. I decided to call their bluff and said, "Okay, here; take my rifle. You do it."

"Um, no . . . that is okay . . ." Suddenly, when it came time for them to pull the trigger and end someone's life, they weren't so sure. And with that, we went back to bed.

The next morning, I intentionally diverted our patrol more to the south so I could show Lieutenant Aziz that the farmers were indeed working in a field, which was right where I said it was. I drove the point home by asking him where the road was that he was talking about. He became quiet and walked away from Ali and me.

But the one good thing about Captain Shafiq Ullah blessing us with his presence on patrols was that whenever he came out on patrol, nothing ever seemed to happen. He either had a snake charmer's hypnotic effect on the enemy, or it was the fact that he refused to go to the only place we knew the enemy actually hung his hat—behind the mythical 29 Easting on the map, off to the west.

We had been patrolling to the north, east, and south, but had only skirted around to the west, just far enough to get around the base, but still always within shouting distance of it. Clearly, in their handover the ANA had talked about Captain Stephens's patrol (the one where they'd been ambushed and were all lucky to have survived), so the word had spread, and the mythical 29 Easting would be safe from our patrols until the ANA were ordered to go there, or I could somehow *mentor* them over.

The next day we got permission to run a small-arms range at the south-west corner of the base. The ANA would be firing against targets we'd set up against a ten-metre-high sand wall, with both the OMLT artillery and infantry teams acting as the range safety officers. The warrant said we should probably find out now if their weapons would actually fire or not.

Some of them were carrying the Canadian C7/M-16 rifle, while most still sported something from the Kalashnikov family. As the senior officer there, I was in overall command, and I was bricking it, big time. "Neil Diamonds" (negligent discharges) could happen on Canadian ranges. Accidents happened back home. But here? *What were we thinking? I mean, who actually signs up to get shot?*

To say it was a complete and utter gong show would be a gross understatement. Only my fellow Canadians' professionalism and ninja-like reflexes stopped the Afghan soldiers from killing themselves, us, even some camels that came too close to the fence. I had never done drugs, but I felt like I'd just inhaled something hallucinogenic and then sat two inches away from a Salvador Dali mind-bender painting. As we finished up (much sooner than originally planned) and walked the long slope back to our barracks, we swore to each other that we would never discuss it again, nor would we ever sign up to *lead* a range again. You can only tempt fate so many times in a war zone, and our luck couldn't hold out forever. *Point taken. Lesson learned. Never again!*

Lieutenant Aziz took us out the next morning, eager to show us that even though Captain Shafiq Ullah was *technically* in command, Aziz was the guy who possessed the skills and drills that paid the bills. He was keen to head back to the small village northwest of our base, where we'd seen the flying kite and rooftop FAMs during our first patrol. I was keen to see it as well, thinking, it may be northwest, but it's still west.

We were on a joint patrol with one of the Canadian platoons, and the plan called for them to set up in a line to our east and provide fire support if necessary. We would patrol in to the village from the north, then march through to the south. We knew where the Canadians were set up, and they knew where we were *supposed* to be, that is, until Aziz developed a "Haley Joel" (a sixth sense) and began to see ghosts.

We had patrolled up to the large village and some of us had crossed over a narrow single-log bridge over a deep stream. I watched as Fourneau and a few of the ANA took a longer route off to the side, for fear of falling in. We then patrolled through some narrow, dusty streets, while I gave the CP and Canadians off on our flank regular sitreps (situation reports). After marching through the top end of the village, we stopped to talk to a large group of villagers who were having a town social. I noticed a young guy, leaning against his motorbike, trying to look cool, hard, and non-Talibanesque, all at the same time.

I asked Aziz if I could give the guy a GSR test and he said, "No, he is not from this village." *Well, that's sorta the point, good buddy.* I tried to explain that was all the more reason to do it, but he wasn't having any of it and started patrolling down the middle of the village, heading due south, all by himself until we caught up to him. Aziz could be incredibly petty at times.

We marched for a few minutes and were almost at the end of the village, when he cried out, "Over there!" and took off at the speed of a thousand gazelles. Now, I had never seen an Afghan do that before, so at the time, I thought he'd legitimately seen someone suspicious. All of the Canadians fell in behind him as he gave chase. At one point, I got caught up in the chase and thought I saw a wisp of fabric as someone rounded a corner. We ran into compounds, around houses, through gates, into small alcoves, and down alleyways. The ANA were so far behind that Fourneau and I ended up clearing most of the compounds ourselves. Every compound or street we ran down Aziz was convinced he could make out the guy, just *a bit* ahead of us, but that we'd catch him soon.

"It's Dick, boys! Thar be Moby Dick! Death, death to the white whale!" I cried, laughing away at my own cleverness as I passed Aziz in a dead sprint and rounded a corner. I stopped laughing the moment my face smashed into a mud wall, and then like a bunch of Keystone cops, everyone smacked into the back of me. I spit out blood from my fat lip and started to say, "How could *one* guy get over a wall like—"

Ali cut me off, translating for Aziz who was dictating between ragged breaths, winded from his sprint. "You must smash it down, Captain Rob. We cannot all climb over!"

"How in the hell am I supposed to—"

"You must hurry, Captain Rob. He will escape!"

I wanted to shout, "Who *will escape, you mad bastard? There's no one even there!*" but decided to take it on the chin and do something I'd always wanted to do, namely, kick down a mud wall whilst in hot pursuit of a suspect.

Images of a hundred cop shows and, for some reason, *The Littlest Hobo* flooded my mind. I handed Fourneau my rifle and said, "Don't get all gropey!" as I started delivering vicious front kicks like I'd learned at the Ninja Dojo of Inner Wisdom and Sacred Pain back in Saskatoon many years ago. *If only the Hard and Soft Masters could see me now!*

The Canadians and Afghans alike formed a protective half-circle around me, but instead of watching their arcs and scanning for the enemy, everyone was facing in toward me as I really laid into that wall, boot stomping it with everything I had. I began to hum the theme song from *The Littlest Hobo*, or as my wife called him, *le chien qui sauve le monde. There's a voice, that keeps on callin' me / down the road, that's where I'll always be / every stop I make, I make a new friend . . .*

SMASH! SMASH! I was making some progress, but in the heat, I was really starting to feel it too. Sweat was pouring off my face by the time I finally got the wall kicked down to where it was only four feet high. I grabbed my lead chucker back from Fourneau, shouted, "Follow me—I'm bulletproof!" and leaped over the smashed blocks, eager to win my Roman legion its first *corona muralis* for being the first soldier over an enemy wall. I had always been a big history buff, and sometimes the oddest thoughts would pop into my head. I immediately scanned left and right, my weapon tracking everywhere I looked, just like I'd been taught.

I shouted "Clear!" when I realized I was alone in a courtyard. I quickly told the guys over the PRR the layout of the fields, but I hadn't cleared *them* yet, and so far there was no activity. *Don't really like being alone. . . .* I looked back at Fourneau, who was struggling to get over the four-foot wall. I was on my own until he came over, but I couldn't just sit around and wait. *Timothy was getting away!*

We were in a farmer's field surrounded by high walls, so I immediately began scanning down each row until I had made it to the end. The ghost we'd been chasing was nowhere in sight. I ran up to a shoulder-high block of mud and hopped up onto it, slung my rifle, then jumped up another couple of feet and gripped the edge of the wall and pulled myself up, until my chin was peeking over the edge.

I saw some fields and more huts, but no one running for his life, nor any civilians, period, so with a grunt I pulled myself all the way up and threw a leg over each side of the high wall. I thought everyone must be at the town meeting at the north end of the village.

Aziz ran over and jumped up next to me. He was surprisingly agile. That, plus he had about eighty pounds *less* gear on him. Fourneau was next and quietly said, "I'll never make that, sir."

"Sure you will. Jump with everything you've got, and I'll muckle onto you and pull you up!"

"Sir, I don't think—"

"Get the fuck up there, Fourneau, *right now!*" The warrant shouted at the back of Fourneau's head, startling him in his moment of self-doubt. The Wizard had jacked up Fourneau a few days ago for not being able to follow me over a wall, and now it was happening all over again.

Fourneau leapt and floundered, but I had a death grip on his tac vest shoulder, and no power on earth could make me let go. "I'm not . . . going to . . . let you fall." I said, remembering *Cliffhanger*, one of Stallone's seminal movies.

The warrant got beneath him and gave a healthy shove and that was all I needed to hoist my fire team partner up beside me. I looked at Fourneau and smiled. "Told ya. Now you get scanning, I gots to do the occifer thing!" I quickly checked my GPS and sent up a locstat and sitrep. I asked the Canucks to our east if they'd seen anything, but they had zero activity to their front. *Aziz really* was *seeing ghosts.*

I helped get everyone up and over, and then slowly slid down the wall, careful not to land with too much of a thump. Just letting yourself fall to the other side was a quick way to make the front page of *Safety Digest* (the CF's magazine dedicated to tales of admonishment), so I tried to hug the wall and slide down, but it didn't matter. I landed with a good, hard *thud*. When you wear that much kit, you're going to land heavy, and like my Brit Para instructors always said, "Sometimes you just got to take it. Nuffin' ye can do!" I knew to breathe out, though, so at least I wouldn't wind myself.

I scanned around but there was no one to be seen, although Aziz had seen another ghost and took off again at a dead sprint.

The warrant shouted behind me as I gave chase. "Enough's enough!" He was right. It was easy for the ANA to sprint around; they were carrying two mags each and that was it—no body armour, maybe a helmet, maybe not.

I jogged up next to Aziz as Ali struggled to keep up with us. We came to an intersection, and I guess we chased the ghosts to the *other side*, because Lieutenant Aziz was finally satisfied. Our exorcism was a success. He collected his men and marched us to the southwest of the ville, where we entered into the deep grape-field trenches.

I got on the net, thanked the Canadians for their patience and for coming out to play, and said the ANA were satisfied and now heading back to Sper. The Canadian platoon gave me *roger* and made their way to the road to head back in, probably to check the culverts at the same time.

I heard some choppers in the air to our north, and radioed the command post to find out what was going on. The CP sergeant said, "American general's ground convoy. Heading to Masum."

We were cutting through the grape fields when Ali ran up to me and said, "Sir, they are talking to each other on Icom, and one of them asked the other if the ANA searched him or his motorbike, and he said, 'No, they only talked to me, and then let me go!'"

Holy crap! We had only seen one motorbike all day, back at the town shura. "Please tell Lieutenant Aziz that!" I told Ali.

He translated, excited like me to finally have some solid int, but Aziz saw the barn and, like a good trail horse, was on his way back to his stable.

"No, I do not believe him. That is not the same person," he said over his shoulder to us.

And how the hell would you know that? I wondered. "But Lieutenant, we're only one hundred metres away; we could go back and still catch the guy, and search him and his motorbike and—"

"No, we have done much running today, and we have not had any water since three o'clock this morning, so we must go back now."

I could understand about the water; I had easily drunk at least two litres so far, and they had had nothing, *but we were running around like idiots because of you, jackass!* We never got any solid int leads like this, so it was a fantastic opportunity, and he was just letting it slip through his fingers. And that was that. He continued marching and I tried not to pout, but I was not impressed.

We followed a ditch and then marched into a deep wadi, or dried-up riverbed, and then followed it until it led us to an open patch of ground. I looked around and realized we had all marched out into the open and Aziz would need to disperse his men; we were one big gaggle of troops, waiting to get mowed down or killed with one RPG or IED. The ways the enemy could kill us were almost limitless, *so why make it easy for him by bunching up?*

"Sir," Longview said quietly, and then much louder, "SIR!"

I spun around to see one of the American Kiowa helicopters, high up in the air in its over-watch position of the convoy, make a slow, half-circle in the cloudless sky until it was in line with us, about a kilometre away. It was now flying in our direction and covering the distance between us a little *too* quickly. Everyone around me stopped dead in their tracks. We all realized at the same moment that thirty-five *armed* men had just popped out of a wadi and were now huddled up in one big group, *just* like the Taliban would do!

Co-lishun' furces would-unt bunch up like thaht! I could hear the American pilot saying to his gunner, in a thick Texas drawl, as the gunner's thumb clicked up the red switch to make his guns hot.

"Nobody run, nobody move . . . " I said as calmly as I could. "Ali, tell the Afghans not to move or run, or the chopper will kill us for sure. Everyone wave!" The gunship's nose dipped and its engine screamed with the strain. He was commencing his strafing run!

"Big, friendly waves!" I shouted. "Wave, wave you sons of bitches, WAVE LIKE YOUR LIVES DEPEND ON IT!" I had packed a Canadian flag for just this sort of occasion, but try as I might (and I was *really* trying), I couldn't get my side pouch open without using both hands, and my sense of self-preservation told me every guy and his dog needed to be waving at that exact moment with both arms.

It must've been a ridiculous sight: thirty-five fully grown and splendidly bearded men, armed to the teeth, waving like a bunch of kids on the playground, trying desperately to get the quarterback's attention: *Throw it to me, I'm open! I'm open!*

When his nose dipped and his engine began to scream, my heart dropped into my ballbag. I felt sick to my stomach and thought, *This is it. This is how I'm going out: a blue-on-blue, killed by my own side, by a guy from Skokie, Illinois!*

The pilot must've been a big fan of theatrical suspense, because he waited until the last possible moment to get his guns off before he turned his chopper on its axis, making it bob left and right as if to say, *Hi, you're all pretty damn lucky!* and then he veered off, going back to protect the convoy and scare the living crap out of somebody else.

"Jesus wept for the city of Jerusalem!" I whispered, and suddenly, everyone was laughing hysterically. I felt like an old man who had to wipe his eyes and blow his nose after a good guffaw. The adrenalin monkeys were riding us like crazy and we felt high the whole way back. But after a moment like that when the adrenalin is surging through you and making you feel invincible, when your body starts to finally come down off that natural high you hit the pavement pretty hard, and usually face first. Suddenly you can't keep your eyes open anymore and you just want to pass out and sleep for three days.

When we got back to our shack, Fourneau dropped his kit in a heap and collapsed on his bed, and I knew exactly how he felt. I would've liked to crash out too. The angry father tore him a new one, insisting that he get up out of his wank pit and top up his water and brush off his weapon. I followed my own SOP, and then began writing the report as the warrant went to the computer, Fourneau went back to bed, and Hetsa fired up the Xbox. I wasn't quite sure how to write this one up. That whole situation had been sort of novel for me.

I thought of something after our near-death experience, so I asked Captain Shafiq Ullah if I could speak to his men. He agreed and got Lieutenant Aziz to assemble them. They stood neatly at attention, but it was brutally hot and they were still observing Ramadan, so I wanted to do this as quickly as possible.

I asked Ali to do his terp thing as I got their CSM, Khan, to stand the soldiers at ease. I shouted in my best General Rommel voice, "Soldiers of the Afghan National Army, all of the Canadians are very impressed with you. It is an honour to be here, fighting alongside all of you. We can only imagine how hard it must be to patrol, every day, in this heat and dust with no food or water. We are amazed by your strength.

"I want you to remember what I am about to tell you, because one day, it may save all of our lives. If we are on a patrol, and you see some Canadians, the British, or Americans, but they have not seen *you*, your life is in danger. Sometimes, the soldiers the coalition countries send over here are very young. Many times, it is their first combat tour. Many of them have never been shot at before, and they are scared. If you pop out of a wadi, or from behind a wall, and they are not expecting you to be there, they may fire at you and kill you, or call in a jet, helicopter, or artillery. That is why, what I am about to say, you must remember . . ." I waited a few seconds to increase the dramatic tension.

"*The Taliban don't wave!* To give a big, friendly wave—this is surely blasphemous to them! So, because the coalition forces know the Taliban don't wave, *if* you ever find yourself about to be shot at, by a soldier or a helicopter, do not run! Do not take cover! If you do that, they will think you are Taliban for sure, and they will fire on you. The best thing you can do is before they shoot, stand perfectly still and give a big, friendly wave, and keep waving until they wave back. Just like what we did this morning. Obviously it worked, because we're all still alive."

The Afghans began laughing as I shouted, "Like this!" and gave a huge, flamboyant wave. I got the Afghans to copy me, and although we were all laughing and having fun, I was dead serious about what I had said. And I didn't know it at the time, but the Taliban-don't-wave trick would save all of our lives, many times over.

* * *

Later after we'd showered and had lunch, I went to the command post to use the encrypted telephone. I called Sean, our 2 I/C, at the OMLT HQ in Masum Ghar. We called each other all sorts of nasty names, as was our custom, and then I got down to it. I explained how Fourneau's fitness had been lacking as of late. I mentioned the patrol a few mornings back, where the ANA wanted to patrol to a small village called "Little Reggae" to the south of Sperwhan. They had gotten lost and confused when they could no longer see it as we passed through a small village, and the warrant had to take their recce guys by the hand to extricate them from the village. But that wasn't the problem. The issue arose when we came upon four hundred metres of open ground between the small village we were in and the one we had to patrol to.

Captain Shafiq Ullah was completely convinced we were going to get fired on from Little Reggae, so he said we'd have to sprint across the open ground, like soldiers at Gallipoli. I considered requesting smoke shells to screen us, but our guns were currently firing to the north, so someone needed them a lot more than we did. We began to run across the open ground, and had probably gotten halfway across when the warrant started shouting at Fourneau over the PRR. I spun around and realized that I had lost him. I asked the captain if we could halt to let Fourneau catch up. Shafiq Ullah said, "He is only one man," and I could see his point, if indeed we were being fired at. In a situation like that we couldn't risk everyone's life for the one guy who couldn't keep up, but that wasn't the case here.

I said we really had to go firm, to let him catch up. The warrant shouted at him again over the PRR: "You'd fucking better catch up to the sir, right now!" Fourneau ran up to me and smashed into the ditch beside me and started apologizing, but I cut him off and said we'd talk about it later, because right now we had to get going. I gave him a minute to catch his breath, but we were all terribly exposed so we had to move. We continued running, and again, Fourneau fell behind. The warrant ripped another big strip off him.

I relayed the story to Sean, and mentioned how Fourneau, on a couple of different patrols, had left me to climb small walls or cross streams on my own, while he would go out of his way to try and find an easier route.

"Now, to be fair to him, some of the walls were quite high, and the bridges narrow, but we have to follow where the Afghans lead, and Fourneau's ten years younger than me, and twenty years younger than the warrant, so he should be able to keep up," I told Sean. I also mentioned that after the first time he'd ditched me to find another route, he was told to never do it again, and in the future, I told him to let me know any detour plans and I would go with him. I just didn't want to turn around and find him gone. That tends to violently age a commander, especially when the enemy would love nothing better than to capture a Canadian alive so they could cut his head off on the six o'clock Al Jazeera news.

"So what you're saying," Sean replied, "is you're a bad leader and you're putting his life at risk with your unnecessary heroics?"

"Yes, that's exactly what I'm saying, ya got me!" I snorted.

"No, I get it. He's becoming a force-protection issue. He's not covering you, he's not going the same routes, and he's leaving you exposed."

"Yeah, but he's not doing it on purpose. I mean, he's not being malicious, and it *is* incredibly hot here. Of course, you wouldn't know because you can't leave the safety of the Batcave to go on patrol, because you're too important to the cause, but... He's a good guy, he's just struggling on the PT side. Everything else, he's doing great. I don't want to get rid of him, but, well, you know what I mean."

"Yeah, I know. You live in a world of fear, and he ain't helpin'. How are you holding up?" Sean uncharacteristically asked.

"Aw, you know me. My tour 'stache and adamantium-laced bones will protect me! Give it some thunk, all right? Thanks for nothing, out. *Ksscchh!*" I hung up on him before he could get the last word in, as was my custom.

I cornered Fourneau that afternoon, and he said he was really sorry for letting me down. I accepted his apology, but then said we needed to seriously discuss what had been going on over the last couple of weeks. I told him I considered him to be a very good and bright soldier, but his fitness was letting him, me, and the rest of the team down. I explained that I knew he was trying, and I was happy with him, overall, but his fitness level had put all of us at risk the other day.

He started to cry. That took me a bit by surprise, so I sat down next to him and put my arm over his shoulder like a big brother, and told him we just had to get his fitness level up.

He explained that he wasn't crying because of his fitness, but because he felt like he was letting down the memory of a couple of his friends who had come to Afghanistan on tour and been killed in action. He went on to say that the only reason he had come to Afghanistan was to try and honour their memory, and now he was letting them down too. I felt terrible for the guy, but I had been to the Stan before, so I knew what to expect. He told me he believed me back in Canada, when I said how tough it would be, but until you've experienced heat like this first-hand, it's too hard to imagine. Again, I knew exactly what he meant.

I asked him if there was anything I could do. Fourneau told me that he thought he could do the job, but he was having a really hard time. He was visibly exhausted, both mentally and physically. Every night, he would go on the computer and play a video game, and it didn't take a crack team of Viennese psychiatrists to realize he was doing it to escape.

I asked him again, what would he like me to do? He asked if he could get transferred to work in the storeroom back in KAF. He wanted to stay in the OMLT, but the constant patrolling was taking its toll on him, and he was finding it too much. I said I would see what I could do. I felt for him, I truly did, but he was quickly becoming a liability, and he knew it. And things, as they so often did in this, the world's saddest place, were about to get worse.

* * *

After our close call with the American chopper, the ANA, under Shafiq Ullah's leadership, decided to take another admin day. The Canadians took advantage of the opportunity to clean our weapons, change all of our batteries, and dry out our kit. There were a couple of washing machines on the base, something I'd never had before, so we'd combine our clothes, seriously overstuff the poor machines, and then hang our kit up to dry, but always with a guard posted nearby, lest our clothes magically grew legs and walked away. I'd been told that Afghanistan was a place of strange voodoo magic, so we took no chances.

That morning, I invited the ANA leadership over for *chai*, coffee, and fruit after lunch; we hadn't had them over yet, nor vice versa. Stephens said he had supper almost every night with his Afghans, so maybe I wasn't doing something right, 'cause so far, no invites.

I asked the cooks to put together a hospitality plate of cheese and fruit, and they didn't let me down. They provided a huge platter topped up with some great finger food, and not surprisingly, the Afghans were on time, for once. We offered them tea and pop and they were immediately smitten with the kiwi fruit, having never before seen any. We sat down on the comfy couch and all of the westerners remembered to only reach in and take food with their right hand. In Afghanistan, the left hand is considered unclean.

I asked them how they felt the patrols were going and they quickly responded, "Great, no problems." I asked them if we could start training their troops in modern techniques and SOPs, after they had a chance to approve our training syllabus, of course. After Ali translated, they looked at me like I'd slapped their moms' faces, right in front of them!

"Captain Shafiq Ullah says that is kind of you to offer, but it will not be necessary. They already know everything," Ali translated.

Longview began to violently choke on his drink. I couldn't help myself and blurted out, "They already know *everything?*" An awkward silence ensued. *Well then, I guess our job's done and we can go home!*

After that, there wasn't a whole lot left to talk about. We discussed some minor things, and then thanked them for coming over. They thanked us for having them, we all shook hands, and they quietly left.

We waited until they were out of earshot before we snickered at their "expertise."

"We can stand down, boys," I said. "Our job's done! We've mentored them to a level where they know everything, and we can finally go home!" Fourneau got up from the table and went to the porta-potty, so I had a window to speak quickly to Hetsa and Longview about something that had been bothering me.

I put on my serious officer face and said, "Guys, from now on, please open your mail only in your bed space where no one can see you, okay?"

Hetsa looked indignant. "Why's that, sir?"

"Because, Hungo, the other day you got a three-by-three-foot box with enough kit—including a new Xbox, video games, and magazines— to open your own Mac's store in the village centre. The warrant's getting mail almost daily from his harem from all over the world, and I'm getting care packages from home too. But guess who *isn't?* When I collect the mail after the morning BUB, I can't help but notice the only mail Fourneau's getting is from the bank back home. He's getting bank slips for his mail. Can you possibly begin to imagine how much that would suck, if that was the only mail you were getting, in a place like this? So don't ask me *why,* okay? Just do it."

They both nodded in agreement and I went back to my computer before Fourneau could walk in and interrupt our witch's coven. I felt really bad for the guy, he was having a rough go, and I wanted to help him out where I could. *But will it be enough?*

Chapter 9

No matter what the ANA leadership said, somehow we doubted their claim to omniscience. We were proven right the next day when, as if on universal cue, the ANA promptly burned their kitchen to the ground.

After we'd taken another day off, again for admin issues, I was working on the computer when someone began beating down our front door. It didn't help that it was already literally swinging on its hinges. I guess the Afghan repairman hadn't been around since, well, since *ever*. I walked over to the door and opened it to find Ali and the ANA artillery commander, a guy Stephens had berated for wanting parachute flares from the OMLT a few weeks ago.

"Good morning, sir. Can we talk to you about something, for only a minute?" Ali asked, in his usual overly polite English. It didn't matter how many times I told him to stop calling me *sir*, he couldn't drop the habit.

"Of course, Ali, you can always talk to me. Would you like to come in?"

"No, sir. There is something happening and we need to tell you about it."

"Okay, what's going on?" *This should be good.*

"Fair, sir," was all he said, and then looked at me as though I would know what the hell he was talking about.

"Fair, Ali? I don't understand. What do you mean, *fair?*"

"You know, sir. Fair . . . fair!" He began to look nervous, fearing I wasn't getting his point.

"No Ali, I don't know." I was becoming tired after the last couple of weeks, and my temper was beginning to fray a bit. "Fair? As in, 'Fare thee well?' Is the Rankin Family here? Is there a *fair* in town? I don't know *what* you mean Ali, but I'm pretty sure you don't mean 'fair.'" This wasn't like Ali. His English was usually very good and he didn't normally make mistakes like that. Unless it wasn't a mistake, and the Rankin Family really was at the base, about to perform. Usually you'd hear about those sorts of things, but not always.

Ali looked over his shoulder and started speaking in rapid-fire Dari to the artillery commander. After a heated exchange back and forth for a good minute, Ali tried again to get his point across.

"You know, sir. Fire." Ali looked pleased with himself for finding the right word.

"Fire?" I shouted. "Something's on *fire*?"

"Yes, sir," Ali proudly stated. "The ANA kitchen is on fire."

"The ANA's *kitchen* is on fire?"

"Yes, that is right, sir. Their kitchen is on fire and soon the whole building will be on fire, and probably the other buildings too." Ali looked over his shoulder to let the agitated commander know that the point had gotten through my thick skull and help would be on its way, hopefully *sharpish* if the look on his face was anything to go by.

"Okay, thanks Ali. I'll call the command post and ask them to send the fire brigade."

"Very good, sir. Thank you. I am sorry, sir, that I did not say the word correctly." Ali didn't seem overly bothered that their kitchen was on fire, but more troubled by his poor interpretation skills.

"Don't worry, Ali," I said. "That was my fault. I'm very tired." I shooed him out the door. "I'll get help, okay?" With their mission complete, the two of them calmly walked off.

I was a firm believer in the old army saying "trust, but verify," and that was never more true than when you worked with the ANA. So I poked my head out the door and looked in the direction of the kitchen. Their storeroom was blocking my view, but I could easily make out a huge plume of grey-black smoke quickly rising into the air, where their kitchen should be. *Holy crap!* This was serious! The Afghans left live ammunition and grenades all over the place; we'd been trying to mentor them out of the habit, but weren't having much luck. Leaving grenades and RPG rockets right next to a large, open firepit in their kitchen wouldn't bother them in the least. *Do we even have firefighters at Sperwhan Ghar?*

I picked up the field phone that was connected to the command post. The CP was manned twenty-four/seven, maybe not necessarily by Mike Company's best and brightest, but the guy in charge at least was always switched-on. The phone was picked up and a corporal identified himself.

"Hi there," I said, in my non-panicky voice. "This is Captain Semrau with the OMLT. I guess the Afghans' kitchen is on fire. Is there anyone on the base who acts as firefighters?" There was a long pause on the other end.

"Sir, I don't know if you're being serious or not," the corporal quietly said.

"Hells yeah, I'm serious! I'm not joking around! Seriously, their kitchen building really *is* on fire. Can you guys muster some people to come and fight it?"

"Yes, sir, we've got people tasked for that. I'll mobilize them and get them there ASAP."

I hung up and ran over to the kitchen. Smoke and flames were billowing out of it as the warrant and Ali were desperately trying to stop the ANA soldiers from running back into the burning building to save their kit. We found out afterwards that they would've been held fiscally responsible for any lost or damaged kit, fire notwithstanding, so they didn't want their children's children to have to join the army to pay off *their* debt. They were literally running back into a burning building, smoke was everywhere, and it looked like the fire was going to spread to the other buildings because they were only a few feet away.

Suddenly our army cooks (who apparently were also moonlighting as professional firefighters) arrived, dragging long fire hoses with them. When I told them about the possibility of rounds going off from the fire, they never wavered for a moment; instead they gave the signal to a guy back at the water bladders and began fighting the fire with everything they had. They were nothing short of heroic in their efforts, and after a good thirty minutes they had the fire in check. But unfortunately, all of them had suffered smoke inhalation. For their bravery and dedication to saving the buildings (and making sure we didn't get blown up when the Afghan explosives went off), I believed they all should have been "gonged" for gallantry, but I don't know if any of them were officially recognized.

Longview and I joked afterwards, saying "Canadian army cooks: not only do they make an amazing chicken curry, but they can fight fires, professionally!"

They had what the old cowboys in western movies called "sand." No doubt about it, and their bravery was unquestioned by the ANA and OMLT.

An hour later an American Humvee jeep, painted in many different shades of desert camouflage (as was the Afghan custom), pulled up and a very large, blustery Afghan general and his party of hangers-on disgorged themselves. The general had turned up to see the damage first-hand, and in all probability, demand an answer from Shafiq Ullah as to why he hadn't sacrificed every soldier he had to save the ANA's Vietnam-era radios and crockery.

Game face, Rob, game face! It was go time. I quickly strode over, putting on my field cap. Even though people had laughed at me for carrying it around with me, I had known, in my heart of hearts, that someday the Afghans would undoubtedly set their own kitchen on fire and I'd have to personally intervene to try and save my fellow captain.

I wish I could say my motives stemmed from a sense of compassion, but I felt it was better to try and save the devil I knew in Shafiq Ullah. I'd hoped I could keep him around, instead of getting some complete wing nut as his replacement, who might get us all killed. Shafiq Ullah wasn't going to single-handedly defeat the Taliban, but he also wasn't going to light the fuse that blew up the world.

I grabbed Ali and confidently strode over to the general and jumped in front of him. He came to a stop so suddenly he almost plowed me over. I snapped out my sharpest salute and said, "Sir, my name is Captain Rob. I am the mentor for the Afghans here. I want to tell you, sir, that I was amazed by the personal bravery of every Afghan soldier here. They kept running back into the building, even though it was on fire. One soldier was even *on* fire. They wouldn't have stopped, sir, they would have died to save their equipment, but when the firefighters got here they ordered everyone to stop running inside so that they could put out the fire. I was very proud of them. *You* should be very proud of them, sir. I am honoured to fight alongside them! Thank you, sir." And with that, I saluted sharply once more.

At the beginning of my spiel I could tell he wasn't impressed that I cut him off mid-stride, but as my words were being translated, a smile began to form around the corners of his mouth. Then he started beaming with pride. *I think I pulled it off!* He spoke to Ali in dignified tones and then saluted me back. He clapped me on the shoulder like a father, and went up to Captain Shafiq Ullah. Ali told me the general said, "Thank you for your kind words. I am glad they were brave."

The two Afghans saluted each other, and then Shafiq Ullah called his men to attention. The general walked to the front of the men and started pacing back and forth. Ali began translating for me. The general was berating them for starting the fire, but then he said he was proud of their bravery. He explained that the Canadian mentor told him they were *ordered* to stop their kit retrieval, and therefore it wasn't *their* fault they had lost some of their equipment. The soldiers all breathed a collective sigh of relief.

The general thanked them once again, Shafiq Ullah returned to the front officer position and saluted, and the general turned to leave. As he passed in front of me, I saluted, and he smartly returned the salute. Shafiq Ullah dismissed his men and rapidly walked over to me.

"I will never forget what you have done. Thank you, Captain Rob, for speaking to the general on our behalf." He seemed genuinely moved. I guess it'd been a long time since someone had helped him instead of blading him.

"We share the same dangers," I laughed, "whether it's on the battlefield, or when generals come to visit." I smiled, hoping he'd get the joke.

"Yes, it is more dangerous for us when generals come to visit, is it not?"

We both laughed at that. I'd seen how our visiting Canadian generals could put some soldiers in a real panic, so I knew how he felt. Although I'd never actually set my own kitchen on fire . . . yet.

Shafiq Ullah continued, "I will have my sergeant major fill out the Mod 14 form and give it to you as soon as he is done."

"Thank you. I will send mine up the chain of command the same time as you. I'm sure you will have the missing equipment you need by tomorrow." The second I'd said that, I wished I hadn't. I immediately felt terrible, like I'd kicked the captain when he was down. It was widely acknowledged that their Mod 14 system of kit replacement was completely useless, but he didn't need *me* to rub it in.

I became serious again and said, "Hopefully when we send the forms up our respective chains of command, we'll find out where the order gets stuck and we can get it fixed. *Inshallah*."

"*Inshallah*," he repeated. " And thank you once again."

"*Sabah al-khair*," I said, trying to pronounce "good morning" properly.

"*Sabah al-khair*." He placed his hand over his heart and turned to leave.

Ali and I walked off toward my building. "Thanks for the good translating today, Ali. You did a very good job, as per."

"Thank you, sir. I will see you tomorrow."

"*Inshallah.*"

Ali laughed, "Of course, sir. *Inshallah.*"

About a week later, the ANA stood in a group, anxious to see the kit and crockery that the general was sending to them as replacements for the things they had lost in the Great Afghan Kitchen Fire of Oh-eight. They were shocked to find even older radios, which were completely dysfunctional, along with rusted ammunition, Chinese grenades with no fuses, and for the *crème de la crème*, several children's playtime tea sets, replete with miniature plates, knives, and forks. They were livid, as any man with an ounce of pride would've been. I didn't know what to say.

It was like a sick practical joke. The ANA told me that their logisticians had taken the money meant for cutlery and plates, pocketed it, and went out and bought kids' tea sets instead. I guess they thought the troops in the field wouldn't notice they'd pulled the ol' switcheroo on 'em!

I immediately radioed my chain of command to let them know what had just happened, but Captain Mike, our OMLT logistics officer, who would normally have tried to sort out the problem, was in the doghouse himself. He had spent the better part of the last three days trying to explain to the interpreter he had insulted, and the ANA, *and* his boss, Major Hobbles, that he was only *joking* when he said *sangai* (*hello*) to an interpreter in Pashto and then thoughtlessly added "motherfucker" in English.

Everyone from North America knew that Mike wasn't actually accus-ing the terp of having intimate, carnal knowledge of his own mother, but of course, the Afghans weren't from North America. An unholy brouhaha of shouting ensued, entirely one way, and death threats quickly followed. For the time being, Mike was *persona non grata*. So my Afghans, due to the ridiculous insensitivity and corruption of their own logistics system, would just have to play tea for the next few weeks, until we could go on an operation and confiscate some crockery from the Taliban. Which is, of course, exactly what we did.

* * *

The next few patrols were milk runs, and you didn't hear 72A complaining. I had been watching the guys from the start, monitoring their behaviour and attitudes for signs of stress. Longview was the gold standard for us, always switched on, always good to go. Hetsa was really starting to act like an old vet; he'd seen some action and was beginning to swagger, maybe a bit too much for the angry father. Fourneau was a different matter, and I was becoming quite concerned. At the end of each patrol, he'd perform the mandatory water top-up, dust off his weapon, and then crash out hard on his bed space. Clearly he hadn't made peace with his version of the Almighty, and no matter how hard he tried to hide it, it was obvious he thought he wasn't going to survive this tour.

I talked to him privately on several different occasions, and did my best to reassure him that he was going to be fine. I took him with me to the gym, I took an interest in his video game progress, and I started a 72A SOP of watching *Battlestar Galactica* (the new series) after every patrol, knowing he was a big fan of science fiction. We had fun with it, and wouldn't start the show until everyone on our team was seated on the comfy couch.

One thing was for sure, we'd all lost weight. Of course, we'd been sweating like damn pigs for the better part of three weeks, but there was more to it than that. Living in a state of near-constant stress begins to wear you down, degrade you, and make you less combat-effective, and sadly, less *normal*. The things you would've found funny back home don't make you laugh as much anymore, and you begin to lose interest in the things you once enjoyed. I recognized the effects of constant wariness and stress on myself and the team, but recognizing it *and* finding a way to stop it were two different things. Slowly, everything began to feel grey.

It didn't help that the ANA artillery was beginning to fire their heavy rounds into the mountains to the south. They were meant to call the CP, who would then call everyone to let them know it was the ANA firing, and to not crap themselves when they heard a massive cannon shooting only metres away from their shack. As so often happens in war, the message never got properly passed, and we would literally jump inches off the ground when they fired, our hearts beating out of our chests for a good minute.

Someone would shout "Sonofabitch!" and we would all nervously laugh, not really finding it funny. Our whole building would shake and dust would fall all over our kit. The first time it happened, I flinched so violently I twisted my neck out of whack. On top of that, the Canadians would be firing their howitzers too, at all hours, and again, with usually no warning given, so you couldn't prepare your heart not to freak out.

I had some extra fun thrown into the mix because, at least once a week, I'd wake up to a mouse climbing up my arm or on my face as I slept. I'd shout

"Gaahaaaa!" and violently shake until it was bucked off of me. *There was just no need for that....*

* * *

Captain Sean often radioed me to see how we were doing and if we needed anything. "Yeah," I'd respond, "a 2 I/C with a functioning spine!"

I liked to give Sean the gears, but I credited him for acting as a great shit shield between me and Major Hobbles.

It probably didn't help Sean that I liked to remind him that this was his first combat tour. Whenever I would rudely point that out, he'd tell me that he'd been to Bosnia. Then I'd tell him *that* tour didn't count. I'd go on to tell him that within the Canadian military, none of those so-called tours before Afghanistan counted, for anything. If you hadn't been to the Stan before, you were a nobody, and nothing you had done previously counted for squat! I was only joking, but I knew a lot of people within the CF actually believed that crap.

"Numbnuts," he opened with over the secure net, "next time you go on patrol—that is to say, *if* you ever go back on patrol and stop screwing the dog with all of your admin days off—check out the local area and see if you can find a good place to set up a donkey pen, over."

"HA! Good one! Over, *ksscchh*!" I laughed. Sean had a great sense of humour.

"No, I'm serious, someone in KAF has a full-time job of trying to get donkeys to the Afghan army. They're meant to start using them for long-range resupply missions, over."

"Donkeys? *Donkeys?* In the year 2008, when we've got this marvellous invention called the four-stroke internal combustion engine, they want to try and convince the ANA to use *donkeys?* I thought we were trying to get them *out* of the twelfth century? Over, *ksscchh.*"

"Well, I saw the officer myself when I was back in KAF; he calls himself the Assman. It's his full-time job, trying to get donkeys to the ANA. I'm serious, so quit screwing around and try to find a suitable place to put a donkey pen, out."

"You don't out *me*, I out *you*! Out! *Ksscchh*!"

"Hey dickhead, have you been making the '*ksscchh*' radio static noise this whole time?"

"Don't know what you're talking about, 72A, OUT! *Ksscchh!*"

Lieutenant Aziz found me later and asked if I'd heard anything about donkey pens. It seems his HQ had told him the same thing: to find a suitable location to begin maintaining a crack team of donkeys that were earmarked to resupply the ANA over countless klicks of hostile enemy territory. We both thought it was some sort of a practical joke.

Later that afternoon I saw the ANA artillery officer, the one Captain Brannon (the OMLT artillery mentor) was advising. He was the ANA officer who had been pestering Stephens for parachute flares, and Stephens (being so close to catching his "freedom bird" home at the end of his tour) sort of snapped at him, telling him he wasn't an effing supermarket for the ANA. I approached him and through Ali, I said I'd found some para flares, and if he could find some time, I'd give him a demo on them.

Without a word he silently abandoned Captain Brannon and followed me over to my OMLT HQ, where I radioed the command post to tell them we'd be test firing para flares, and they shouldn't be alarmed.

We fired a few until he got the gist, then I handed him several and told him, "Good hunting. Oh," I added, "and of course, try not to use them all at once." That was akin to telling a kid on Christmas day, "Don't open *any* of your gifts."

Tears welled up in his eyes as he shook my hand vigorously and thanked me. Of course, that night several para flares could be seen drifting lazily in the sky over Observation Post Brown, where he was stationed at the T-intersection north of Sperwhan Ghar, and I think some non-affiliated Taliban donkeys were mercilessly gunned down in the confusion, but what the hell. If he wanted to use them to kill Taliban (and hopefully not any more donkeys), then I would find some for him. We literally had huge ISO containers (giant steel shipping containers) full of them back in KAF that no one seemed to be using. And I didn't know it at the time, but I had done my good karma deed for the day. That one would come back to help me, not haunt me like some of the things I had done in my lifetime.

Chapter 10

As if on fatalistic cue, Strong Point Sperwhan Ghar was attacked for the second time since we arrived. This time we were sitting at the picnic table as Ali was giving us a Dari lesson, when rounds began to crack overhead and smack into the cement of our buildings, pinging and ricocheting around the barracks. Suddenly a dull THUMP came from the hill as mortars began to fall onto it. An RPG warhead screamed over the buildings, flying just over our roof.

"Stop your grinnin' and drop your linen!" I shouted as I held open the door to our shack for Longview, Hetsa, and Fourneau. "Go go go!" I shouted as I slapped them on their butts like Coach Green, my old high school football coach, as they ran past. I ran over to the field phone as the snipers were talking over the net, picked it up, and told the CP that Sperwhan was under attack (and if the vapour contrails of the RPG rockets were anything to go by) from the west.

We quickly kitted up, a very sombre tone falling over the team as we struggled into our vests and gear. We knew this attack was a lot more serious than the last one. Last time it had been a few village yahoos taking potshots, but this was different. Now there was a lot of incoming machine gun fire, rockets, and mortars. I shouted, "Dress me, Hetsa!" and then led the team into the mélée.

ANA were running everywhere in total pandemonium, shouting and cursing. Ali poked his head out from around a corner and I shouted at him to go back to his building and get on the ground and stay there. No interpretation was needed; the situation was remarkably clear. Find the enemy and kill him, before he killed us. Simple really, as long as we weren't killed before we could even *find* him.

I spoke into the PRR as we took off running towards the sandbags, the sound of rounds snapping into the buildings and overhead. "Wizard and Hungo break right, Fourneau on me; hard and fast into cover!"

I sprinted out from between the buildings and into the open area, and suddenly all hell broke loose. Rounds whizzed and cracked all around us; mortars exploded on the hill as RPG rockets screamed overhead; the snipers on the hilltop were returning fire with their high-powered rifles; an ANA soldier with a PKM light machine gun was blasting away into the village to the west, shouting at his number two on the gun to find more ammo.

I was running as fast as I could, but it felt like I was in a bad dream; my legs were kicking and pumping with everything I had, but the smooth stones were being churned up as I ran and it felt like running in thick sand, as the sickening CRACK CRACK sounds passed over and in front of my head. I almost fell over but righted myself as time slowed down. Multiple RPG warheads flew over top of us as rounds snapped and cracked in front, overhead, and behind us.

It seemed like something out of any of the hundreds of war movies I had watched in my life, but *this is real, this is real*, I had to keep telling myself, because it all seemed so incredibly surreal. You could hear the enemy shoot, then when you heard a *snap* sound it meant it's close to you, but when you can hear the *crack* of a bullet, you know it's *too* close; the cracking sound is the bullet breaking the sound barrier, right next to your head. The louder the crack, the closer it was to freeing you from your mortal coil.

I was running toward the sandbag emplacement. I could see the berm; it was only a couple of feet away now—*c'mon, c'mon!*—and I made it, slamming into the wall. I looked back, and Fourneau was still twenty feet away. "*Move*, damn it!" I screamed at him, scared I was about to watch blood spray out of his body as bullets tore through him. I suddenly realized the best way to help him was to get my rounds downrange to suppress the enemy and force Timothy to get his head down.

I peeked over the berm and scanned the village. A ghostly haze was hanging over it, and I couldn't see anything. No movement from behind the walls or in the alleys—just haze and dust. Finally off to the right I saw movement and a long-barrelled weapon—*there!*—and I brought my rifle up and over the berm, sighted on the movement, and started firing. I shot a quick, three-round burst, and went to fire again, but all I heard was the dead man's click. No bang, no recoil, nothing. *Stoppage!* I tilted my weapon to the right and saw an empty shell casing half-sticking out of the breechblock. With my left hand I racked the slide back to clear it, then I rammed the forward assist, took aim, and fired again and again. A couple of ANA soldiers ran up next to me on my left and began firing their AKs over the berm and into the village.

I ducked behind the sandbag wall and looked back to see if Fourneau had made it. I saw his arm and leg hiding behind a wall at the back, thank God.

"All right, you sons of bitches!" I heard Forrest Gump's momma say in her loving, motherly tone. "If anyone ever tries to kill you, you try and kill them right back." *Good advice.* I moved four feet to my left, noticed the ANA were hiding behind the berm, and popped back up over the sandbags, quickly scanning for the enemy.

Incoming rounds began snapping all around me with a sickening SNAP SNAP SNAP! CRACK CRACK CRACK!

I looked to my left and saw that the Afghans were still hunkered down as a line of automatic fire was being punched into the sandbags, only two feet away from my face, getting closer with every snap, until the *crack* sound happened right next to my ear and sand spit into my face, little rocks pinging off my ballistic glasses.

Now anyone with any real experience getting shot at would've told you the best thing I could've done was immediately drop my head as quickly as I could. But I had never been shot at that closely before and I'm embarrassed to say, even with all of my training and some good experience under my belt, my brain began to play the circus song—*doo doo dudda dudda doo doo, doo doo*—with a nature show voice-over narration: *The human eye is attracted to movement...* So even though rounds were passing danger close to my face and kicking up sand all around me, my brain said, *If you move slowly, you won't attract their attention,* so I slowly, very slowly, slithered down out of view, and took a few breaths. *What the hell just happened there?* Obviously I already had their attention! *Idiot!* The ANA soldiers to my left looked at me and pushed their palms to the ground as if to say, *Stay down, moron!* And when the Afghans have to mentor *you* to take cover, you know you're doing something terribly wrong!

Okay, I thought to myself, *until my brain stops working against me, maybe I should send up a contact report.* I hadn't heard anyone do that yet. As rounds continued to smack into the sandbag berm all around me, I hunkered down and broke out my map, GPS, and compass. I looked at the Afghans, who were hunkered right down, not budging, and I guessed they had decided to wait until Timothy took an interest in somebody else.

I quickly sent the contact report over the net so the rest of the base would know the enemy's grid location on the map, his strength, and what he was doing (*trying to kill us*), and what the OMLT team was doing (*trying to kill him back*), as well as the start time of the contact. The CP said, "Roger, ack," and went back to doing their thing.

I radioed Longview on the PRR and asked how they were doing on his side. He and the dirty Hungo were good, and I could tell from the shooting and sound of outgoing 40mm grenades from the warrant's weapon that he was having a right ol' cockney knees-up. *The Wizard, finally gittin' some!* Longview had told me at the start of the tour that one of his war to-do list points was to fire every weapon in the CF and Warsaw Pact arsenal. *Well, that's two out of the way.*

The enemy fire continued; snapping and cracking noises screamed through the air as incoming rockets and mortars splashed into Sperwhan's hill. I was peeking over the top again when something gave me a *tap tap* roughly on the shoulder. I spun around and found myself staring down the barrel of a massive boom-stick.

My eyes slowly tracked up the barrel from its pointy end all the way to its middle, where Lieutenant Aziz, wearing nothing but camo pants, flip-flops, and his green army shirt, was carrying the massive stovepipe Russian Spig 9 recoilless rifle firmly on his shoulder. It was called a rifle, but it was really a cannon: the damn thing was over eight feet long, and there he was, carrying it on his shoulder like it was a hockey stick. I looked at him and smiled. He had used the loaded Spig 9, with his finger on the trigger, to tap me on the shoulder to get my attention. *Well, you got it!*

Still holding the cannon, he motioned with it, as if to say, "Kindly get out of the way."

"Yeah, just let me . . . get out of . . . the way here. No problem," I said. "You want to kill Timothy by firing a weapon from your shoulder that's meant to be mounted on a freaking truck, then be my guest!" The weapon he was nonchalantly carrying around was designed to kill tanks!

In World War II the Germans had their dreaded 88mm artillery guns and tank cannons. Well, the cannon on Aziz's shoulder was a 90mm! I squatted out of the way and went over to the side to find some hard cover at the end of the emplacement when I bumped into Fourneau, who hadn't budged (as far as I knew) for the whole firefight. He was sitting on his bum, his rifle under his shoulder, his hands resting on his thighs.

"Fourneau—what the hell?" I shouted. "We need every gun in this fight, what're you . . ." Then I remembered that Aziz was about to fire his nuclear missile at the enemy, and would undoubtedly be showering Fourneau and me in melting hot backblast and dust. The Spig 9 was supposedly a "recoilless rifle," but this was an oxymoron, because you still didn't want to be anywhere near its so-called *recoilless* backblast. Once fired, the rocket would fly out one end, and a molten lava propellant (backblast) that would melt your face off flew out the other end of it.

"Move, move!" I pushed Fourneau around the corner. We were still in cover from the enemy, but now relatively safe from any backblast.

Aziz walked stoically up to the berm, swung his BFG (big f-ing gun) over the sandbags, and took aim. *Holy crap, he's really going to do it!* I flung my body over Fourneau's back to cover him as we both hunkered down, "Breathe out! Backblast backblast!" I shouted as a massive KERBAAMMM! reverberated through the air. We were instantly struck deaf from the noise, blind from the dust, and mute from the backblast, which sucked all the air out of our lungs. I had been winded before from sports, fights, whatever, but this was unlike anything I'd ever felt; it was like an elephant had just trampled on my chest. All I could hear was ringing in my ears as I checked Fourneau to make sure he was okay. I pulled his head around to see his face, and all I could make out were his lips silently moving to say, "Holy shit."

I shook my head then squat-walked over to Aziz, who was still standing above the berm, completely exposed to incoming enemy fire, but not worried in the least. I shook my head again to try and get some hearing back and soon realized the incoming firing had died down considerably. Now there were only four or five guys left still shooting at us.

I got up and walked the last few feet over to Aziz, looked over the berm, and saw a huge mushroom cloud forming in the village, right around the spot I had been shooting at. I thought mushroom clouds were the exclusive domain of nuclear weapons, but after that, I realized if an explosion was big enough, it would always suck dust up into the air.

Captain Jay, the outgoing Canadian artillery observer on top of the hill, shouted over the radio, "The Afghans have just fired their cannons into the village!"

I could see why he would think that, based on the unholy amount of dust the explosion had just kicked up, but I had to correct that erroneous report so I spoke over the net and put the record straight, since Brannon, the OMLT artillery captain, was nowhere to be seen.

I looked at Aziz. He was smiling like Ares, god of war, marvelling at his handiwork. He stood fully exposed, staring over the berm like a hawk on a high perch, looking for any signs of life or movement.

"Crap, he's doing it again," I remarked as Aziz evidently saw something he felt was worth shooting a massive anti-tank round at, and began to quickly reload his BFG. I shouted, "Backblast, backblast!" as I ran around the corner again and draped over Fourneau again. I was scared he would get up to see the action and then get turned into a fine red mist as the backblast washed over him and made him literally disappear. "Breathe out, breathe—"

KERBAAMMM!

Fourneau and I were readier this time, covering our ears and breathing out. We choked on the dust kicked up in the air for about thirty seconds, and then I walked over to the berm to check out Aziz's impressive, but highly dubious, shoulder-gunnery skills. *How in the hell had the blast NOT knocked him flat on his ass?*

Obviously, he was a salty vet and had lots of TI firing tank-killer rounds from the shoulder. It was dumbfounding because a) anyone even half-sane would never fire a cannon from the shoulder, and b) it totally worked, because within a second of his next shot, the incoming firing on our base dwindled down to nothing, and then silence hung over the entire area. No one was shooting anymore. They *couldn't* shoot at us because Lieutenant Killer had turned them into shredded meat.

"You did it! You killed them all!" I shouted excitedly as I thumped him proudly on the back. His stern, patrician facade weakened a bit, and then he began to smile. When he realized he had almost single-handedly stopped the Taliban attack on Sperwhan Ghar, he began to grin like the Cheshire cat. Ali came running up to us when the TIC (troops in contact/ firefight) had come to a dramatic conclusion, and I told him to tell Aziz what a great shot he was, and how his firing the rockets had probably killed a lot of the enemy.

Aziz smiled proudly and shrugged. *Just another day at the office*, as far as he was concerned. I asked him if he would mind if I started calling him "Lieutenant Killer" from then on, and he said he would be proud to be called that by me. He went on to say he wasn't sure if he had actually killed any of them, so I cut him off and said, "Trust me, you just killed them all." I got on the radio and basically said, "Well, that takes care of that." We marched back to our shacks, completely free from any more incoming enemy fire of any kind. We were elated to still be alive, with no casualties on our side, and happy to know Timothy would have a large burial party detail to take care of before sunset.

As we walked back to our shack I congratulated the warrant, Fourneau, and Hetsa for getting their "gold combat badges," for engaging the enemy with their personal weapons, just like I had. The warrant smiled, but Hetsa and Fourneau both looked at the ground. I had a sneaking suspicion that Fourneau hadn't fired his weapon, but I didn't realize Hetsa didn't get a shot off either. I asked him why he hadn't fired and he coldly said, "I didn't have any targets. I couldn't see anyone." I could relate to that. The haze draped over the village had made it tough to see anything. I dropped the matter and brought everyone in for high-fives.

I looked them in the eyes and said, "I'm proud of you fellas. You all kept your heads on a swivel and that's what you gotta do when you find yourself in a vicious cockfight! But seriously, congratulations guys, on our first *proper* firefight. We're all alive, two of us belong to the 'righteous and sacred order of the gold combat star,' and Timothy had his front teeth kicked in from Aziz's boot-stompin'." *A good day out.*

I asked Ali to monitor the Taliban Icom radio traffic, to see if we could get any int regarding their KIA (killed in action) and wounded, or figure out where they would be taking their injured fighters. Aziz was walking next to me, still proudly bearing his anti-tank cannon on his shoulder, so I asked Ali to question him as to where he thought Timothy would take his wounded.

"Pakistan, obviously," Aziz responded. "They will flee across the Registan Desert to the south and cross the border into Pakistan. That is what they do." As we rounded the corner back to our building, several of the ANA were gathered around Lieutenant Mujahedeen, who was obviously telling a funny joke because everyone was laughing it up. I asked Ali to find out what was so funny and report to me later.

I went back inside and started writing my contact report on the computer when, after a few minutes, Ali called me outside. He told me the joke, but I didn't find it funny, not at all. He went on to say that the ANA were spreading it around like wildfire, and soon everyone on the base would know. I thanked him for letting me know, and then I walked across the narrow alleyway and knocked on the OMLT artillery guys' door. Captain Brannon answered, and I asked him if we could talk in private outside.

I took us around the corner and then quietly said, "Brannon, I know you're artillery, and no one expects you to get involved in firefights." *Although technically speaking, the defence of the base is everyone's responsibility,* I thought to myself. "But what you absolutely cannot do, is get all kitted up, ready for war, and then *not* come out to fight with the rest of us."

He snapped back angrily, "What're you talking about?"

"Brannon, I don't want to get dragged into a scrap, okay? I'm just trying to help. As an OMLT mentor, you know how the ANA pride themselves on being a warrior culture, and if one of them, namely Lieutenant Mujahadeen, sees you peek your head out your door, sniff the wind, decide the firefight isn't to your liking, and then duck back inside, they're going to mock you for that. So like I said earlier, if you don't want to come out and get your gun off, that's entirely up to you. But don't get kitted up, poke your head out, let them see you mentally debating the pros and cons, and then go back inside. That's a shameful thing to them, so for your sake, don't do it again."

Brannon swallowed and quietly said, "Fine."

That was all I had to say, so we walked back to our respective buildings in silence, and I made a few mental notes.

Ali told me later that night the Taliban had been talking on their Icom radios after the firefight. They reported they were firing on the infidels and doing just fine, and even had *us* on the run, until someone fired a cannon shell at them killing three men outright and wounding several others. The Taliban were still fighting the good fight, but the infidels fired another cannon shell, and this time it killed four guys, including the local Taliban area commander, and wounded several more. After that, they'd had enough, cut their losses, and fled to parts unknown (a.k.a. Pakistan).

* * *

The ANA, as expected, took the next day off for admin issues, so just for fun, I went down to the interpreters' building and taught them how to play the kid's card game Uno. The OMLT weren't the only soldiers with their own interpreters. The battle group had around five or six working just for them. I took an Uno deck with me wherever I went in the world, and the interpreters loved it because it helped them practise their English. They were good guys, and happy to be working with Canadians, but they all lived under a terrible shadow of death, and worse, hideous torture, if the Taliban ever discovered they worked for the infidels. But they came to work every single day, always smiling and cheerful. Of course the pay was very good and they couldn't make that kind of money working anywhere else, but there was more to it than *just* money.

Every single interpreter that I met believed with all of his heart that we were there to help, and they all wanted to help us in any way possible as we tried to improve their country's security. Sadly, it often seemed to me that the terps believed in us more than we believed in ourselves.

Chapter 11

One morning in mid-September, 72A and about fifty ANA under the always "stellar" leadership of Lieutenant Aziz were summoned from on high to join a British battle group made up of Royal Marines for a week-long op—Operation Array—in Salavat, a large town southwest of Kandahar city.

Naturally, hilarity ensued.

We drove into Masum Ghar that afternoon with no electronic counter-measures package on our RG because it had never worked and we couldn't find the time to get it into KAF for repairs. It was meant to stop the IEDs from exploding, but since we didn't have one, we'd just have to rely on the Wizard's magical protection spells!

Once there, we were quickly briefed on the plan and then, later on, watched *Braveheart*. That night, 72A had to sleep under a parachute jerry-rigged between some buildings, since there was no room at the inn. We talked for a bit and then dozed off, but I was awakened by the sound of a cat getting torn apart and then dragged off by a mongoose, right under the table I was sleeping on.

The next morning we joined a huge convoy of armoured vehicles and watched as our engineers' bulldozers smashed through about three klicks worth of farmers' walls and fields in order to get us to the LD (line of departure).

"Hearts and minds, boys," I said as I waved to the angry farmers who were cursing us. "Hearts and minds."

Our column split in two, with me and the lads heading north to join the Royal Marines, while Captain Rich and his merry band of Afghans broke off to the south with November Company as part of the Canadian battle group going to a town called Nakahonay. I mentally wished Rich good luck and sent him and 72C, a.k.a. call sign "Dead Man's Bread," some good vibes.

We formed a vehicle leaguer (from the Afrikaans word *laager* for "camp") and circled our wagons, then one of the Royal Marines cleared his vehicle-mounted .50-calibre heavy machine gun and had a Neil Diamond right next to a fellow soldier's head, making him deaf in one ear. I walked over and checked on him, and gave him the only thing I had to ease his pain: some Aspirin. I thought to myself, *You know what they say about Royal Marines—they're not Paras! Poor deaf bastard.*

That evening as we prepped for the next day's patrol into Salavat, we heard a massive KERTHUMP in the dirt behind us, not really sure what had just happened. We shrugged our shoulders, said good night like the Waltons family and then hunkered down for some sleep, or like we used to call it in the Paras, "gonk." I had created a fashionable hobo blanket out of a long cardboard box that I used to keep myself off the dirt. There was no room in the RG, so we slept next to it, under the stars, and wondered if Timothy was stalking us as we tried to sleep.

The next morning we discovered what had made the *kerthump* sound. I saw a howitzer carrier shell from an illumination round stuck nose-end in the dirt. It had just missed our vehicle. *Huh. Fancy that.*

Seven Two Alpha and our ANA joined up with a platoon of Royal Marines and patrolled into Salavat. Our mission was to clear the town of Taliban forces, but it was eerily deserted, which gave the Royal Marines captain a bad case of the heebie-jeebies. Lieutenant Aziz invited himself into a compound where he was confronted by some angry FAMs. They told him there were no Taliban in Salavat. Aziz told me he believed them. When I asked him why (every single piece of int on the subject pointed to a contrary hypothesis), Aziz said, "Because they are good Muslims, so they would not lie to me about that." *Really? Seriously? Wow.*

As we walked out of the village (because according to the good Muslims, all the Taliban had left), Ali ran up to me and told me the Taliban were talking about us over their Icom radios.

"Really?" I asked, all intrigued. "What are they saying?"

"Well, sir, it is actually very funny. One Taliban asked the other Taliban if we were still in the village, and the other Taliban said, 'No, they have left.' Then the first Taliban said, 'Ho, ho, ho, they are so gay!' and the other Taliban said, 'Yes, they are so very gay!' The Taliban have called you 'gay,' sir," Ali finished, and began to laugh.

Well, now it's official: the Taliban have called me gay. I looked at Ali and said, "If they mean 'gay' like in the Old English definition: as in carefree, fun, full of joy; then yes, Ali, I'm very 'gay!'" Although I didn't quite think that's how Timothy had meant it.

On our way out of the village, some Brit snipers hiding up on Salavat Mountain saw two FAMs running with weapons take cover in a compound near us. The snipers guided us in as Aziz led us into the suspect compound, where his men performed their usual half-assed search, and as per, came up with nothing. The Brits weren't satisfied, so they started shooting the locks off of the civilians' locked boxes or "tickle trunks" with their 9mm Sig Sauer pistols. They'd obviously watched too many movies, because trying to shoot off a big lock with a 9mm round just doesn't work. Ricochets began to whang around the compound with every shot.

BANG! WOOOO! BANG! WEEE!

Aziz, never a big fan of the Brits, flew into a rage and demanded the Brits stop this shameful thing. He had asked the homeowners if the Taliban were there and they had said no, so why were the Brits trying to shoot off locks? To Aziz, it just didn't compute. I had to think quickly, *Who do I piss off—the Brits or the ANA?* It was a Brit op, but I had to continue to patrol and work with the ANA.

I had a moment of clarity and came up with a solid idea. I asked the Brit captain if he knew the old good cop/bad cop routine, and when he said he did, I told him to whisper to his men over their PRRs to hurry up. Then I really tore into the Marine captain with every combination of the F-word I could possibly imagine. Hell, I even made up a few for good measure. I knew it was the only swear word the ANA understood, and after thirty seconds, Aziz was so embarrassed over the loss of face the Brit captain was suffering from my frothing mouth, that he quickly collected his ANA and left the compound. The Canadians and Brits in earshot had to turn their backs to my swear-fest because they were afraid of bursting out laughing.

The Brits finished their search, found nothing of interest, and packed up to leave. I concluded with a "Fuck, fuck, fuckety-fuck!" and stormed out of the compound in a fake rage. I was instantly swarmed like a hockey player whose goal had just won the Stanley Cup. The ANA were all around me, shaking my hand and slapping me on the back, for courageously standing up to the imperial Brits, with their posh once-upon-a-time-we-ruled-the-world attitude, and putting them back in their place. Even the normally stern Aziz marched over to me and said, "Thank you, Captain Rob, thank you," and vigorously shook my hand.

Later on I got the Marine captain to come over and "apologize" to Lieutenant Aziz, which he graciously did, placating the ANA. The captain was a good sport. A lot of guys would've told me to go to hell, but he was game and I appreciated that.

That night in the leaguer I approached the friendly Canadian captain who had been assigned as an LO (liaison officer) between the Canadians in the south and the British with us. He hadn't been able to get me a Brit radio, and I couldn't communicate with the Brits during the entire operation because their radios were encrypted differently and they weren't allowed to give me one. Top secret, don't you know, *what what!* Nor had he sent up my patrol report to my major in the south. I politely asked him a few more questions, and then I got a sinking feeling. After pondering some of the other things the LO *hadn't* done, I said, "Look, I don't want to seem like a prick, but do you even *know* what an LO is supposed to do on an op like this? Do you know what your job is?"

He quietly replied, "No . . . can you please tell me?" So I spent the next ten minutes explaining what an LO was supposed to do on an operation with different coalition forces working together. It was hard to be upset with a guy who was so honest.

The next morning the Brits didn't want to come out to play guns, so as we marched past them, I raised my right shirt sleeve so they could see the glorious 2 Para cap badge tattooed on my shoulder. I shouted loud enough to wake the dead, "That's right you crap hats! You stand down while 2 Para does the biz!"

"Fuckin' 'ell," they shouted back, "we've come 'alfway round the world, only to get slagged off by a feckin' Para!" They hooted and hollered at us as I continued to proudly show off my tattoo of the "cap badge that meant something," unlike their crap-hat badge!

We'd only been patrolling for a few minutes when we saw two FAMs observing us, not far from the leaguer. The ANA banged off some warning shots and we gave chase as they fled back toward a large compound. Somehow the suspected Taliban youths managed to escape, but inside the large mud hut we found several sleeping bags, some rice, a few grenades with some PKM ammo (for a Russian light machine gun), and a teakettle still boiling. We'd just missed capturing Timothy with his knickers down. The Canadian LO radioed me to let me know the Brits were coming to join us after all. *How kind.*

The ANA immediately began pillaging anything of worth (they had to recoup their losses from the Great Afghan Kitchen Fire of Oh-eight), and before their major could order them not to, the Marines lobbed in some thermite (sort of like white phosphorous) grenades that burned at a thousand degrees and set the sleeping bags on fire. *Good old Willy Pete!*

That got the ANA's blood up and they went to check out another suspicious two-storey building to the south. Warrant Longview went inside and found a victim-operated IED that Aziz, after scrutinizing it, said was "saw blades, used to cut wood." *Hmm, yes. They're saw blades all right, and once someone or something steps on them and the two steel blades touch each other, they complete the necessary electrical circuit to make the attached explosives go "boom." But well done, Aziz. Good effort.*

Lieutenant Aziz. Good kid, tries hard. Bottom third of his class.

The ANA rounded up a half-dozen sleeping bags, a couple of hundred rounds of rusty PKM ammunition, some Chinese grenades, a copy of the Quran (which the occidentals were very careful *not* to touch), a couple of bags of tea, a large bag of rice, a small bag of marijuana, and about twenty pounds' worth of plates, knives, spoons, forks, cups, and a brand-new pressure cooker, all pillaged to replace the kit they'd lost in their kitchen fire. The ANA began backing up their Ranger trucks to load their booty.

Ali walked over to me and quietly asked, "Sir, what should they do with the things they are not stealing?"

"That's not called *stealing*, Ali," I quipped. "In war, that's called *liberating!*" *Or is it pillaging?* I then asked him, "Isn't it obvious? Burn it. Anything the ANA aren't taking, they're going to burn, to deny its use to the enemy." He cringed and quietly asked about the yellow water jugs. Surely they couldn't be used to hurt anyone?

I cut him off with, "We're leaving them with nothing they can use! Burn their sleeping bags, burn their sandals and water jugs, *burn everything!*" The

ANA were way ahead of me. They had already made a large pile of the leftover belongings and were pouring cooking oil over it. Then, one of the soldiers ran up to the pile and lit it with a cigarette lighter. The pile of Taliban gear quickly went up in flames, and it felt good to watch Timothy's possessions burn.

He would IED our soldiers from over a klick away, and no one would even see him do it. He would shoot at us and try to kill us, and then as we were closing in on him, he would drop his rifle, pick up a shovel, and suddenly he became a farmer, and there was nothing we could do about it. He would line up innocent civilians against a wall and gun them down. He would hold kangaroo court sessions, but with deadly consequences, where he would prosecute and convict people for listening to radios or flying kites, and then bury them in the sand until only their heads were showing, and then force their neighbours to throw stones at their faces until they were dead.

If Timothy came back to his hut and found his sleeping bags, tea, food, water jugs, and spare sandals in perfect condition, right where he'd left them, then he'd get a good night's sleep and just go back to trying to kill us the next day.

This way, when he came back to his safe house, he'd find his food gone, his ammo and IED components confiscated, and his sleeping bags, water jugs, and sandals all torched. Now he'd be cold, hungry, thirsty, tired, and without any ammunition, and most importantly, he'd be scared. He'd be scared because we knew where he lived. Now he'd be in no condition to conduct operations. Now he'd have to go far away to get resupplied again, and he couldn't kill us, because he'd be too busy trying to find food, water, ammo, and a new safe house. It only made sense that the ANA would burn his things. If the ANA had asked me, I would've happily torched the pile with my own Zippo lighter.

We collected up the gear from the safe house and made our way back to our leaguer. That night, 72A ate Taliban rice for the first time, and since it had been only recently pillaged, it was still amazingly fresh. The ANA macerated it in their own blend of liquid herbs and flavours, and then boiled it to perfection and added raisins at the end for effect. It was incredibly aromatic and delicious. They offered some to the Brits, who devoured it. I told everyone since it was Taliban rice, the reason it was so delicious was because of their secret ingredient—hatred.

* * *

The next morning it was decided by the Brits to leave Salavat alone, even though we hadn't cleared a single compound inside of it. *But that was neither here nor there.*

We drove our vehicles over to the east of Salavat and formed a leaguer next to some Afghan Bedouin. We muckled onto our Afghans and patrolled into the nearby village of Fathollah, and you would be hard pressed to find a "more wretched hive of scum and villainy."

It was one of the birthplaces of the Taliban, so obviously, it was a *bit* dangerous, and not really the sort of place you just wandered into. Once we were inside its twisting alleys and high walls, the ANA (to a man) all sauntered off, and then Fourneau decided to join in the fun and promptly left me. I turned around at one point; I couldn't find my fire-team partner, and Ali asked me, "What?" I tried desperately to suppress my panic and started looking all over, but I couldn't see Fourneau. It was just me and Ali, as the warrant and Hetsa were with the recce element to the east. I had climbed a small wall, and Fourneau had decided he would find another way around it, and just took off without letting me know.

When I realized he was gone, I was absolutely terrified. Images of him with an empty sandbag over his head, a single dangling light bulb barely illuminating a propaganda banner behind his beaten-up body, and a guy holding a rusty saw standing at the ready behind him, limbering up his sawin' arm to begin slowly cutting off Fourneau's head for the Al Jazeera six o'clock news flooded my mind, threatening to choke me out with panic. *Must not fear, fear is the mind-killer!* I told myself as I suppressed the panic threatening to drown me.

I ran to a nearby rooftop and started scanning and asking the rest of the team over the PRR if they had seen Fourneau, when suddenly he rounded a corner, unperturbed by the heart attack he almost gave me. I, on the other hand, was *quite* perturbed, so I explained a few things to him through the use of expletives and frothing at the mouth, and together, as a fire team, we moved out.

On our way out of the village, we came under small-arms fire, and as the ANA returned it, I had to run up onto a roof to find out why the Brits weren't joining us. They were supposed to be to our south, ready to act as a QRF if we needed them. If they had run up to join us, they could've acted as a fire-support base while the ANA flanked the small group of Taliban, but the Brits hadn't so much as budged.

I was a bit angry, so after the ANA had scared off the Taliban, I walked over and asked the Royal Marines captain, "What the hell just happened?"

He told me his major had denied him permission to come up to join us. That night at the major's O-group (orders briefing), I asked him why he had denied his men permission to join me in the TIC, and he arrogantly replied, "The days of soldiers charging to the sounds of the guns went out with the Napoleonic Wars."

I replied, "For some, maybe." His men couldn't make eye contact with me; they knew they'd left us high and dry.

That night, as I slept peacefully under the stars on my hobo blanket, I heard a strange noise to my left. I sprang up and grabbed my rifle and reached for my night-vision monocle. I scanned around, but couldn't find the source of the weird noise. I then looked to my immediate left and realized it was Hetsa, shivering in the cold night. I had told my young Jedi apprentices to pack some warm gear for the op, but Hetsa, being the salty vet, knew better, so now he was freezing in his sleep. I got up, took off my American-issue Ranger blanket, and draped it over him and whispered, "Good night, son."

*　*　*

Early the next morning, the Brits decided we would move our leaguer back to where it was at the start of the op, just above Salavat. As we patrolled through the western edge of Fathollah to clear it for the vehicle convoy, the ANA with Warrant Longview caught out the Taliban and fired on them before they could detonate their IED. I heard their gunfire so I hopped over a wall and ran to join them, where the warrant had to give me an impromptu satellite map-reading lesson under enemy fire, which was probably a first for both of us.

I sent up my contact report to the LO to give to the Brits, then I traced the detonating wire (which Lieutenant Aziz, God bless him, had already cut) back to the wall. I stood by the wall, saw where I thought the IED was buried in a nearby culvert under a small bridge, and then I sent up my IED contact report. I found out two days later that the wall we had all been hopping over had about four hundred pounds worth of IED explosives buried in it. The wall *was* the IED. *GEEEWWWW!*

An American Apache helicopter gunship turned up, but for some odd reason, wasn't allowed to disintegrate the Taliban currently shooting at us. I found out later it was because he was in a British AO and our Royal Marines major on the ground denied him permission to engage the enemy. What would've taken the Apache five seconds took us close to twenty minutes of shooting—and getting shot at—until Timothy had enough and fled into a wadi. The Americans, bless their socks, decided to act as a mobile spotting platform and chased the enemy all the way to a large compound, about two hundred metres away to the southwest, where they quickly went to ground.

I ran and told the Brits the ANA had a cunning plan to give chase, if the Brits would be so kind as to set up on the southern flank and act as a mobile cut-off, ready to kill any Taliban we chased out of the compound. They were game and wanted to discuss the plan at great length, but I said, "I've gotta go; the ANA are hard chargers and I don't want them to leave without me!" I took off shouting, "2 Para leads the way!" as I sprinted over to the HMCS *Tippy Canoe* (our RG) to retrieve my driver and gunner. At the start of the day, Fourneau and Hetsa were manning our vehicle in the British column move through Fathollah, but now the plan had changed considerably, so I told them they were more than welcome to come and join the flying circus. Hetsa was game, but Fourneau said he'd rather stay with the RG. *Hmm.*

I was about to order him to abandon ship when I realized he hadn't made eye contact with me once during my entire speech about the newly developing situation. I didn't press him—Phobos the Greek god of fear had obviously gotten a good hold of him, so Hetsa and I ran over and rejoined the warrant and Aziz while Fourneau opted to stay with the British vehicle column.

When the warrant found out that the Fornicator was missing out on a once-in-a-lifetime combat opportunity (we'd never known before with one hundred per cent certainty where the enemy was actually hiding), he was beyond livid and threatened to drag Fourneau out of his metal security blanket by his short, dark curlies. I asked the warrant to let it go for now, as we had more pressing matters, like leading the ANA on a flanking assault on an enemy-occupied compound.

I told the Wizard and the dirty Hungo to go schtum as I lied through my buckteeth to Lieutenant Aziz, telling him the Brits wanted us to take it back to the old school and do a hard-knock entry on the compound while they covered us from the south. Once Aziz (who put the "Q" back in "Quisling") heard that the plan came from a major, he was all for it. I thought to myself, *Hey, he's probably thinking, as long as a higher rank can take the fall if it goes sour....*

Aziz quickly briefed his CSM and sergeants on the plan while I told Ali to stay close to me and to do what I said. I reminded him I had promised his mother I would take care of him. Then I turned to my Canadians and told them what my peewee hockey coach always said at times like this: "Keep your sticks on the ice and your heads up in the corners!" I clasped them both on the shoulders. "This is who we are . . ."

"So say we all," Hetsa and Longview said back in perfect unison.

I told them that if they had any questions, to make it quick. They said they were good to go, so I said, "Okay then, it's the old army classic, 'hey diddle-diddle, right up the middle.'"

We started marching with some ANA in front of us when suddenly we heard laughing and shouting behind us.

We turned around to see an Afghan soldier with something in his hands running between his friends, all of them reaching at his arms, desperately trying to steal something from his grip. He got closer and ran by us with a large bunch of grapes (recently liberated from a farmer's field) in his mouth, another bunch in each hand and, for the *coup de grâce,* a pretty white flower hanging from the front of his beret. We shook our heads and kept marching toward the compound with the angry Apache Dragonfly buzzing over top of it.

We were only twenty metres out from the compound when we found ourselves with open ground between us and its nearest wall, so I shouted, "Run for it!" as every Canadian and Afghan sprinted across the dry field, fully expecting the sickening snap and crack of incoming fire to ruin our family fun run.

We made it to the wall without taking any fire and began to round it, heading toward the compound's front gate. Somehow I ended up as lead man on the assault, but there was no time to shoosh some ANA out in front of me, so I had to act quickly. I turned the corner, my weapon on my shoulder, and quickly made out an old man standing next to the compound's open front gate. He beckoned us in, but we didn't budge until Ali got him to lift his shirt so we could see he wasn't packing a fifty-pound IED suicide vest.

We had heard of this happening before. The Taliban would go into a village and grab a senior citizen or a mentally challenged child and strap a suicide bomb to him. To the child, they would make it seem like a fun game—"Run up to the soldiers and say hi." To the elderly man they would say, "You're almost dead from old age anyway; this way, you can serve Allah. Do this, or we'll kill your whole family." Then they'd hold his family hostage until he detonated himself. He raised his shirt and showed us he was clean, so we gently pushed him out of the way and snaked into his compound.

He had a massive bruise forming under his right eye and tears began to flow down his cheeks as he began pleading with Ali, begging us to leave his village. It was as I'd feared. The Taliban had run from the chopper into the nearest village, found out who the elder was, punched him in the face, and told him, "We now belong to your village. In fact, we're your nephews from Fathollah. If you tell the coalition soldiers who we are, we'll come back and kill all of you, tonight." It wasn't an empty threat, and the old man knew it. Completely innocent civilians found themselves in these hopeless situations every day in the warring provinces of Afghanistan, and as in every other war since the beginning of time, it was always the civilians who suffered the most.

I began to feel very angry. *Those fucking savages! They don't have the guts to stand and fight, but they're pretty fucking brave when beating the shit out of an old man and threatening his life and the lives of his family!*

All of the ANA soldiers had stopped in the middle of the compound and began chatting amongst themselves, asking villagers the odd question, but not overly concerned by current events. Even though there were several fighting age males, covered in dust and sweat and shooting us terrible stinkeyes, the ANA just couldn't seem to get the concept that the chopper had followed the Taliban right to this *very* compound. *Damn it all to hell!*

I advised Aziz to politely ask his men to start policing up all of the FAMs, searching them properly and putting them under armed guard, and then to start searching the compound for their weapons. He thought about it for a good minute and then slowly turned and told his men to get busy. The ANA slowly started herding the FAMs over to a wall beside me, but didn't bother to search any of them, just casually told them to go over and stand next to me. *Yeah, thanks.*

Suddenly an Afghan shouted something and opened up with his PKM belt-fed machine gun right next to me, shooting over a wall toward a small farmer's hut in the middle of a grape field about a hundred metres away. I followed the trail of his rounds and thought I saw movement and a long-barrelled weapon, so I shouted, "Fire!" and suddenly the world erupted into a hellish cacophony of gunfire and outgoing rockets. I switched to fully automatic on my assault rifle and said, "Git some, git some!" over and over as I shot at Timothy, who so brazenly had called down the fires of hell. Outgoing rockets, RPGs, PKM machine gun fire, AK-47s, M-16s; everyone opened up on full auto with everything he had, trying to kill this guy, who in hindsight, I wasn't a hundred per cent sure anyone had even seen.

I saw one ANA soldier throwing grenades; he'd never make the distance, but by God, it was on his war to-do list! The ANA gunner immediately to my left was screaming "Ahhh, ahhhhh!" as he sprayed his whole belt of ammo downrange. Hetsa was to my right, his Minimi belt-fed machine gun pumping out hundreds of bullets, the burning hot brass of his expended cartridges falling all over the suspected Taliban youths who had ducked down behind the wall next to us when the firing started.

Ali asked me if he could shoot and I said, "Why not?" and watched him closely as he shot off the rest of my magazine. I took it back and Ali wandered off somewhere as I put my rifle on full auto, and began putting mag after mag downrange, when I felt Ali's hands stuffing something into my drop bag (which was usually reserved for empty rifle magazines). When I asked him what he was doing, he told me he'd found some corn, so he was shoving it into my drop bag (which he felt was perfect for the task) so we could have a good ol' corn roast that night. I told him that was called stealing, and from the *very* farmer we were trying to protect, but he assured me it wasn't stealing if we *actually* ate what we took. PKM rounds, RPGs, C8s and C9s on full auto, M203 grenades firing: it was pure unadulterated madness! Thousands of rounds and dozens of rockets turned the poor farmer's field into the mother of all firefights!

Then, to make matters worse, the Brits to our south decided to get in on the fun and started firing their vehicle mounted .50-cals, GPMG machine guns, and a 40mm automatic grenade launcher. All this for one guy who had long since fled to Karachi!

I started shouting for everyone to stop when we heard a massive KA-WHOOSH!

We looked south to see an $80,000 Javelin anti-tank missile soar high into the sky, and then come screaming back down to earth. BOOM!

A deafening explosion reverberated across the grape field as the missile found its target—the poor, defenceless farmer's hut. Dust kicked up into the air and formed a small mushroom cloud over the hut as a shattered wheelbarrow performed lazy cartwheels in the sky.

Now I am become Death, the destroyer of...wheelbarrows.

The billowing mushroom cloud finally signalled everyone to draw our little firefight to a close, and soon some of us were shaking our heads as others were doubled up laughing. *How freaking ridiculous had that been?*

After the dust had settled and I had made sure the Brits weren't going to kill us, I led the OMLT team and some ANA over to the hut to see if we'd gotten the lone gunman. No blood, no tattered weapon shot out of his arms, just a single sandal abandoned on his flight to safer pastures. When we returned to the compound, we found out that Aziz had let all of the Taliban suspects go. When I asked him why, he merely shrugged and said, "They did not look like Taliban," and then walked away.

Of course, we were extremely frustrated, but what could we do? That was just how the ANA operated. To take the FAMs into custody would've involved work on Lieutenant Aziz's part.

I got Ali to apologize to the old village elder for putting a massive hole in his hut wall, and asked him to please address his damaged property issue at the next *shura*. I assured him the coalition would pay for the damages. He thanked us and was very glad to see us leave.

That night we dined on roasted *stolen* corn, lovingly prepared by Ali, and he was right: it *was* delicious. We raised our mugs and toasted the bravery of the lone gunman and hoped he'd find a matching sandal in his local bazaar, probably back in Peshawar.

We did a few more patrols as part of Operation Array, but after that firefight, everything seemed pretty tame in comparison. The ANA had eaten their British halal 72-hour ration boxes in the first six hours of the operation, so they had officially run out of food. We patrolled back into Fathollah to try and get a shop vendor to open up for us when Aziz "recognized" a Taliban safe house.

Aziz had two soldiers adept in the ways of the ninja, so they quickly hopped the compound wall and let the ANA in to find some rice. I told Aziz I knew perfectly well what was really going on, but he became indignant and denied any wrongdoing. Then he cooked up a doozy and told me he'd just received an int hit from the NDS (Afghanistan's National Directorate of Security), notifying him about the Taliban safe house. Coincidentally enough, we didn't find any weapons or IEDs, just two huge sacks of rice. *Hmm, fancy that.* I put it down in my report, but nothing ever came of it.

That afternoon the Royal Marines had another Neil Diamond on a .50-cal, and this time they almost took off the top of some guy's head. I saw the poor bastard later; he was still pallid, terribly shaken up, *and* deaf in one ear. Again, I shared my Aspirin with him.

Finally it was time to bring the flying circus to a close, so we began to re-org our gear and get everything strapped onto our RG, when a high-explosive shell screamed into the ground about thirty metres outside of our leaguer. It was close enough to scare the living hell out of us, as shrapnel whistled over our heads. I ordered everyone inside our tin can and started doing some quick mental math. I then transposed it over my map, and realized it was probably a Canadian who had fired the round. It wasn't artillery, and it wasn't a mortar or rocket round, so that left a *tank* as the culprit. Everyone was madly running for hard cover as I dismounted and sprinted over to the Canadian LO. I told him to get on the net and ask the Canadians just to our south if they'd fired on anyone recently, as they were departing *their* leaguer.

They came back with, "Yeah, we just fired on a spotter. He was dicking us by talking on his phone, so we turned him into a red mist with a tank shell." I then politely informed the LO to make sure, in the future, that everyone in the battle group did what every kid who's given a BB gun has to do before he shoots: namely, think about *target and beyond*. The tank had turned the Taliban *target* into a red, gooey paste, but we were *beyond!* The LO gave them our ten-figure grid and thankfully there were no more close calls.

And as though that week hadn't been fun enough, on the ride back we were told to keep our eyes peeled for an Afghan National Police (ANP) truck that had just been stolen and was now being driven by a Taliban suicide bomber who had a thousand pounds of homemade explosives in the back of his cab. *Nice. Couldn't just be a simple drive home, could it?*

After half an hour we saw an ANP truck matching the description, perpendicular to our convoy, just watching all of us as we passed. If it was Timothy, he changed his mind when every single coalition weapon on a mount, swivel, or turret spun around and pointed straight at him, tracking him as they passed. He knew if he so much as revved his engine, that would've been it for him.

* * *

Back in Masum Ghar after the operation, Rich told me that when our TIC got started with the lone gunman in the north, everyone on the Nakahonay op in the south got "stood to," which meant they were told to get kitted up and ready to come and save us. Because they were so far away, they couldn't tell if all of the shooting was incoming or outgoing fire—it had all rolled into one massive noise and sounded like the world's biggest TIC. When the guys to our south heard the Brits start firing anti-tank missiles, they knew things had gone terribly Pete Tong wrong for us, so they didn't even wait for our distress call, they were going to mount up and come to rescue us! *Damn good of 'em,* I thought to myself.

"How many Taliban were you up against?" Rich asked. "It sounded like Armageddon had kicked off up there!"

"One guy," I said, with my best poker face.

"One guy? All of that, for *one* guy?"

"Well, he looked really mean, and he had this stick—with a nail in it—so, uh . . ." I started laughing. *Yes, all of that—for one guy.*

* * *

It was time for us to go so we said goodbye to our friends at Masum and mounted up. The trip back to Sperwhan was delightfully uneventful. We had a quick hot wash (after-action review) where I asked for any points or comments and, after that surreal week, the guys had plenty of things to add to my report.

After we were done debriefing, I took Fourneau with me for a walk and apologized for accidentally reading a letter he had been writing in his field message pad. I had opened up what I thought was my FMP, but turned out to be his.

But I told him I *had* read part of it, and I wanted to talk to him about it. He said everything he had written was true—he hated the place, and he desperately wanted to go back home. He asked if I'd made any progress on getting him placed somewhere else, and I told him the truth. When I'd mentioned to Warrant Longview about moving Fourneau to the artillery OMLT and bringing Ginge or Swede (Captain Brannon's two fit and switched-on infantrymen from 1 RCR who got roped into helping with the OMLT artillery) over to replace him, the angry father had lost his mind, and he and I had a good back and forth over Fourneau.

In decisions like these, Longview had just as much say as I did, and his position was that we could never just swap Fourneau out for someone else—it was terrible for everyone's morale. "Even if they don't want to be in the infantry OMLT anymore?" I asked him, and Longview said, "He signed up; he made his choice." I then explained to Longview how Fourneau had "pulled the chute" and no longer wanted to be on our team. Longview basically said it was too late, and that was that. I told him I disagreed, and had already talked to the OMLT company sergeant major and Captain Sean about it, and they were looking into the matter and trying to find the best option for everyone. Longview wasn't happy with me, but we agreed to disagree. I'm sure he thought I was meddling in his senior NCO business, but I had seen this type of thing before and thought Fourneau was on a slippery slope; one that could ultimately see him shooting himself to get off the tour. It wouldn't be the first time it had ever happened.

Fourneau looked very downtrodden when he learned that our plan had been kiboshed, and I started to wonder if maybe the warrant was right. In certain things, I wasn't even supposed to be getting involved—that was for the warrant to take care of. But this was sort of a grey area, where we shared equal amounts of responsibility. But I felt bad for Fourneau; he was a good guy, and I knew he was having a very hard time on the tour. I told him I would keep trying, and reminded him that he could talk to me anytime.

The next morning, Ali told me he had received permission to go to a wedding near Kabul, but I knew right then and there I would never see him again. He assured me he would come back, but sadly I was correct—he never returned. He was one of the best terps I'd ever worked with, and even though I was angry, I couldn't say I blamed him. I would've liked to have gone to a wedding and never come back, too.

His replacement from the battle group pool of terps, a young guy named Max, could barely speak English.

Chapter 12

After a few days off, we got told to prep for a major operation in Helmand Province, over to the west of Kandahar Province. Helmand was in the British AO and they had their own OMLT, just like us, so we weren't exactly sure why we were going.

I spoke to Captain Shafiq Ullah, who told me that about forty ANA soldiers were on a bus going home on leave when they were forced to pull over at an illegal vehicle checkpoint and then were kidnapped en masse by the Taliban. We were joining the ANA on a hostage rescue mission. *God help the hostages—and us!*

We packed up and joined a battle group convoy under Major Obermann heading to Masum. Once we got there, thankfully without incident, I was gobsmacked when I realized we'd forgotten our new terp, Max. I told Major Hobbles, who just stared at me when I related the news. I accepted full responsibility, and he told me to quickly go and grab another terp from the pool of OMLT interpreters at Masum. Froggy, the interpreters' boss, recommended another terp, also named Max.

Sean and the major collected int throughout the day and it was decided we would travel with our ANA early the next morning to Helmand. Rich and I hung out and wondered what we were getting ourselves into. Usually with an operation like this, weeks of planning were put into it, but we guessed if it really did turn out to be a rescue operation, time wasn't on the side of the ANA hostages.

Later that night, we were told the plan had now changed: it was no longer a rescue op (apparently our operations guys had fallen victim to "the whispers game": there were no hostages, and nobody had been kidnapped off of a bus!). Instead we'd be taking the full complement of First and Third ANA companies—along with OMLT call signs 72A and 72C, and an HQ element made up of the major, the CSM, a medic, a FOO/FAC (forward observation officer/forward air controller), plus a few signallers—to Helmand to conduct an operation to relieve the besieged provincial capital of Lashka Ghar from Taliban forces who had been firing on it almost daily. We were told there were hundreds of Taliban just across the river from the capital, and for once they were going to make a stand and fight it out with us.

We hatted up and headed out early the next morning with three RGs from the security force (sec-for) group out of KAF. They were fearless men under an excellent captain named Ross, whose sole purpose in the Stan was to do convoy protection and VIP close protection throughout Kandahar. That meant they were in RGs and on the roads all of the time, constantly risking IEDs. We all admired their sand. It wasn't a job any sane man would want!

We muckled onto our ANA, and our six-RG convoy and thirty ANA vehicles rolled out the gate of Masum, surprisingly on time. En route, Ross's rucksack fell off his RG next to a small ANP outpost and, before he could dismount to grab it, it had been scooped up and taken inside their base. Major Hobbles said we'd try and get it back on our return trip.

We got a flat tire, quickly repaired it, and after a full day's driving, we rolled into a British base in Helmand province called FOB Tombstone, surprisingly on time and thankfully in one piece. We spent the night, and the next morning Stamps (Rich's driver) and I were ordered by Hobbles to do an interview with an American marine who worked for the US military's *Stars and Stripes* newspaper. The marine, who actually had a video cameraman with him, forced us to do retake after retake until he finally got the positive feel piece he was after. Afterwards, we all mounted up and drove to an RV point outside of Lashka Ghar (Lash).

At the RV point, we debated whether or not to remove our tall radio antennas off of the top of our RGs, but the Brits were on time for the RV, so we got told to leave our tall antennas up, and we quickly took off, following the Brits into the city. Then we stared like mesmerized children at the spectacular fireworks display of popping sparks and streaking lights as Ross's lead vehicle, with its high antenna *still* up, ripped down low-hanging power line after power line.

I waved to the gathering angry mob on the side of the street as we drove past them and their blacked-out apartments and said, "Hearts and minds, boys. That's what it's all about—hearts and minds! We're here to help you . . ." and the warrant finished my sentence with, "and take away your electricity!"

As the OMLT was single-handedly causing the Great Lashka Ghar Power Outage of Oh-eight, the Brits took off once they saw an ugly riot brewing. We quickly lost sight of them as they burned off and we accidentally turned down a very narrow alley which, of course, came to a dramatic dead end. And to make matters worse, three of our RGs were hauling long, heavy trailers behind them.

After half an hour of successfully completing 140-point turns, we managed to extricate ourselves and rolled into the ANP station, our new home away from home, only a few minutes late. The ANP stared slack-jawed as Ross's vehicle pulled up to their gate, dragging a hundred feet of electrical wire behind it. *Don't look at us,* I thought to myself, *it was like that when we got here!*

We spent the next day liaising with our ANA captains, Shafiq Ullah and Ghias, and began re-orging our kit, getting ready for the upcoming operation. Major Hobbles took Rich and me to the British HQ in Lash to get an up-to-date briefing, and the major was politely offered a seat at the adults' table while Rich and I gratefully sat off to the side. We were stunned when we realized that the Brits had the entire operation already fully planned out, and at no point did they consult our major to see if the ANA were willing and/or capable of pulling off their audacious plan.

It called for an almost twenty-kilometre-long patrol through heavily contested ground the first day, and another twenty-plus-klick patrol the next day, until we finally arrived at an isolated, beleaguered British forward operating base called Bermuda. We would be the first troops to make it to them on the ground in over a month. They were in contact with Timothy daily, and all of the resupplies to their FOB were through chopper only.

That evening Major Hobbles met with Colonel Morris, the ANA officer he was mentoring, and they discussed the plan, making some small changes. Hobbles told us Colonel Morris said he wanted to manoeuvre a force of ANA with their OMLT mentors to create a blocking position south of the expected enemy positions. That way, when Rich or I patrolled south with our ANA at the start of the mission, one of us would engage the Taliban at the front and then chase them toward the other OMLT commander, and then we'd old-school "hammer and anvil" the enemy to death. *Not a bad plan, but the enemy wasn't just going to sit still and watch as a group of Canadian OMLT mentors and a full company of ANA troops drove by them, waving away, and then let us set up a blocking position to the south of them on their six o'clock.*

The major rightly pointed out that if we *did* set up a blocking force, we would take casualties. It would be unavoidable. If we blocked Timothy, he'd fight to the death to get through the blocking force, and our men, both Afghan and Canadian, would be heavily engaged and would surely take wounded and KIA. The colonel listened, pondered, and then decided against a blocking force.

Hobbles then called everyone in for his O-group. No matter what a person could say about the major, he always delivered an excellent set of orders.

The plan was changed so many times that it had already passed through its A through F iterations. The latest plan ("G") called for Rich and call sign 72C to be on the eastern flank with the Third Company ANA, just on the other side of the river that separated the Taliban from Lash. Seven Two Alpha and the First Company ANA would be on the western flank, paralleling 72C as we both moved our companies to the south.

Opposition was expected to be very heavy, with the Taliban having vehicle-mounted heavy machine guns in support of their ground troops. They were expected to fight to the death. Int also said these particular Taliban fighters were experts at setting up three-sided ambushes, and that they preferred initiating their contacts with IEDs.

The major, the CSM, the artillery FOO/FAC, and Laddah the medic would be travelling with some sec-for guys as the major stayed next to Colonel Morris, one tactical bound behind us (anywhere from fifty to two hundred metres). That was the plan, anyway.

The next day's operation would be officially called Op Atal-28, because there were twenty-seven previous Op Atals. *Fair enough.* Major Hobbles asked if anyone had questions; a few were asked and quickly answered, and we walked back to our rooms on the fourth floor of the empty police barracks.

* * *

We woke up very early the next morning and had a quick breakfast, washed our faces and pits with wet wipes, and began to take our kit down to the RGs.

We were told to leave our rucksacks at the ANP station and to pack only a sleeping bag and a few things we wanted into our sleeping-bag carrying sack. No big rucksacks would be taken. *Travel light, freeze at night!*

I was carrying kit down to the RG when I noticed the ANA mounting up in their Rangers, getting set to quickly head out the gate.

"Switching to Plan H now now now!" I shouted as I ran back into the building to find the major. When I told him what I'd seen, he shouted, "Aw, what the *fuck?*" and ran out of the building to find Colonel Morris. I ran upstairs and told everyone to pack the RGs quickly because we had about five minutes to get kitted up; the ANA had decided we'd *now* be travelling by vehicle to the LD. Plan G had seen us marching to the LD with the ANA, but that was *yesterday's* plan—basically ancient history.

We stuffed the vehicles, put the machine guns back on top (but had no time to align or sight them), ran back upstairs, and got kitted up. *Nothing like hurry up and wait.* The major had zero luck getting Morris to change his mind, and since we couldn't take our RGs because we'd need our gunners and drivers to join us on the march, we were forced to leave them behind. We couldn't just abandon them at the LD.

Major Hobbles jogged over to me and said, "Disperse your call sign in the ANA trucks and we'll all meet up at the LD." I thought to myself, *There'll be hell to pay if someone gets IEDed and the CF finds out we were riding in old Ford Ranger trucks instead of in our armoured vehicles.* But I knew the major's hands were tied and he was doing the best he could. No one had told him about the change in plan; it wasn't his fault.

I quickly briefed the boys on Plan H and we mounted up between the ANA in the back of their trucks. They were singing and laughing away, having a good old time. I made sure everyone in 72A had a vehicle to ride in, and we quickly zipped through the town, crossed the only bridge to the west, and drove for another klick before we came to a screeching halt. We dismounted and then mingled around on the highway, in between rows of bazaar shops.

Another bunch of Afghan trucks arrived, and they disgorged some ANA troops the likes of which we'd never seen before. They were wearing old American urban-camouflage uniforms, all of them were sporting thick beards and long hair that flowed past their shoulders (looking like Afghan versions of Jesus), and most of them were barefoot. They had their boots tied up and slung over their shoulders. Some carried their weapons like baseball bats; some didn't even *have* a weapon. I'd patrolled through enough marijuana fields in Afghanistan to realize I was allergic to pot, and as I got closer to the long-haired friends of Jesus, my nose started to twitch.

Oh no, don't tell me ...Yep, they were totally, inexcusably, high.

They began passing around what could only be described as King Kong joints and started puffing away, their glassy eyes not really taking anything on board (but they did like to smile a lot and giggle to themselves). Hobbles arrived and I brought them to his attention. He said they were Afghan Border Police and followed up with, "Yeah, but what are you gonna do?"

I knew if I was back in Sperwhan I'd immediately call off the patrol, but this wasn't *just* a patrol. It was a two- to three-day operation, with a lot more working parts involved than just a bunch of high border police. I pointed them out to Rich, who just shook his head and said, "Savages. Goddamn savages."

Our ANA companies got in line and faced toward the south: 72C was on the left, 72A on the right. Rich and I looked at each other. Sweat had already begun to trickle down our faces; it was much hotter in Helmand than in Kandahar Province.

"Good luck," he said.

"Strong is Vader, mind what you have learned, save you it can!" I shouted back. Rich gave me the finger as his men moved off first, just the way my ANA captain would've wanted. Captain Shafiq Ullah then gave Rich's group a five-minute head start before beginning our trace (projected route) to the south.

We had gotten maybe twenty feet before the first rounds were fired into the air. I couldn't tell if it was our ANA or Rich's who had fired. It seemed to be outgoing. *Maybe they were warning shots.* Nobody said anything over the net, so we continued on as if nothing had happened. After marching about fifty metres, Shafiq Ullah flew into a rage and started shouting something at Lieutenant Aziz over their radio. Aziz was up front with Longview and Hetsa for the duration of the patrol, but after about a minute, they marched past us and walked all the way back to the highway, moved a few poxy metres to the east, and then took a different trail heading south. I asked the warrant over the PRR what was going on, and he said Shafiq Ullah was probably buying more time, so that Captain Ghias in charge of the Third Company and 72C would be the first to spring an ambush. *Figures.*

We patrolled south for a couple of hundred metres when all hell opened up farther to the south. It sounded like either the Brits or Americans had stumbled upon some Taliban hiding in ambush. It was a two-way range because rounds would periodically snap high over our heads. It lasted for a few minutes and then died down.

I tried to reach Warrant Longview for a locstat but his radio was dead. I found out later that his radio had dumped its crypto, meaning it had just chucked out the encryption codes necessary to communicate over our net, leaving him with no radio for the rest of the day. *Fantastico!*

Ross spoke over the net and sent up a grid, but his numbers were all wrong. I talked over the net and corrected him, and then knowing everyone in the OMLT could hear me, I said it was too early in the morning to start making those mistakes and we had to switch on, the day was only starting. I told him later I hoped he wasn't pissed at me for what I said, but I stood by it. He said it was a good admonishment to have made, and I appreciated his maturity.

We knew the Afghan intelligence service (NDS) was out on the ground, trying to gather real-time int for our operation. (I found out later, during my court martial, that they had about twenty operatives dressed as Taliban walking around the area we'd be patrolling.) We'd gone maybe six or seven hundred metres from the highway when the NDS radioed the ANA call signs, warning them the Taliban had sent out suicide bombers to target the coalition forces.

Hey, great news!

We patrolled for maybe a klick when the NDS came over their net again, warning the ANA that the Taliban were planting IEDs and mines on the roads behind us, effectively cutting us off from Ross and our vehicles if we needed them for fire support or medevac.

Perfect!

Another half an hour passed, when suddenly Rich and his ANA were in a TIC with rounds snapping all over the place. We could tell by the volume of fire that the ANA were giving better than they were receiving, but it was our first official contact of the day, and Rich handled himself very well. He was calm over the radio and quickly delineated the forward line of his troops, in case any Apache gunships were coming over to help him out.

I was distressed to see Captain Shafiq Ullah completely clam up, unsure of what he was supposed to do. *Maybe if you'd actually patrolled with us, instead of issuing orders from Sperwhan hill through a set of binos, you'd know what to do!* Rounds snapped and the odd one cracked over our heads as we took cover behind a wall.

I sent up my locstat, eager to let Major Hobbles know where 72A and its ANA were, in case an Apache did come in. I didn't realize it at the time, but I had lost comms with 72C and I interrupted Rich right when he was giving an important sitrep. Because I was carrying the spec ops MBITR (multiband inter/intra team radio), my transmission capability was more powerful than his, so I accidentally cancelled him out during mid-sentence.

After twenty minutes 72C and their ANA had won the TIC and were carrying on. Our side had no wounded, no KIA, so it was a good action for them. They found blood trails all over the place, but no enemy KIA or wounded. But I didn't like a trend that seemed to be forming—Captain Shafiq Ullah never offered to help. In fact, he never even budged from behind his wall. Seven Two Alpha's ANA had gone completely to ground. Shafiq Ullah gave Rich's call sign enough time to get well ahead of us, again, and then we slowly moved out.

After about another half an hour the sun was starting to get really hot. I was going through my water and realized I'd have to ration it out. The day had just started and we were nowhere near the twenty-odd klicks we had to cover before nightfall.

A TIC started over to the southwest, with incoming and outgoing fire. It sounded more serious than the last one, with rockets and heavy weapons firing. It seemed about seven or eight hundred metres away. I radioed the major to let him know (of course thinking he was behind me), and he calmly said, "Yeah, that's us. We're in a TIC. I'll get back to you." *Geeewwww!*

I said, "Okay . . . well, good luck and keep your head down," and listened as his firefight raged for another couple of minutes. Later that night, I found out that Colonel Morris, the officer he was mentoring, got it into his head to cruise down a road, farther to our west, and parallel our companies as we patrolled along. But Morris didn't account for the fact that he was in a vehicle, travelling quickly, while we were on foot. So in very short order he was literally behind enemy lines, about a klick and a half farther south than us. The major, realizing the ANA and OMLT HQ elements had inadvertently become the recce team, tried to mentor the colonel back to the straight and narrow, but Morris liked his position, *dangerously* way ahead of his own troops, and he wasn't going to budge.

The CSM was about to have a massive coronary, when suddenly RPGs flew over the hood of their truck, rounds cracked into their vehicle, and all hell opened up on them. They smashed into a wall and dismounted, and returned fire as best as they could. But they did great, because after a few intense minutes, they'd chased away the Taliban. By a complete miracle, they took no friendly wounded or KIA, even though RPG rockets had sailed over their bow. They mounted up, drove over to a nearby hill, where Hobbles sent a message over the net to let us know they were still alive. The ANA HQ then put out a defensive screen and stayed there for most of the day.

We patrolled through some corn and grape fields, hopped a few walls, and continued the trace through some compounds. Suddenly it sounded like Longview and Hetsa were in a TIC as outgoing rounds filled the air. We moved up but took cover as Fourneau, Shafiq Ullah, and I heard the ominous CRACK CRACK CRACK over our heads. We got behind a wall, but I couldn't see anything. I tried to reach them over the radio, but we had no net comms, only PRR with Hetsa, and their range was notoriously short. After a few minutes the TIC died down, and we continued on the trace. I couldn't rightfully send up a contact report, because it was the warrant who should've called it in. Of course, at the time I had no idea his radio had crapped out on him.

The ever-present dust swirled through the air as we patrolled along, watching for ambush points and sending up locstats to the major. He was up on his hill at this point, so we had pretty good comms for the rest of the day.

Suddenly, over to our front and left, the firefight to end them all kicked off. My call sign took cover because incoming rounds were snapping and cracking all around us, and we weren't even the target! Rich and his ANA had just sprung a major ambush. RPGs exploded as rounds cracked and snapped all over the place.

Rich shouted over the radio and his voice sent shivers down my spine. They were getting hit—hard. All of the rounds sounded like incoming. After a minute he shouted over the noise of incoming fire that they'd been caught in a three-sided ambush and were so suppressed they couldn't poke their heads out of cover.

I found out later that the ambush started with an RPG rocket that exploded so close to 72C's Warrant Smith it had flung him ten feet through the air like a rag doll. He landed on his head, shook the dust and stars out of eyes, and sprinted over to a wounded Canadian, pulling him into cover. Rich had dived into a shit ditch, and could only raise his rifle over his chest and "pray and spray" on full automatic. He couldn't even raise his head to look, because incoming rounds were kicking up dust all around him and passing between his arms and his rifle. They were in a desperate situation.

And Shafiq Ullah wanted nothing to do with it. I knew it could be very dangerous for us to just sprint up and try and relieve them, but we were on a different axis of advance. As long as we ran up to help and stayed on our proper axis of advance, our fellow OMLT and ANA call signs knew where we were *supposed* to be. Was there a good chance Rich's ANA would fire on us? Possibly, but the alternative was to sit where we were, do nothing, and listen as our friends were slaughtered. At least if we advanced, we could come up next to them, and either draw some heat away from them, or actually kill the Taliban who had them trapped in a three-sided ambush. *Kill the ambushers! But we'd have to move, now!*

I walked as calmly as I could over to Shafiq Ullah and asked through Max, "What would you like to do?"

"We will stay here."

Okay… "Captain Shafiq Ullah, listen to that gunfire. That's almost all one-way firing. Our friends, as we sit here, are being shot at. If we stay here, and do not go to help them, there's a good chance they'll all be killed. If we leave, right now, we can still help them, it *might* not be too late!"

He listened to Max translate and said, "No, we are good. We will stay here."

I wanted to scream in his face, "You cowardly *bastard*!" but instead stormed off. I looked at Fourneau who quietly said, "Sir, maybe we *should* stay put—"

"Oh for fuck's sake, Fourneau! Those are our friends! LISTEN TO THAT! They're being shot to shit, and you want to *stay put?*" *I couldn't believe what I was hearing.* If the roles were reversed, I knew Rich would've been running at full sprint to save us. *Son of a bitch!*

I couldn't hear anything Rich was saying over the net; I'd lost all comms with him. I spoke quickly over the radio, trying to reach Major Hobbles. I couldn't reach him either, but thankfully Ross spoke over the net and said he would act as a relay station for me, sending Hobbles my message. I told him to get Hobbles to have Morris radio Shafiq Ullah and give him a damn kick in the ass! We were just sitting there, cowering; we had to move if we wanted to help Rich. Ross got the message and quickly passed it on. I couldn't hear Hobbles's response because he was out of range. Rounds continued to snap over our heads, and we could hear RPG rockets being fired and detonating all around Rich and his men.

After about five minutes of pacing back and forth, I made up my mind to grab Fourneau, go forward to find Longview and Hetsa, grab Lieutenant Aziz, and try to go help out 72C. Suddenly an Apache helicopter gunship startled us as it flew in low over top of us, and after thirty seconds of hovering in the air, cut loose with its 30mm chain gun, spitting high explosive death into Timothy. *Thank God! Rich might still have a chance!*

Rich told me later he'd crawled to where he could see his ANA and plotted their grid on his map under extreme enemy fire, as Warrant Smith crawled down a ditch to throw red smoke in front of the ANA, delineating their forward-most troops so the Apache wouldn't engage them by accident. Again, it was sheer heroism on both of their parts. No one would've blamed them for going firm and taking cover, but they put their own lives at extreme risk to make sure their ANA weren't going to be lit up by mistake.

We were only about four hundred metres away, and the Apache's guns sounded like a chainsaw. They were so loud that Captain Shafiq Ullah lost face by diving headfirst into a ditch when he heard the noise. Fourneau and I didn't budge, and I told Max to explain to the captain that the sound was Apache outgoing fire, not incoming Taliban fire. Shafiq Ullah was very embarrassed and argued the point for a few seconds and then slowly climbed out of the ditch and dusted himself off. The Apache hovered over the battle space and periodically cut loose with a loud burst of 30mm. We could hear his rounds detonating all over the ground, tearing the Taliban apart.

Finally Rich spoke over the net to say the Apache had cleaned house, and they were able to continue. He said over the radio they had one wounded Canadian and an Afghan, but he didn't give the nature of the injuries. My heart dropped into my stomach. *Who got hurt? How badly?* I listened as Rich passed up his nine-liner, the military's radio report for wounded personnel, and realized it was a wounded Afghan and a Canadian with an injured knee. They would both need to be extracted. I could hear Hobbles again. He said the area was too difficult for the RGs to get to; would Rich be able to extract his wounded to a point farther south down the trace, more suitable for a pickup? Rich said they could, and carried on with the mission. The Apache was "Winchester" (out of ammo), so he flew off to the south to re-arm and refuel.

Shafiq Ullah got a steaming message from Colonel Morris, and suddenly we were on the move south again. There was a haze lingering in the air, and it smelled strongly of cordite. Warrant Longview, Hetsa, and their ANA were far ahead of us, over to the right.

My combat antenna started going off. *We're being watched....* I scanned around but could make out only tall cornfields, in every direction, as far as the eye could see. *That's not good. They're probably hiding in the corn.*

I knew Rich's wounded man was probably only a few hundred metres away, so I asked Shafiq Ullah if he could get some ANA Ford Rangers to come down the road and pick him up. He almost shouted back at me and said, "The road has been mined, remember? The Taliban have been planting IEDs on the road behind us!" *So that's a big "No!" then.* As far as the ANA were concerned, we were cut off.

We came out of a cornfield and I took in a scene of utter devastation. The Apache had just loitered over the enemy and ripped him apart with 30mm high-explosive rounds. Shrapnel damage was all over the place, gouges of earth were torn up, and branches were on the ground from where they'd been shot out of the trees. My eye caught on something dangling from a tree branch and my brain said, *Cannot compute, cannot compute.* I thought to myself, *What the hell are sausage links doing in a tree?* Then I realized they were human intestines. I looked at the ground and saw big pools of blood, with smaller blood trails leading off in different directions and into the cornfields.

It was readily apparent that any Taliban who had fled from the battle could easily be hiding right next to us, in the tall corn. I tried to mentor Shafiq Ullah to send some clearance parties into the cornfields, but he strongly refused. I guessed he was afraid I was right and there were still Taliban hiding all over the place in the corn.

What happened next was hotly contested during my court martial for second-degree murder. Depending on who gave testimony, a few different versions played out. One soldier said we came across a wounded insurgent that some ANA soldiers had just finished kicking and spitting on. He had a small, fist-sized hole in his stomach, a partially severed foot, and an injured knee. Another soldier said he thought the insurgent was already dead, with a hole in his stomach the size of a dinner plate. Captain Shafiq Ullah said the man was torn apart, had lost all of his blood in a nearby stream, and was ninety-eight per cent dead. And although they differed in their testimony as to the manner and what was said before and after the incident, two witnesses basically agreed that I had shot the insurgent two times, in what was later dubbed by the international press as a mercy killing.

As a Canadian citizen, I had the right to remain silent during my trial. I could not be forced to testify. I chose to remain silent during my murder trial, and I never gave testimony on the stand, nor did I make a statement for the police. The truth of that moment will always be between me and the insurgent.

The ANA were ordered to continue on their patrol to the south and we passed two more torn-apart insurgents, laying in the cornfields. The Apache had been absolutely devastating—it was like the hand of God had come down and just ripped the legs and arms off of people. Shafiq Ullah approached the two bodies and said something to Max.

"Pakistan," Max said. "They are from Pakistan."

"He can tell, just by looking at their dead faces?" I asked.

"Yes, and I can tell too. It is obvious to us."

We patrolled for a while until we came alongside a road, and I saw some blood trails leading off in different directions. It also looked like the Taliban had put some wounded into vehicles. There would be a large pool of blood, and then nothing, like they were picked up and moved. We came up to a large compound, and I saw bloody handprints on the walls. It was very eerie to see blood everywhere—sometimes in big pools—but no bodies. I remembered hearing that in the Vietnam War, Charlie would drag away his dead, wanting to give them a proper burial. Timothy was apparently the same. The Taliban's religious beliefs said their dead had to be buried before sunset.

Fourneau called me over to a wall and showed me several empty boxes of Winchester ammunition, with a "made in Michigan" stamp on them and a bunch of brass cartridges littering the ground. They were deer-hunting rounds for a civvy rifle, but they would work in an AK-47. I got Fourneau to take a picture and zoom in on the lot number on the boxes; maybe they could be traced back to their source. Shafiq Ullah came over and said, "See? We told you the Americans were supplying the Taliban!" Almost every ANA soldier I met would swear on his family's lives that the Taliban were being secretly supplied by the States. I had gotten into a heated debate one day back at Sper on the subject and tried to show them how ridiculous the theory was, but when we found boxes of American ammunition, in the middle of Helmand Province, I was fighting an uphill battle. Later when I was at FOB Mushan, we patrolled into an Afghan civvy compound and found a huge stash of American medical supplies, and of course, nothing I said could convince the ANA that America wasn't secretly in cahoots with the Taliban. I didn't know if the ANA thought it was all part of the American military-industrial complex or the Tri-lateral Commission making business from the war, but there was no changing their minds.

We decided to take a lunch break, and made our way onto a strip of grass near a compound. I was just digging my spoon into an MRE (meals ready to eat, a.k.a. "meals rejected by the enemy") pouch when an incoming round cracked loudly in the space right between Captain Shafiq Ullah's head and my face, missing my nose by an inch. I automatically flung myself backwards and lay on my back for a while, with my legs still crossed underneath me. Fourneau asked if I was okay and I replied, "Fine; just wanna stay like this for a bit." I asked him how he was doing, and he said he was fine too.

"How's your water, do you have much left?" I asked as I stared up at the cloudless sky, pondering my own mortality.

"Yeah, I'm good for a while, sir." Fourneau just looked down at me.

"Let me know if you need any; I packed extra just in case you guys ran out." I slowly picked myself off the ground. *That was a bit too close. Clearly they didn't want the son of Jor-El to become a Jedi! They feared my "medicine."*

The ANA picked up stakes again, and we could see Longview and Hetsa off in the distance. We gave a big, friendly wave and they waved back. I hoped they were doing okay.

* * *

We realized we wouldn't be able to make the required distance that night, so the ANA began to look for a suitable place to make a patrol base for the night. Major Hobbles and Colonel Morris had gone ahead, again, and found a nice compound that would suit our purposes, right next to a hill.

I saw Rich a few minutes later. His company had marched a bit too close to mine, or more accurately, Shafiq Ullah had patrolled closer to them, hoping they'd keep up their shit shield routine for us. I gave him a big, happy wave and he waved back, shaking his head. I could hear his voice in my head: *Savages. Goddamn savages.*

Our call signs split up again and we patrolled farther along, until the ANA decided to stop and pray at a mosque. Fourneau and I took some cover and just sat down. It had been a very long, hot day, but I was proud of the boys. We'd marched close to twenty klicks in one day, and even though Fourneau looked exhausted (I'm sure I did too), I think he could've kept going if he had to.

The ANA and Max finished their prayers, and I was anxious to get moving before last light. The sun was starting to go down and we still had about a klick left to go to the patrol base. Suddenly my combat antenna began to buzz, so I told Fourneau to go firm. He was about to crest a small hill past the mosque and cemetery, but I wanted him to let the ANA with us go first. He walked over and joined me as we let an ANA soldier, the PKM gunner Adam Khan, pass us and go slightly over the crest.

Suddenly hundreds of incoming rounds cracked all around us, showering us with dirt and rocks as they smacked into a wall behind us and the crest in front of us. I threw Max to the ground and quickly dropped behind the crest, into dead ground where the enemy couldn't see us. I crawled to the crest and peeked over, looking for Adam Khan, absolutely sure he'd be lying dead in a pool of his own blood.

I got to the edge and then saw him standing tall, giving a big, friendly wave to the shooters over by the treeline, just like I'd taught him. But I told them to wave *before* the shooting started, not *during*! He wasn't fazed by the hundreds of rounds cracking into the rocks and sand all around him, passing over his head and kicking up sand between his legs. He just kept waving, knowing that the Taliban don't wave, trying to get whoever wanted him dead so badly to kindly stop shooting at him.

"Adam Khan, *pro-at, pro-at*, get down, get down!" I screamed, as the incoming rounds began to slowly taper off and then stopped completely. It felt like five minutes had gone by, but it was probably closer to ten seconds, when I quickly crawled to the edge, and looked to see who was shooting at him. I saw about thirty of the high friends of Jesus, the Afghan Border Police, hanging out by some trees around fifty metres away. I guessed they were *still* high if their poor marksmanship and target identification were anything to go by. *As if this freaking day hadn't been crazy enough, to now almost get killed by the Afghan Border Police!*

Looking at Adam Khan, at the bullet holes in his shirt and pants, and at the dust kicked up all around him, it completely reaffirmed my belief in the concept of "when it's your time, it's your time," because clearly, it *wasn't* his time. He didn't have so much as a scratch on him, let alone a hundred bullet holes through his thin body! It was nothing short of divine intervention that he hadn't been totally ripped apart by the amount of incoming fire, all directed solely at him. I wanted to reach out and touch his Wookie ammo bandolier, hoping his mojo would rub off on me and keep me safe, but he just shrugged and kept walking down the slope, leading the way. *Inshallah.*

As we passed by the border cops, Shafiq Ullah shouted something derogatory at them and they shouted something back. We marched over to the hill and then into the compound, where we'd be staying for the night. We cleared the compound to make sure no one was hiding in the back, and used a broom to sweep a bunch of used hypodermic needles into a corner. A bunch of old heroin pods littered the ground. Obviously, the compound was used as an opium den and someone had been shooting pure heroin oil with the needles. We grabbed some water from the ANA trucks and topped up. I looked over at Fourneau and realized he was absolutely finished, both physically and mentally. But I couldn't blame him. I wasn't exactly feeling a hundred per cent myself.

We finally reunited with Longview and Hetsa and I gave them hearty slaps on their backs, happy to see them alive and well. They looked the way I *felt*. I found out the warrant's radio had crapped out at almost the very beginning of the patrol, but I'd figured as much. But the warrant and Hetsa seemed good to go. I was confident if we had to, most of us in the compound could've kept going, and that was a real testament to the Canadian soldier, because it had been a very long march through crushing heat, with lots of TICs thrown into the mix.

A big cheer went up as Rich and his men arrived in the compound. We all ran over to greet them and help them with their kit. Warrant Smith looked absolutely hilarious! His helmet was askew, he had dust and dirt all over his face, and he looked like he'd been through the damn wringer. Of course, at the time I didn't know he'd been caught in an RPG explosion and launched ass-over-teakettle in the air like a rag doll. I found Rich and gave him my seat and handed him a coffee I'd brewed especially for him.

"How you feeling, champ?" I asked, smiling away.

"Fuck me, Rob. Holy shit, man." His thousand-yard stare had improved considerably. He now looked like he could see through time.

"I know, brother," I said as I handed him the brew. "Have some joe. Don't talk, just take a sip." After a minute he really began to open up and told me the story of their two firefights. It sounded incredible and hard to believe at the same time. I said I was sorry I couldn't get Shafiq Ullah to come and help them out, and I told him I felt really ashamed by what happened. I felt like I'd really let Rich down and it bothered me a lot. Rich called me a dickhead and told me they probably just would've ended up killing *us* too. Maybe he was right.

Hobbles called an O-group and gave out some good pointers. Everyone took the piss out of me when they explained how I had cut off Rich during the middle of his contact report to give my locstat, earlier that morning.

Hobbles turned it into a cautionary note for all of us, and it was a lesson I'd never forget. He also warned me of the dangers of being *too* eager to go and help out a buddy, and he explained it from his perspective and it made total sense. But he was a klick and a half away, and I was only five hundred metres away, listening to Rich's voice as he shouted on the net with all hell breaking loose around him, so my perspective was different as well. But I could see his point and took it on board.

He wrapped up the O-group and, as was his custom, insisted that everyone make at least one point, even if it was only to say, "No comment." I liked that idea; it was sort of Chinese Parliament–inspired. Our wounded Canadian had a banged-up knee, so he'd be sitting the rest of the foot patrol out with Ross in the RGs. It was an absolute miracle that we only had one guy with a sore knee, after the day we'd just had.

A real festive mood overtook the compound as everyone realized how close we'd all come to being killed. Rich was on the sat phone with his missus when Hobbles fired off a full mag of AK tracer rounds into the air, trying to bring the other ANA vehicles into our leaguer. Rich had to explain to his concerned girlfriend that it was fireworks going off. *Oh how we lie and lie!*

I went over to the ANA HQ truck and asked Colonel Morris how he was doing. It had begun to get cold, and he didn't seem to have anything besides a small blanket. We talked for a while and he asked about me and my family. He had come to visit us in Sperwhan once, and when he opened up our OMLT door, he immediately began speaking to Hetsa (who was resplendently bearded) in Dari, asking Hetsa to introduce him to our team. He began to get frustrated until Hetsa finally broke his silence and explained he wasn't a terp. We had a good laugh and he talked for over two hours with us that night, getting to know all of us and just having fun.

I knew I had my sleeping bag, and my outer "bivvy" bag to protect the sleeping bag and add extra insulation, so I offered Colonel Morris my Ranger blanket from the States. He seemed very grateful, and when he tried to return it the next morning, I told him to keep it. I didn't know at the time, but I had made a friend for life. Later when I was in FOB Mushan, he would radio the ANA on their net and tell his captain to go and get me, just to talk and ask about my family. He was just that type of guy. I think it burned Major Hobbles pretty good to see me getting along so well with the officer *he* was mentoring.

When my turn came for the sat phone, I called home and reached Amélie. We talked for a few minutes and it felt great to hear her voice, especially after the day we'd had. I was still giddy with the adrenalin monkeys still riding my back, because we'd almost been killed a dozen times over in *one* day. Amélie was the best, and she understood what was going on, without me having to say anything. She was the rock that kept me grounded in that terrible place with her love, strength, and patience.

We could only talk for a couple of minutes because everyone needed a turn, so I handed the sat phone over to the next guy in line and found Warrant Smith. I shook his hand and told him how glad I was that he was still with us. I described how he had looked walking into our compound with his helmet all askew, and we had a good laugh. He told me all about his "unplanned space flight," and it was an incredible story. I told him he was lucky it was an RPG anti-tank round, the conical shaped one, because if it had been an anti-infantry round, he'd be suntanning in the Elysian Fields. We just hung out and shot the shit. I really liked talking with him, and I learned a lot from him later in the tour when we were together in Mushan.

I checked on my team and made sure everyone was doing okay, then we said good night *Waltons* style, as was our custom. I heard the other call signs snickering at us, but we didn't care. Traditions were important. That night, we all slept like the dead, grateful we hadn't joined them.

Chapter 13

The ANA took a few days off from the planned mission for admin reasons, and nobody really complained. We were all terribly dehydrated from the first day's patrol and welcomed the chance to get topped up and rested a bit. We changed all of our batteries, cleaned our gear, and then started patrolling in the local area. On one patrol, my team found an IED in the middle of the street, not buried but just waiting for us above the ground. We set up a cordon with the ANA, who quickly grew bored with the whole thing, and then casually picked up the IED and just threw it into the back of a truck. We also had some incoming fire whanged at us. Just to *harass* us. *All very normal.*

After two days of local area patrols, we woke up early on the fourth day of the op and headed off to the LD, the start line for the day's patrol south. We marched for twenty minutes, before a visiting Afghan general named Bashir called everyone back to the LD and switched my ANA's position on the trace with Rich's ANA. For no apparent reason.

So after some under-the-breath-cursing, we started up again, and we'd been marching for a half an hour when we came across an American vehicle convoy of army troops, waiting outside of a narrow village. We said hi and kept walking. Rich and his crew broke off to the west while 72A started to enter the village. Longview and the dirty Hungo passed through it with Aziz in the lead, and Fourneau, Shafiq Ullah, and I were just about to go through a narrow alley when—CRACK! CRACK! CRACK!

Incoming rounds began to scream down the narrow alley choke point. I threw Max behind me as we all took cover at a right angle to the alley. I heard Warrant Longview and Hetsa open up, and quickly broke out my map. The next village down the road was allegedly a Taliban stronghold. *Must be coming from there.*

I pulled my head back as rounds snapped and cracked into the wall in front of me and continued down the alley. The Americans scrambled into their vehicles and started them up, ready to move. I knew Rich and his guys would be finding cover on the other side of the village.

I tried to peek down the alley but the incoming fire was too intense. I looked left and right, but the walls were too high for us to jump over. There was nothing for it—we'd have to go down the alley. *Hey diddle diddle, right up the middle.* I suddenly remembered the words of a Para instructor of mine back in England who said, "The worst thing that can happen to you is you'll die." *Hmm. Poignant.*

I turned to face Fourneau. "We can't do any good here; we've got no SA [situational awareness]. We've gotta sprint up and join Warrant Longview and Hetsa. Do you want to come with me or wait here?"

Fourneau looked terribly insulted. "I'm coming with you, sir!"

"Good man." I continued, "It sounds like big incoming rounds, like a crew-served weapon. We'll wait until they reload, and then take off at a dead sprint." I quickly peeked around the corner. "It's going to be twenty metres. Hey, you should be happy I've been working out, 'cause I'm massive! I'll make a great meat shield for ya!"

A big grin spread across his face. I looked over at Max and told him to stay put. We wouldn't need him, not yet anyway. "Please ask Captain Shafiq Ullah if he would care to join me, up at the front, so we can actually see what's going on."

"No thank you; he says he is good here." The incoming fire had begun to die down a bit.

"Yeah, I thought he might say that. Okay Fourneau, stand by. In four, three, ready, steady, GO GO GO!"

I pushed off the wall and rounded the corner at a dead sprint, giving it everything I had to cross the open ground down the narrow alleyway. I could see Longview behind a wall, now only fifteen metres away, ten metres, five metres, *RUN RUN RUN!* I slammed into the wall next to Longview and spun around to see where Fourneau was. He was only five metres away and pounded into the wall right beside me just as the Taliban machine gun began firing again.

SNAP SNAP SNAP! CRACK! CRACK!

The incoming rounds tore the air over our heads as we ducked behind the wall.

I asked the warrant what was going on and he pointed to the village to our south, the one we'd been warned about. I looked all around and took in some ANA behind the wall to my right, ducking and shooting back, and some American Humvee vehicles, part of the convoy, strung out and disappearing back into the village.

Suddenly Rich shouted over the net, "Charlie, Charlie! You are engaging us, you are engaging *us!* CEASE FIRE CEASE FIRE CEASE FIRE!" I scrambled to look left, right, and behind me, trying to find the friendlies who were shooting at Rich. I couldn't see anybody shooting toward him in the west; everyone around me was shooting where they should be, to the south, at the Taliban stronghold.

I spoke quickly over the net, "Charlie, Alpha, there is no one around this call sign engaging you, over." I looked again, but still couldn't see anyone shooting in Rich's direction.

"Charlie," Rich shouted, "run around and tell everyone to stop shooting—the Americans, the fucking Afghans! Get everyone to *stop* shooting!" I suddenly realized how stupid it was to be arguing the finer points of friendly fire with the guy *getting* shot at, so I ran up to the nearest American Humvee and found a major standing behind it, using it as cover. He started to say, "Hey, I was thinking—"

But I cut him off. "Get all your call signs to stop shooting; someone's engaging my other call sign to the west. Get everyone to stop shooting, NOW!"

"But we're not—"

"DON'T ARGUE! Just get all of your American call signs to stop shooting!" I had gotten through to him because he quickly ran up to his vehicle, opened the door, and started barking the order over his radio net.

Ten seconds later Rich told us the incoming friendly fire had stopped. Major Hobbles picked up the radio conversation and said, "Seven Two Charlie, you owe me one, out!"

I told the American major to get a grip of his men; they'd almost killed my friend and his Afghans. He didn't have anything to say back, so I rejoined Longview, Hetsa, and Fourneau over by the wall.

"Hey, sir," Hetsa said, "check this out," and pointed toward an Afghan border cop (judging by his long hair, flowing beard, and shoeless feet). He was out in the open, carrying a large Spig 9 recoilless rifle around on his shoulder, just like Aziz had done when Sperwhan got attacked the second time. The border cop was high as a kite, singing and waving the eight-foot-long cannon tube back and forth, up into the air, and then clunking its barrel down into the dirt. All of the Afghans shouted their version of *"Geeewwww!"* as he'd swing it around and point it at them, as if it was a funny joke. Naturally, his finger was on the trigger the whole time.

Finally a buddy of his, who was equally high by the looks of him, stumbled over and helped him point his BFG in the right direction, toward the Taliban village. The rocketeer shouted something, then casually aimed the Spig at the village. But at the last second his inner-ear problem must've kicked in, because he pointed the Spig up into the sky at a sixty-degree angle, and fired his round off into space.

KERWHOOSH!

I thought he must have taken a personal dislike to the Taliban base on the moon, or something. As his intergalactic missile launched into space, the stoned border cop disappeared behind a wall of dust kicked up from his launcher's backblast.

Everyone started howling with laughter, because after about twenty seconds when the dust started to settle, the cop walked out of the eye of the dirt hurricane, dropped his Spig 9 roughly on the ground, and promptly collapsed in a heap. *Good a time as any to take a little nap.* One of his fellow cops walked over to him, swiftly kicked him a few times in the ribs, and then started laughing again. *Was he alive or dead? And really, who cared?*

I had to wipe tears from my eyes, it was hands-down one of the funniest things I'd ever seen in my entire life. Then Captain Shafiq Ullah decided to finally join us as his ANA began to move out toward the village. Rich and his crew would carry on to the west and hit the village to our front from the flank, supporting us as we attacked it with a full frontal assault. *Pop smoke, full frontal! Airborne!*

We marched along but before we were even close to the village, some of the high border cops ran out of a wood line to the east of the village, stormed the main gate, and began room clearing on full automatic.

"Whaddya think, sir?" Longview asked me over the PRR, as hundreds of rounds snapped and cracked from within the village.

"Let 'em clear it themselves. It would be pure suicide to go into the village while the high friends of Jesus lay down the law!" *No thanks!*

We patrolled up to the village and then quietly passed it. As we walked next to a twenty-foot-high wall, I heard a long burst of AK fire. I looked around but nobody else seemed to notice because there were so many rounds going downrange. We were becoming dangerously inoculated to gunfire and that *could* lead to complacency, and that *would* be the end of us.

We passed the Taliban village and took a breather in the shade. The CSM and his FOO/FAC and medic/mobile reserve unit joined us. I asked how they were doing and they were good to go. It had been a while since any of us had to patrol over twenty kilometres under enemy fire. I reminded myself to watch everyone more closely because heat exhaustion would be a real threat on a day like this. *Yeah, if the stoned border cops don't kill us first!*

We marched on and laughed as the omnipresent, perpetually high border cops "liberated" a motorbike from the Taliban, put four guys on it, and tried to zoom around, much to the delight of everyone present. *These guys should open their own circus.* They zoomed down a very steep ditch, smashed into the bottom of it, went ass-over-teakettle, and sprawled all over each other. We passed them on the road and looked down at them, all crumpled one on top of the other in the ditch, moaning in pain. One guy seemed to be unconscious. Of course we laughed at them as we marched past. Who wouldn't? They were quickly becoming our mobile comic relief.

Some ANA troops called me over and pointed out a possible Taliban compound. Then they asked me if I could call down artillery on it, thereby denying its use to the enemy—and they were serious. I asked them what they planned on doing with all of their fellow soldiers who were still inside the compound.

"They will move," an Afghan officer, whom I'd never seen before, smartly replied.

"In time?" I asked.

"Sure. Can you do it right now?"

"Are you going to get them out of there, *right now?*"

"Sure. Hey, *hey!*" He began to shout at his men to vacate the premises so that I could call down artillery (but most of his Afghans remained inside, probably still liberating items from the Taliban).

I waited until the ANA officer walked back over to me, then I pretended to press my radio button, and moved my mouthpiece closer to my lips as

I said, "Roger Young, we have an official request by the mobile infantry to commence bombardment of Planet P; how copy? Affirmative, that's a big rog. Covenant ground forces are attempting to fire the Alpha Halo!" I called Max over and said, "Please tell the officer, 'Negative, Fleet has other plans for Planet P,' but welcome home." Max looked at me quizzically not understanding the *Starship Troopers* movie and Halo references, then tried his best to translate my mad ramblings. The Afghan officer thanked me anyway and then strolled off.

We continued on the patrol, our feet kicking up the ever-present moon dust, an ultrafine dust powder that settled onto everything like a blanket. As we'd pass farms and compounds, several times the Taliban DEWS alert would begin to bray, letting us know we'd been compromised and Timothy was on to us. *Damn donkeys!*

We patrolled for another half an hour when a massive TIC kicked off to our east. But it was all outgoing fire. And it seemed to be travelling south down the road. I found out later that night, after talking to a few Americans, that their guys had been doing spec fire (speculation fire), which meant they would fire at anything suspicious. So that explained why the TIC seemed to be moving down the road, as they travelled south. I could just see our American cousins, riding up in the Humvee turrets: *No siree, I don't like the look of that rock!* BANG BANG! *Nope, that wadi looks suspicious.* BANG BANG BANG!

* * *

After a few more hours of marching in the terrible heat, with the odd angry shot snapping and cracking over our heads and making us flinch, we finally met up with Rich and his boys. I shouted at them to "Get back! I don't want your death wish rubbing off on my call sign!" We had a few laughs and Rich told me he had a good story for the campfire that night.

The ANA then decided that if they continued patrolling through the fields, sooner or later they might actually come across the Taliban. And since no one wanted that, they decided to stick to the main north-south road. So that's what we did. We left the fields and dirt paths and began marching only along the road, and never left it once. If the Taliban were going to plant IEDs anywhere, it would most likely be on the main road, but that thought never crossed the ANA's collective mind. I politely mentioned it to Captain Shafig Ullah, who merely replied, *"Inshallah."*

After about five klicks, Rich's ANA officer, Captain Ghias, had had enough. He radioed for a truck to come and pick him up. After ten minutes a Ranger pulled up beside him, and he lazily chucked his Dragunov sniper rifle in the back and hopped into the box. *Must be nice!* He waved at Rich and offered him some prime real estate next to him, but Rich angrily shook his head no and continued marching with the ANA of Third Company.

I asked if anyone needed water, and Hetsa said he'd gone dry. I reached into my day sack and gave him some of my spare bottles and, for a morale booster, a bottle of Gatorade I'd brought along from Sper.

We came across the American convoy from the east, which I had affectionately labelled Spec Fire Force Five, and I politely asked if they could spare any water. *Maybe I shouldn't have taken the piss if I was going to beg them for water later.* They took one look at us, and then offered us all we could carry. We thanked them and topped up our CamelBaks and water bladders. *Damn good of 'em.* Despite my apprehension about their spec fire, I loved the Americans, I really did. Sure, everyone knew they would try to kill you from time to time, but on the modern battlefield, you just came to accept that.

But they would also sacrifice themselves to save you, and they certainly brought a lot of toys to the party, and because of that, most of the other coalition countries were extremely jealous of them. The Americans never rubbed your face in this, but you always knew that you were the poor kid on the block compared to them.

But if it wasn't for that Apache the day before, Rich and his team would've all been killed, no question. We asked the convoy for water, but they also offered us food. If we had needed ammo or grenades, they would've just handed that over as well, no questions asked. They were just like that; they would literally give you the shirts off their backs. Many Americans later told me they were happy to have allies they could trust in Afghanistan, unlike in Iraq, where they felt like it was only the Brits and Aussies who really watched their backs.

Around dusk we entered the town next to FOB Bermuda. Some guys said we'd marched close to twenty-eight klicks, other guys said it was more like twenty-three, but regardless, we'd hiked well over twenty klicks, each soldier packing on average a hundred pounds of kit, in forty-degree-Celsius heat. Shots had snapped and cracked around us all day, and once again 72C, a.k.a. call sign "Because I could not stop for Death," had almost met a horrific end, only this time at the hands of our allies. *Feel the love!*

We set up in an abandoned school until our recce element could find the exact location of the FOB. Rich and I walked into the school and found thousands—literally thousands—of man-turds in neat rows in every single classroom. The civvies apparently used the school as a community toilet.

I was amazed by the tight rows and patterns they had somehow managed to maintain. Laddah, the medic, walked over and said, "Well, we can't stay here tonight; we'd all get sick."

I snapped back with, "Thanks, Tips!" and instantly regretted it. The heat was really doing my nut in, but that was no excuse for being a prick. I apologized to him and he said to forget it.

Soon our recce team came back to the school and led us to the Brit FOB on the outskirts of the ville. We must've been quite a sight. We were dirty, dehydrated, tired, hungry, angry, and armed—a somewhat dangerous combination. The Brits greeted us warmly, happy to see ground troops after a month of being cut off. They took us upstairs and showed us to our room, a big, thirty-by-thirty-foot cement floor. No beds, no blankets, but we weren't expecting any. We'd been cut off from our vehicles all day, so we had no sleeping bags or warm kit. I had my toque, dry shirt, and gloves from my day sack, and that was it. And when you'd been sweating bullets all day in plus-forty heat, and the temperature dropped to near zero at night, that change was absolutely devastating. As our OMLT unit's self-appointed "morale officer," I took it upon myself to sort us out for the night. I dumped my kit in the corner and went to find the Brit in charge—a sergeant wearing an Airborne shirt. That was a welcome sight; I knew the Airborne Brotherhood always took care of its own.

"Allo, mucker," I started off with, slipping into my best cockney and Para slang. "We've tabbed over twenty K to git here, mate, and we've got no warm kit, yeah? It's turnin' Baltic and we're absolutely gippin'. We had to dump kit and go OTR back at nutter central. Now things've gone Pete Tong and our jack wagons can't git to us, yeah? You've probly sussed we're completely chinned, Hank Marvin, need some serious gonk, and just wanna get our fat swods down, an' maybe have a lie-in on the 'morrow, and I don't mean a furry thing with claws! Can ya screw the nut for us, mate? An' where's a colonial git take a slash round 'ere?"

"Course mate, no worries," he said. "How many are yuh?"

"Sixteen mate; cheers for that!"

"Right, two shakes an' we'll sort ya out."

"That's absolutely pucker, mate; good on ya, cheers. Name's Rob," I said.

"Daz; no worries. You meat and veg?"

"Aye mate, 2 Para. Did a stint and got kicked out when they sussed me mum and dad were married and *not* first cousins!"

"Ha! Figures, mate. Wait one, I'll be right back." Daz took off and collected some of the lads and spread the word to collect some warm kit for us. One of the guys, when he found out we'd marched with no follow-on vehicles or warm kit, said, "That's a bit schoolboy, innit?"

"Oi!" I shouted from behind Daz, who got out of the way so I could address the ignorant git. "Fuck me, mate! We just tabbed over twenty klicks through multiple Timothy contacts to get here! We had a choice between packing water and ammo, or warm kit! And since we figured youse twats would actually like some company, we chose the ammo!"

"Yeah right, sorry mate," he quietly said. Daz then sent them off, and ten minutes later the Canadians had more than enough warm kit to get us through the night. I took the massive haul upstairs and said, "The good book doth verily say, 'Ask, and ye shall receive,'" and like Père Noel, I began hand-ing out softy jackets, long-sleeved tops, fleeced bottoms, thick socks and gloves, watch caps, and toques to all the good little children. To top it off, Daz walked upstairs with a five-by-five-metre-square sheet of Hessian sack that would cover all of us quite easily. We donned our warm kit, and went downstairs to talk with the Brits and grab some fresh soup and crackers.

After we had eaten our fill, Rich and Major Hobbles told me over a warm cup of joe what had actually happened that afternoon, before Rich started "panicking" on the net. He and his ANA had broken off to the west, that part I knew. But Rich, who would surely be one of the lone survivors of a zombie apocalypse, had a bad feeling just as he was about to walk between two buildings. So he peeked around the corner just in time to see an American Humvee, with some young kid up in the turret, swing its mounted light machine gun around and open up on Rich and his ANA. The major cut in to say that apparently the gunner was a seventeen-year-old reservist, who wanted to be the first kid on his block with a confirmed kill. He saw brown troops and probably figured anyone brown had to be Taliban, even though they were in ANA uniform, wearing helmets, with badges and flags on their sleeves, etc., etc.

Rich picked up the story again, in his Cape Breton accent. "Well, the ANA don't stand for that kind of nonsense." So the Afghans, having been shot at countless times before and therefore possessed of much more clarity of mind, decided they'd been fired on too many times by white folk and began to shoot back. Joey from Podunk, West Viriginia, in the Humvee turret, shouted "Hot damn!" and really started to pop some caps at the ANA. Then the

ANA started manoeuvring to get better firing positions on the Humvee they *knew* was occupied by Americans! Poor Rich was losing his mind, because he was trying to get everyone to stop firing on each other, so he shouted it out over the net.

"But Samroo," he mocked, "goes 'doo, doo, doo, we're not shootin' at no one round here, yuk, yuk' and does nothing to help!"

"Hey Rich," I smirked, "I'll tell ya what: take out your compass and shoot a bearing of twenty-four hundred, then march on it until you find somebody who gives a shit!"

Major Hobbles cut in and said, "I decided I couldn't leave it to Rob, obviously, so I looked and quickly realized there were American Humvees much farther back, way down the line outside the village. So yes, where Rob was, no one was shooting, but four hundred metres back, out of view, was Joey from, where did you say? Podunk? Anway, he had decided he wasn't getting the kill tally he wanted with his M240 belt-fed machine gun, so he swung it out of the way and was about to bring his 40mm grenade launcher to bear on friend Richard, when I jumped up, ripped Joey out of the turret, and shouted, 'You killed a lot of good people with your fucked-up fire mission!' and then literally made him cry."

We all had a good laugh at Rich's expense, ate some more soup, and then hunkered down for the night. For someone not used to the OMLT and its ways, it would have been a strange sight—sixteen soldiers, many of whom had almost been killed a dozen times over, wearing borrowed clothes and using their tac vests as pillows, lying side by side, laughing and farting, under a big burlap sack.

I joked and said, "Everyone, hands above the Hessian, please and thank you!"

Rich shouted out, "Remember everyone, what happens in FOB Bermuda *stays* in FOB Bermuda!"

"The hell *it* does!" everyone shouted back.

Chapter 14

The next morning, Major Hobbles was told by his boss that where the ANA went, the OMLT would follow, and mentor accordingly. So our major explained we'd just been signed up to join our ANA as they were about to cross the desert to get back to the ANP station in Lashka Ghar. We would've been ambushed and IEDed to hell if we had tried to go back the way we'd just come, so that left us only one choice: we'd have to cross the desert to the east, then loop back up to Lash.

In the dead of night, our sec-for guys pulled up to FOB Bermuda with our RGs, so 72A and 72C would be losing their drivers and gunners to the RG convoy, while the warrants, captains, and some of the other lads would be accompanying the ANA as they did their Cannonball Run through the desert.

We said goodbye to our wheelmen and automated turret gunners and were about to leave the FOB when Warrant Longview had a sinking suspicion. He went back upstairs and found that Fourneau had forgotten his day sack and Hetsa the spare barrel for his C9. Hetsa's sin against the gods of war, forgetting his spare barrel, was actually a chargeable offence, but the angry father said he'd deal with it properly when we all got back to Sperwhan.

We thanked the Brits for their hospitality, and I collected and checked off every single piece of warm kit once it was returned to me. Not that

I thought anyone would steal from our kind hosts, but when you're that tired, you just forget things like that. We policed up our gear and marched out the front gate and travelled back to the school of a thousand turds. We muckled onto our ANA compatriots, and then Rich, Smith, Longview, and I hopped onto a big ANA deuce-and-a-half truck and sat down for the most bone-jarring ride of our lives. The Cannonball Run had started, and just like the movie, it wasn't funny.

The big trucks fired up their engines, and after a few backfires, things kicked off. We travelled out of town and then passed through a stream, in which we promptly got stuck. The driver spent the next thirty minutes rocking back and forth. We offered to get out and push, but the offer was graciously declined. Hours passed before all of the trucks in the long ANA convoy made it through.

Then we passed into the beginning of the desert, and the trucks all got stuck at different points in the fine red sand. Hours passed again and soon it was dusk. We'd get stuck, rock back and forth for half an hour, and then slowly move along, until we got stuck all over again. All I'd had to eat was some beef jerky the warrant's girlfriend had sent over from Canada. It was a godsend. We'd been driving in spurts and stops for almost ten hours now.

It took so long because the ANA considered themselves a warrior caste, and manual labour (i.e., digging out a stuck truck) was beneath them. So they would wait until the truck could rock itself out.

Finally, one after another, most of the large trucks all became stuck in a row, so we dismounted and sat back to watch what quickly became the new gold standard for what a gong show looked like. The ANA shouted, screamed, cursed, and finally sat down in the dirt and pouted.

I looked over at Rich and Warrant Smith, who were putting their night-vision goggles onto their helmets. *Good idea.* Every one of us was exhausted from the long, boring, painful ride and we just wanted to curl up and go to sleep, but we had a desert to cross before we could rack out. I looked at my watch, it was now 2345 hours. *Nice.* We had left FOB Bermuda around 0800 hours.

Major Hobbles got out of Colonel Morris's truck with the ANA elite and walked over to speak conspiratorially with Rich and me. "Don't make it obvious," he whispered, "but walk slowly to the front of the convoy. Once you're there, do a head count, and then make a mad dash for it, up the mountain to the north, and down the other side, where some ANA trucks *should* be waiting for you. If you don't get on them, you'll be left behind, like the rest of the ANA."

Rich and I just looked at him for a few seconds before I finally said, "You're not joking, are you, sir?"

"Absolutely not. Run up the mountain, it's probably about six hundred metres, and on the lee side, there'll be a bunch of ANA trucks, but there won't be enough room for everyone. So it's first come, first 'don't get left behind in the middle of a godforsaken desert.' I'll meet you on the other side. Good luck." He turned and walked back to his truck.

I looked at Rich. "This is all *your* fault."

"My fault?" He took a step back. "How the hell is this *my* fault?"

"Don't make me say it. It's bad luck to say it," I sighed, looking at the ground.

"No, I *want* you to say it!"

"Fine. You're call sign 'Bad Karma,' call sign 'Sand in the Teeth of Death!' You're marked to die! Every time I'm near you, bad things start to happen!"

"Well, I hope you've been keeping fit, 'cause that's a tall mountain, and this soft sand is going to be a bastard to run uphill through." Rich was looking up at the slope.

"I was genetically designed at the super-soldier in vitro facility to exceed normal human standards," I smugly replied. "Plus all of those augmentations . . ."

"Good to know, Dingo! C'mon, let's go tell the guys," Rich said, and slowly walked back to our little circle of Canucks. After a bunch of "What?" and "No way!" and some "Fuck offs!" thrown in for good measure, the boys collected their kit and we began nonchalantly strolling to the front of the convoy.

I looked at Longview. "Wizard, use your dark magic to cast a cloaking spell over us, so the trolls can't see us!" He just smiled and shook his head. "Thankfully I've got a plus twenty-six rating for my warrior stamina, so I should be okay," I said, not really believing what was about to happen.

Once there, Rich did a head count and said, in his deep Cape Breton accent, "Right, boys. The major wasn't joking. Once the goddamn savages see us sprinting up the mountain, they're going to know the Canadians have been told something they haven't, so they're going to give chase! We'll stick together, but keep an eye on each other, and make sure no one falls back. 'Cause I'm not going to lie to you . . . *if* you fall behind, you're probably going to be raped—"

"Nice," I said.

Rich kept rolling. "I know, I know, this is pretty hard to believe, even for the OMLT. But if you don't want your ass to be the size of your mess tin, stick with me. Good luck, and I'll see you on the other side." He turned around, and started three-quarter sprinting up the mountain. I fell in beside him, and like a morning PT session with the officers in the front and the warrants in the back, we took off, running up the hill.

I felt like Indiana Jones, sprinting away from the angry natives at the start of *Raiders*. The ANA quickly figured out something was up and started honking their truck horns, sounding the alarm because the Canadians were escaping from Stalag Luft Siebzehn. In my mind I could hear Alsatians barking and angry shouting as spotlights swung around, trying to get a lock on us! *Halten sie! Halt!*

"We've been made! Run for it!" I shouted and began laughing hysterically when I heard truck doors slamming and angry shouting as the Afghans began to figure something was up. We had a good head start, but soon two full companies of ANA were running to catch us, shouting at us the whole time, and quickly closing the gap as we ran up the mountain. We had almost a hundred pounds of gear on; they had maybe ten. It was a race we probably weren't going to win.

"Rich," I said between quick breaths, "you're a fast guy, you'll probably catch up. Step over to the side, go firm, and lay down covering fire! Put some rounds over their heads! Make 'em eat sand and buy us some time! I'll try and hold a truck for you, but no promises . . ." I laughed.

Rich wasn't smiling; in fact, he didn't seem to be having any fun at all as he said, "Don't tempt me. I'll do it! I swear to God, I'LL DO IT!"

After a few minutes we slowed down to a quick jog. We had no choice: with every step we sank almost eight inches into the loose sand and our column was beginning to string out. I looked for Longview and found him right behind me, not even winded. I had forgotten he was carrying his own day sack and Fourneau's forgotten one, so I stepped out of the column and together we carried the extra day sack between the two of us. We each held an end of Hetsa's "forgotten" spare barrel, which we had shoved through the day sack straps. I thought of the powerful scene at the start of *Uncommon Valor*, as the American reconnaissance teams were sprinting to get to the choppers as Charlie gave chase. *But these are our allies we're running away from! The guys we're supposed to be mentoring!*

I looked over at Longview. "Still thinking of letting our forgetful friends off easy?" I panted.

"Absolutely not! I wasn't too pissed before, but I am now!" he snapped.

I looked at my watch. It was now 0003 hours (three minutes past midnight), October twenty-fifth—my birthday.

"Well, that's just great," I panted.

"What's that, sir?" the Wizard asked.

"Not exactly how I thought I'd spend my thirty-fifth birthday: sprinting up a mountain getting chased by Eurasian sodomites, and trying to get a seat on a truck so I don't get left behind in a freakin' desert!" I laughed.

"Yeah, I suppose not. Oh well, what're you gonna do? Happy birthday, though."

"Thanks. We're almost at the top. How ya doing?" I asked.

"Yeah, fine. I hope those trucks are there, waiting for us," he said. *Yeah, me too!*

We quickly crested the hill on the double, and there they were: five Ford Rangers, about four hundred metres down in a small valley. I turned to face our escape committee and shouted, "There they are, boys! Go all out now; give it all you've got!" Then I put on my best Arnold accent and yelled, "*Run! Get to tha choppah!*"

The warrant and I stepped to the side and waited until our last straggler caught up, just as the fastest ANA reached us at the crest. They had finally caught up and were trying to pass us as we sprinted down the mountain to get to the trucks before they filled up. I grabbed an Afghan soldier by the scruff of his shirt, trying to slow him down and use him to pull me a few feet at the same time. He angrily swung his fist and knocked my hand off. *Hey pal, you just made "the list!"*

Our fastest runners had made it to the Ford Rangers. "You guys in the trucks," I panted over my PRR, "get 'em turned around." The trucks were facing *into* the mountain and that wouldn't do us any good. By the time they got turned around, the evil dead would've swarmed us.

The warrant turned on his best parade ground voice (which was incredibly loud) and shouted, "Move it! I said, MOVE IT!" to our slowest guy. I counted heads and realized it was just the three of us left; everyone else had mounted up in the Rangers. Finally we ran up to one of the last remaining trucks with any space on it and I shouted over the PRR, "That's it! We're all on board, tell your drivers to go!" The Canadians began pounding on the roofs, shouting, "Go, go!" to their ANA drivers, who probably didn't speak English but got the idea.

The Rangers churned in the deep sand until they got some traction and began blaring off into the desert. A few Afghans made wild-ass leaps, trying to make it into the trucks before it was too late. Some guys jumped and latched onto the tailgates and tried to pull themselves up. I couldn't quite see from my angle, but it looked like one of the guys trying to pull himself on board just got his fingers rifle-butted by a fellow Afghan. *Did that really just happen? Seriously?* The warrant and I reached over to our clinger-on and helped pull him in.

"*Tasha-koor, tasha-koor.*" He thanked us in Dari, smiling gratefully.

"*Salaamat baashaid,*" I said back, placing my right hand over my heart.

Longview looked at me and grinned. "Some night, eh sir?"

"Definitely one for the OMLT yearbook! The boffins back home should make a training scenario out of that!" I laughed. The poor ANA continued to stream down the mountain in droves, racing to get one of the last seats, but they were too late as our trucks pulled away into the night. Some hung their heads, others cried out in anguish and cursed us as we left them marooned in the desert to an unknown fate. *Probably a long freakin' walk!*

We drove for an hour, not sure where we were heading, and not really caring. Sheer exhaustion had set in and we all began to fall into a fitful sleep, until we'd smash a rock or hit a bump and get violently jarred back awake.

After an hour of driving in what felt like circles, our vehicles stopped on a hilltop and formed a leaguer. We had some good over-watch from the position, and as long as the sentries didn't fall asleep, I thought we should be okay.

Adam Khan, my ANA company's PKM gunner, turned up and rallied us to help him collect some tumbleweeds to make a fire. It had turned Baltic cold and we were still covered in sweat from our run up the mountain. Soon a good-sized fire was blazing away and I began to double-tap—my head started nodding as sleep tried to crush me.

The next thing I knew, Adam Khan was brushing smouldering ashes off of my fat swod because I'd just fallen face-first onto the outer edge of the fire. I smiled at him sheepishly and said, "*Tasha-koor, kaakaa.*" *Thanks, uncle.* He grinned and went off to find more tumbleweeds for the fire.

We got shoulder to shoulder with each other, just like it said in the winter-warfare manual, and although it was a bit *too* close for us alpha-male types, it was no good. All of us began to shiver uncontrollably. I had put on my toque, gloves, and dry shirt, and held my sweat-soaked combat top up to the fire to dry it out, but it wasn't enough. The wind was really picking up and we were on top of a large hill, so that didn't help.

Major Hobbles arrived but never came over to see us. He found a place to sleep in the back of an Afghan ambulance and quickly racked out. *Nice. As long as you're okay,* I thought to myself.

"Right, that does it," I said to Rich. "I'm off to find something, 'cause we won't make it through the night." I got up and began walking around the ANA vehicles, until I finally found a Hessian sack covering a DshK heavy-machine gun in the back of a Ranger. *That'll do.* I quickly untied the knots and took the tarp back to the fire where Rich, Longview, and Smith were the only OMLT guys left; apparently it was now every man for himself as we all tried to stay warm.

We went over to a truck to shelter from the wind, laid down part of the tarp to cover us from the sand, and then hopped in, covering ourselves with the rest of the tarp. "Let us agree to never speak of this night again," I said.

"Agreed!" they all replied, in perfect unison.

* * *

The next morning we set off around four a.m., but before we left, I asked Captain Shafiq Ullah if he'd like to do a head count of his men. We'd been scattered to the four winds after our run up and down the mountain, and it wouldn't surprise me if he had accidentally left someone behind. Max translated for me and replied, "Nah, he says, 'We are good.'" *Fair enough sunshine; if you don't care, I don't care!*

The rest of the day became a nauseating blur of getting whiplashed back and forth in a big truck, constantly getting stuck, and dealing with snapping, fraying tempers. At one point, after an open-backed Humvee driver flew through a deep river and sent a tidal wave cascading over his passengers, one of them dismounted and actually pulled leather on the driver. He pointed his PKM belt-fed machine gun at the driver and we all thought he was really going to do it, but cooler heads prevailed and managed to stop him in time.

After hours of bone-rattling slow motion, we finally dismounted on the outskirts of Lash and RVed with our RG vehicles, feeling terribly seasick. I was never so happy to see my fellow Canadians in my whole life. We drove through the city and pulled into the ANP station without further ado.

We did a quick debrief and then cleaned our weapons and kit. *First my kit, then myself.* I grabbed the towel the Brits had given me at FOB Tombstone and strolled off to find the showers, happy at the thought of finally getting clean again. I saw some ANA milling around a low building, so I wandered over there. I walked through the open door to see an Afghan soldier, naked from the waist down, with both of his feet planted on the edges of a sink as he squatted over it and soaped his cucumber and beets. *Geeewwww! I really, really didn't need to see that!*

He turned from his ablutions and said, "*Salaam.*"

I never made eye contact as I kept on walking to the showers. "Yeah, *salaam.*"

I walked into an open stall and saw rusty, used razor blades on the floor. I skipped that one and walked over to another. Mud, and what was probably human feces, choked the drain, causing brown, mucky water to fill the floor basin. *Nasty! Okay*, I thought to myself, *maybe I'll just skip the shower and have a wet-wipe classic later.*

I walked over to the other side of the building to use the toilet, careful not to look at, or make eye contact with, Mr. "I think it's perfectly socially acceptable to wash my junk in the communal sink." I walked over to the stalls, knocked on the first one with a door, and hearing no response, gently swung it open. My eyes were physically assaulted as I took in the human stool smeared all over the floor, the back of the door, *and* all three of the walls. *Gaagaagaaa!* The stink was overpowering, and I was glad I hadn't had breakfast yet, because I would've lost it. Not that it would've changed the overall ambience of the toilet.

I decided to tempt fate once more and walked to another stall with a door on it, and repeated my polite knock. I opened the door and was instantly showered in the face with spraying water—a hose ripped out of the wall was shooting all over the inside of the toilet. I choked and spit out coppery-tasting muck as I slammed the door shut.

I thought to myself, *Luck be a lady tonight,* and slowly, carefully, opened another stall, expecting God knows what to jump out at me.

No hideous smell or brain-scarring sight met my tired eyes, no terrible-tasting water splashed onto my face. *Huh.* I slowly walked inside and then remembered my toilet SOP: look for toilet paper before you start. I closed and latched the door behind me, and then bent over to check the toilet roll holder. I reached under and felt for a paper roll, but instead stuck my hand into something soft and mushy. *GAAHAAAA!*

Suddenly—horrifically—hundreds of flies began swarming out of the mush under the toilet roll holder, buzzing angrily around my face and arms. "No, no, get back! *Aaaahhh!*" I squealed as I swatted the air around me, with hundreds of flies clinging to my face and hair. I tried to find the latch to let myself out of the toilet, but couldn't grasp it as panic threatened to choke out my reason and dexterity. I boot-stomped the door, ripping it off its hinges, and fled the building, back outside into the hot sun. I shook my head violently to get the last of the flies off of my face and hair. *Seriously, what the hell was that all about?!* I stormed back to the resident OMLT building and warned the boys not to use the toilets. "They're like a haunted house! The ANP toilets need an exorcism!"

But I still really had to go. Thankfully, I suddenly remembered we'd brought along our portable toilet bucket, which was a Gucci piece of kit. Some genius had created a triple-sealed bag full of cat litter, which you would open up and spread over a bucket by its edges. Then you would put a makeshift toilet seat over the bucket, do what nature called, and then zip the bag, wet wipe your hands, and chuck the lot in the garbage. I'd totally forgotten that we'd packed the portable buckets, because if I'd remembered, I never would've risked losing my soul in the ANP toilets.

Later that morning Major Hobbles, as the OMLT rep, got called to the governor of Helmand's palace on the outskirts of Lashka Ghar. He was presented with a strange white-rock trophy, and was told that he and his officers were now entitled to become landowners in Helmand Province.

The governor estimated our combined kill tally of insurgents to be close to one hundred dead, two hundred wounded. Then the governor said that at least two hundred Afghan families had returned to the area we'd cleared in as many days, to return to their homes that were once occupied by Taliban and their supporters.

When the major said that, we all felt pretty good. *Finally, something decent, something important, that we can point to and say, "We did make a difference: we helped the people get their homes back."* To be able to say we had accomplished something tangible on the op was very important to everyone in the OMLT. It was a good thing, something we could be proud of, because we'd had precious few moments like that.

* * *

We mounted up the next day and were leaving the front gate when our vehicle column of Afghans and RGs came to a screeching halt. Wandering into the base, covered in dust and looking like death warmed over, was a small, frail-looking ANA soldier. It seems he'd fallen asleep at our leaguer on the hilltop in the middle of the desert, his friends forgot to wake him up, and he'd been left behind. He'd just walked over forty kilometres in two days through enemy-held territory and strolled up to the front gate. *I don't want to be the kind of guy who says, "I told you so," but …*

The ANA threw him into the back of one of their trucks, gave him some water, and had a good laugh over it. We continued on and drove down the highway until we rolled into a Brit base called FOB Bastion, just north of the Lash. Hobbles and I walked into the command post to let them know we were there. We met a small Dutch major who explained they knew exactly where the enemy was, pointed their position out to us on a large map, and then politely asked if we would be so kind as to go and take care of them.

Hobbles and I looked at each other, and then stared at the Dutch major.

"And what's wrong with your soldiers?" Hobbles asked.

"Well," he started to murmur, "if we go, we might get hurt, and so—"

"Holy crap," I snapped. "What about us? It doesn't matter if *we* get hurt?" Hobbles muckled onto me and we quickly left the CP. *Wow—did that really happen?*

We spent the night and then made it back safely to Kandahar Province the next day. On our way, Ross had wisely taken a ten-figure map grid on his GPS for where he lost his rucksack on the way into Helmand, so we pulled up to the Afghan National Police station and Ross got out to confront an ANP officer wearing a CF army-issued winter jacket on the front gate. Ross's name tag was still on the jacket, so hilarity ensued when Ross asked if he could speak to himself about getting his jacket back. Then he ripped it off of the officer and hopped into his RG, and we fled down the road as the ANP threatened to kill us for stealing *their* jacket.

We made it back to Masum just in time for a late lunch. We began offloading our kit when Major Hobbles declared we were all going to KAF for two days of R&R. It was the best news we'd had in a long time. Visions of finally calling home, drinking coffee and eating ice cream on the boardwalk, sleeping in for once, and eating until we were actually full, filled our exhausted minds. You'd think we'd just won the lottery!

We had a quick after-action review for the road move and any points we wanted to pass on, and then remounted our RGs for our two days of roller coaster fun in KAF! *Yippee!*

The Wizard and I would be travelling with Ross and the sec-for boys in the lead vehicle. Rich offered us a place with him in his RG, along with the rest of call sign "Dead Men Walking," but I wisely said, "*Mon cher* Richard, you—good sir—can stuff your offer. In fact, you can shove it, poke it, cram it, wedge it, stick it, push it, elbow it, and finally, nudge it right up your—"

"Yeah, I get it, dickhead," he snapped. "All you had to do was say no thanks."

I was about to mount up when I saw that the vehicle Hetsa was travelling in had all of its plastic firing ports open. If an IED went off (and didn't immediately kill them) and they had so much as even one port open, they'd all be concussed and deaf. I got their attention and shouted at them to close their ports like good stormtroopers. They groaned and assuredly said something derogatory about officers, but sealed all the ports closed.

The Wizard and I mounted up with Captain Ross and shrugged off the dust from the one-horse town that was Masum Ghar. We were heading to the bright lights of the big city! *Yip-yip-yippee! Bright light city gonna set my soul / gonna set my soul on fire!*

We screamed, "So long, suckers!" as we flew out the gate of Masum and quickly zipped along the ring road south to Kandahar city and then KAF. I reminded myself to stay switched on, but allowed myself to get caught up in the conversation about what we were going to do in KAF once we got there. Everyone was joking and laughing away, and for once, my fear of driving in Afghanistan seemed to have been left behind.

I looked back at the Wizard and said, "Do you think we'll find the suppressors you've been aft—"

KAAA-BOOM!

I looked out the back window. *Oh no, oh no, oh no!* I wanted to throw up. My heart had dropped into my stomach as I saw a huge mushroom cloud begin to billow and form in the sky, right in the middle of the road between our vehicles. *Was it an RPG or a Spig 9 or an IED? Had to be an IED—the explosion was too big to be anything else. We just got IEDed!* Everyone began to talk over top of each other. I couldn't hear any orders coming over my radio. I . . . what . . .

"Shut up!" I ordered. "Everyone be quiet and watch your arcs for Timothy! Listen for orders over the net!" I was expecting a stop and secure order if our friends had been obliterated or too badly damaged to move (we weren't going to leave our wounded or KIA behind), or a "Go go go! Get off the X!" order if the IEDed vehicle could still move. If it could move, we were supposed to get off the incident site, to get off the "X." Secondary IEDs, direct fire, mortars, rockets: they could all be waiting for us if we didn't move, right now!

But no orders were forthcoming. *Maybe Hobbles got hit!* Then it was up to the nearest officer to call the next move. But no one was saying anything. The radio had gone maddeningly silent. *What the hell?* Longview started to open up the back door.

"Close that door!" I shouted, "We haven't been told to dismount! We're waiting for orders; we might be moving off the X." He quickly slammed the door shut and sat back down. I was still staring back toward the explosion. The dust had begun to settle and I could see all of our RGs had come to a complete stop. *Oh no, that's not good. They're too badly hurt to move. We've got to protect them.* "Gunner," I said, talking to the automated turret operator, "what do you see?" He had swiveled his gun around to check out the damage. He was using his optics to cut through the dust.

"Two vehicles back, one RG, missing its .50, with its hood gone, and smoke billowing out of the engine," he stated. *Two vehicles back? That was Hetsa's RG....*

"Is anyone moving inside?" I demanded. *Please, God.*

"Yes! Guys are moving inside!" He shouted. Everyone in our RG breathed out again.

"Sir," the warrant said. We'd been in enough trouble together that I knew what he was thinking.

"You called it, warrant. Move out, dismount dismount dismount!" I ordered.

"Gunner, swivel your weapon around and look for any Taliban in cover; check out the hills to our north and the houses to the south. Ross, I'll be outside, diverting traffic. Get your gunner to cover us after his sweep."

"Roger that," Ross said, listening intently over the radio for some news, for someone to says something, *anything.*

I hopped out and looked down the road as soldiers ran up to the RG and climbed inside. They were doing their job; I had to do mine, which was to make sure we weren't about to come under fire from someone else or encounter a suicide bomber trying to rush through our cordon.

"Do your fives and twenties, boys!" I shouted to my vehicle's dismounts, reminding them to check for IEDs in their immediate area. The Taliban enjoyed planting secondary devices in the same location as the first IED, trying to kill us as we went to help the wounded.

The road we were on was the only major highway to Kandahar from Masum, so civilians were travelling back and forth on it as well. When they saw the explosion, they immediately stopped and wisely began to back up, knowing soldiers were more than likely to shoot first, ask questions *never*! I looked at the oncoming vehicles; they were beginning to pile up behind the lead one.

To our great relief, Rich's voice came over the net and said everyone in the vehicle was okay. They'd gotten their bells rung and some nosebleeds, but they were going to be okay. I wondered why our major wasn't telling us this. *Was he hurt? He wasn't in Hetsa's vehicle....*

I spread out the guys from our lead vehicle and we started conducting traffic in a big loop, away from the incident site.

Once I was happy with everyone's position, I started to walk back to the IED blast site. I ran into Rich, who was running around, trying to get everything organized.

He ran over to me and said "Big effing IED—ripped the hood off of Hetsa's RG. The sheer force ripped off the .50-cal and launched it twenty metres into the desert. Everyone's okay though, nothing serious, lots of headaches and ringing ears." His relief was written all over his face.

"What happened, though?" I demanded. "No one said anything, no orders, no nothing! I snapped at the guys because they wanted to dismount right away, but what happened to 'Get off the X'?"

"I know," Rich said, "that was messed up."

"What about the major—is he okay, is he wounded?"

"No, he's fine, he was—"

"Then what the hell is going on? There's a whole freaking list of things we're supposed to do right after that happens, and we didn't do any of them!" I was really upset. The major enjoyed calling me a *junior* captain, but I knew we didn't just hang around immediately after an IED, not if we didn't have to!

"Rob!" he said, snapping me out of it. "It's not the time for that! Right now, we're off-loading the guys and waiting for the QRF."

"The QRF will take hours to get here, but can the vehicle still be driven? Is it too damaged to move?"

"Besides the hood and the fifty, I think it's fine."

"Well then what the fuck are we still doing here, just hanging out? Rich, I'm not having a go at you brother, but you and I both know we should've left ten minutes ago! It's a total miracle that wasn't an IED-initiated contact, because if it was, the way this gong show has been handled, we'd all be in a right shit state!"

"I hear ya."

I breathed in deeply and stared back at the RG missing its hood. *How weren't they all killed?*

"Orders are: we sit and wait. QRF out of Masum will come and collect us to go back there," Rich said quietly, not wanting to provoke me.

"Well, thank fuck you were there! You were the only guy saying *anything!*"

"Some guys step up, some guys go and stare into IED holes . . ." Rich said absent-mindedly.

What? What did he mean by that? Before I could ask him, he turned around and jogged back to the damaged RG where the guys were being carefully removed.

I walked over to the warrant and briefed him on the plan. He felt the same way I did. Collect our wounded, swap out drivers, grab the fifty, and vamoose!

Some ANP officers came up, and after begging me for some 9mm ammo, they wandered over to the IED blast site and found the detonating wire. They dug it up and followed it about six hundred metres away to the south toward a large compound, where they found a ladder leaning against the wall.

Thankfully Timothy's sense of timing was off, because he initiated the IED too soon, and all he managed to do was rip off the hood and the .50-cal. Had he fired his device at the right time, everyone in the RG probably would've been killed or severely wounded.

The cops did a search of the compound, but once Timothy had seen the ANP following his det cord, he would've lit out, *rapido.*

I walked back over to the IED hole to find Major Hobbles. I saw him standing next to the hole, with a vacant look on his face, staring into it. *So that's what Rich had meant.*

I walked up to him and quietly asked, "You okay, sir?" I could still smell the explosives from the hole.

"Yeah," he snapped, "I'm fine. I'm not the one who got IEDed!" *Well, you're sure not acting like it!* We both looked into the hole. It was huge, easily five feet across. It must have been a large IED.

"Close one, eh?" I asked in a comradely tone of voice.

"No shit! I can't believe how close they came to getting us—half a second later and they'd all have been killed." He continued to stare into the hole.

"Well, thankfully that didn't happen, so now I guess we just wait for the QRF."

He didn't respond but just looked around, in a sort of daze. I let him be and walked back over to my lead vehicle and cordon duty.

After what seemed like an unbearably long time to wait, the QRF from Masum Ghar turned up with a Bison sporting a plow in the lead, bulldozing down walls to create a new route to get to us. It was followed by some tanks, a few LAVs, and a flatbed truck.

They pulled up to the site and loaded up the RG onto the back of the flatbed. *Okay, that's why they called it the QRF.* The RG couldn't move. We mounted up and slotted ourselves into their column for a slow ride back to Masum Ghar.

We pulled into the base and then escorted our guys to the medics. I asked all of them how they were feeling, and besides headaches and ringing ears, they seemed to be doing all right. One of the guys from Ross's sec-for group, whom I had only ever said a few words to, stopped me and said thanks for telling them to seal up their firing-port hatches. I said I was just glad they were all okay (relatively speaking).

We did a quick hot wash and it was obvious the CSM was livid over the lack of orders or any direction immediately following the IED. Everyone stared at the major—the CSM's comment was aimed directly at him. He didn't have an immediate response, but asked, "Any other points?" What did the CSM expect him to say?

I had been in enough scary situations in my thirty-five years to know that a person could be a hero one day, and a total goat the next. No one could be perfectly brave and courageous every single time, in every situation. It was a continuum, and all a leader could do was hope that on any given day he would do the right thing, make the right call, and not get anyone under his command killed. If you were particularly brave, then all the better.

Rich and I talked long into the night over powdered coffee. We had been told to stop using the instant mocha coffee sachets because one of the guys said a medic had told him they were poisonous, but after a day like that, *pfft, who cares?*

Fourneau was on leave and had been choppered out of FOB Tombstone back in Helmand, so it was just Hetsa (with cotton in his ears), the Wizard, and me left from call sign 72A. We slept outside on tables around the BBQ pit, outside the Batcave in Masum. I looked up at a parachute drifting lazily over us; someone had strung it up between the buildings to provide some shade from the cruel sun. I wondered if I would ever jump again. Then I caught myself and wondered if I was even going to make it home again, to do *anything*.

Around two a.m. I was ripped from a deep sleep by the sound of a small OMLT kitten getting torn apart by a wild mongoose, only a few feet away from me. I listened as it screamed when the mongoose began to eat it while it was still alive. I rolled over and fell back asleep.

Chapter 15

The next morning I found Sean hiding in the Batcave, obviously as far away from the wire as he could possibly get. After our usual pleasantries and piss-taking, he told me I would be taking over the mentoring position Rich held with the Third Company, 72 Kandak. The officer I would be mentoring was Captain Ghias, the guy who got tired on the second long foot patrol in Helmand and decided to hop onto the back of a Ranger truck and take off. *Great. Sounds like my kinda guy.*

The Third Company and all of its troops would be part of a huge Canadian resupply and teardown convoy making its way to Combat Outpost (COP) Zangabad, and then on to FOB Mushan, to the west of Masum and Sperwhan. Sean told me I would be taking over for Captain John at FOB Mushan, the westernmost base Canada had in the Panjway Valley.

I would be signing for the RG that was already at Mushan, so I wouldn't be taking an RG out there. Sean had checked my file and realized I was LAV crew-commander qualified, so I was dicked to be in the turret of a spare LAV for the ride out. I hadn't been a "Panzer commander" since phase four officer training, so I was rusty as hell.

Then Sean dropped an A-bomb on my head when he told me I would be taking over as the commander of Rich's Canadian OMLT team, 72C, or as I liked to call them, call sign "Do Not Go Gentle!" *Gaahaaaa!*

"Are you *mental?*" I shouted. "I don't want to die!"

"You'll be fine, relax—" Sean said, trying to soothe my frazzled nerves.

"*Relax?* You don't know! You weren't there! But I saw it, with my own eyes: Death follows them on horseback and then just hangs out, eager to see what they'll get up to next! They have the mark of Cain on their foreheads! Like it was prophesied in the *Necronomicon Ex-Mortis*, 'Woe betide any man that doth willingly stand next to Seven Two Charles in a war zone....'"

"Oh, stop being so biblical," Sean chided.

"I suppose you're right," I sighed, slowly accepting my fate. "I guess Moe Szyslak's dad in *The Simpsons* was right—sooner or later, everybody gets shot."

"You're such a nancy," Sean sneered. "Grow a pair, you'll be fine."

"As always Sean, *your* strength gives *me* strength."

Sean told me to grow up and then said Warrant Smith would be my 2 I/C, but he was already out at Mushan, so I would meet him there. Stamps, Rich's ultra-dependable driver and all around good joe, would also be coming along, as would Rich's gunner, a young guy called Iropolous.

I told Sean thanks for nothing, and got up to go and find the Wizard and the dirty Hungo to tell them the bad news. I found them and said Ragnarök was upon us.

"The Big Green Machine has decided to finally break up our little award-winning team of like-minded individuals. They know that together, as a team, our combined strength was just too powerful, and that we 'threatened the natural order of things!'" I said, trying to keep the mood light.

I thanked Hetsa for his hard work and for keeping morale up with his full beard and great sense of humour, and then I spoke with the warrant alone. I thanked him for his excellent attitude and for watching out for me and not letting me step on my dick, as the expression went. I told him how much I appreciated his looking out for me and the team, over and over again, and for keeping us safe with his magical enchantments.

It bothered me a lot that 72A was getting split up, but with the leave blocks the way they were, we all knew it was inevitable. Everyone, no matter his rank or job, got a couple of weeks of vacation during his tour. And the way our staggered leave blocks were set up, it was unlikely the members of 72A would ever work together as a team again. The warrant said some kind words back, and helped me get ready.

I grabbed a terp (a young guy who, not surprisingly, was named Max) and told Captain Shafiq Ullah the news. I thanked the ANA for ... for uh ...

for coming on patrols every morning and for the great working relationship they had fostered with me and my Canadians. They thanked me back for ... for uh ... for always going out on patrol with them and for being ready to radio for help. I heard the Bellamy Brothers start to sing in my head, *"Just let your love flow like a mountain spring."* Truly, we would all be heartbroken to be working with someone else: me with another group of ANA in Mushan, the ANA with other Canadians in Sperwhan.

Then Max and I went to meet my new ANA. I knocked on their office door and they let me in and introduced themselves, but they were somewhat cold. I shook hands with Captain Ghias and his CSM, a very young man probably no older than nineteen or twenty called Shamsallah. Then we sat down together, but they weren't overly chatty. I guess they were scared I was the new guy who would get them all killed. The ANA could really take their time warming up to you.

I was just about to leave when the door opened and in walked the artillery captain that Brannon was mentoring back in Sperwhan, the guy I gave the parachute flares to. When he saw me in the corner he literally ran over to shake my hand and gave me a man hug, and when Ghias and Shamsallah asked how he knew me, he told them the whole story, and finished with, "He's a friend of *ours.*" Suddenly their defences came down and I was just one of the boys, chatting away and having a few laughs before I had to go back to OMLT HQ. *Now that's some good karma!*

That afternoon, Sean and I sat in on the convoy movement and Zangabad teardown orders given by the tank major in charge of the convoy. Early the next morning we would mount up, take our armoured vehicles and RGs into the dried-out Arghandab River, and then travel west until we were north of COP Zangabad. That afternoon our engineers would tear down the COP, and the next morning we'd hat up again, go back to the riverbed, and go farther west until we were above FOB Mushan. Then our vehicles would form a huge leaguer just west of the FOB, and our engineers would do some maintenance and construction on the FOB while the Canadians and ANA patrolled through the bandit country west of Mushan. It was a good plan, and nobody had any questions.

I spent the rest of the afternoon studying a LAV manual, because I would be in the turret commanding one of those beasts for the move with some sec-for guys as my driver and number two on the turret. Sean would be following along with an RG and then heading back with the convoy, at which point 72C and the Third Company ANA would be left in Mushan, to our own dubious devices.

Naturally, I mercilessly took the piss out of Sean, telling him it was okay to be scared, and to stick close to me because I was a heavily augmented super-soldier: "Spartan-118, UNSC designation: ROB." I assured him if anything happened, I'd take care of him. He countered with some choice words, rife with expletives, and told me to get out of his office.

I fired off an e-mail to Amélie and told her I'd get in touch with her again just as soon as I could. Because of OPSEC I had to be careful not to tell her where I was going or what I was doing, but she was a veteran and knew the drill. Then I wrote back to a class of schoolchildren from Saskatoon who had written some letters to me. My mom's friend was their teacher, so they all wrote fun notes to me, saying things like, "I hope you're having a good war," and "Can you bring your tank when you come to visit us?" My personal favourites were, "I give you strength, I give you power!" and "I hope you don't die." *Yeah, me too!* I took a picture of the OMLT kittens (the ones the mongoose hadn't eaten yet) and attached it to the letter I sent the kids, thanking all of them for their great letters.

I had a great sleep, and the next morning we were up early and quickly on our way. The column we joined was absolutely huge, with at least fifty to sixty different vehicles. We rumbled through Masum and quickly got into the dried riverbed, and even before the convoy's last vehicles joined us, they came under enemy contact. They really did a number on Timothy with their 25mm cannons and 7.62-calibre machine guns. In the hands of a well-trained soldier, the LAV was an incredibly deadly instrument, and our soldiers had been very well trained.

We rambled along, and the whole while our tail-end vehicles were constantly shooting into the walls Timothy was hiding behind. It was incredibly surreal. It was a beautiful day: the sun was up, there wasn't a cloud in the sky, and every now and then an incoming round would snap over my head. Twenty-five millimetre cannons shot death at the enemy as a firefight raged behind me. *All very normal.*

I was riding in my turret, with just the top of my head barely showing out of the hatch, when suddenly the armoured vehicle two in front of me got IEDed. The blast echoed over the riverbed. The major in charge quickly ascertained that the vehicle and its crew were all okay, so we just kept rolling along, like nothing had even happened.

After a couple of hours we turned south and rolled into an open field to the west of COP Zangabad. We dismounted and I went to say hi to Andrew, my friend from 3 RCR who had joined the battalion at the same time as I had. He quickly gave me the lay of the land and assured me that Timothy was most definitely out there, watching us and waiting. In fact, we had pretty much just hopped over his fence and were now hanging out in his backyard.

We didn't have to wait long as the engineers got to work tearing down the small base, and after half an hour, mortars started to fall in the field south of the COP. They were slowly being "walked" (falling increasingly closer) into the COP, but the engineers, in an incredible display of guts, just kept right on working. Only when the mortars started to land fifty metres out could they be bothered to stop their work. Everyone mounted up, battened the hatches on their armoured vehicles, and watched their arcs of fire.

After a while, Timothy must've run out of ammo, because the mortars let up and the engineers got right back to work. I tried to get my new ANA to go with me on a patrol to find the mortar team, but something had them spooked, and nothing I said or did could get them to change their minds. Sean and I discussed some ideas but we decided I would push them for a patrol the next morning. Sean then made a few radio calls, and by the time I went over to see Shamsallah (the CSM) again, he was game for a patrol the next morning. His boss, Captain Ghias, was joining us in Mushan in a few days' time, so Shamsallah was in command of all of the ANA soldiers. That night, we slept next to our vehicles and quickly fell asleep. I got woken up to take my turn on turret duty, but thankfully, nothing happened during the night.

I wondered how Amélie and our baby girl, Caméa, were doing. Cam was only five months old; she was born and then I left three months later. I missed them both so much. I had tried to call on the sat phone back in Sperwhan whenever I could, but it never seemed like enough. But just being able to call them every now and then was an amazing morale booster; I'd never had anything like that on any of my previous tours. I said a silent prayer for them and then went to wake up the next guy on turret duty.

* * *

The next morning I went and found Major Obermann and said I wanted to take my ANA and patrol south. I was hoping to catch the Taliban mortar team completely unaware, before they could start lobbing shells into our perimeter again. He told me good luck and to let them know if we needed help.

I muckled onto Ginge (one of the 1 RCR infantrymen roped into helping Captain Brannon mentor the ANA artillery back in Sper), who joined me as my fire team partner for the COP teardown, and I then broke open my map to show Sean what I had in mind. As much as I took the piss out of Sean, he was incredibly switched on, and although I would never say it to his face, I valued his advice. He said he would take Stamps and go up on a nearby rooftop to act as an RRB (radio re-broadcast) station in case my comms went wonky with Obermann. I thanked him for the good idea, said some nasty things about his fugly face, and then walked over to the ANA who were, to my great astonishment, up and ready to go.

I had a new terp, who would be working for me in Mushan, by the name of Omer. He was a nice guy and seemed really keen to do his job. Together we walked over to Shamsallah and I discussed some ideas with him over the map. He would bring along about twenty Afghans for the patrol. I would've liked to have more, but hey, at least we were going. Memories of a patrol back in Sperwhan when Lieutenant Mujahedeen refused to patrol one hundred metres to a big tree to kill/capture the Taliban recruiting team flooded back into my mind. *Maybe these guys really will be different. Inshallah.*

We set off right on time and began to make our way south of the Zangabad teardown operation, which had started up again as soon as the sun had come up. The sun promised to be hot today. It was only 0800 hours, but already I was starting to sweat profusely. *Situation: no change.*

We followed a wide footpath through a couple of villages, but where there should've been normal village activity, there was only eerie silence. Now that wasn't completely abnormal or anything, especially if we were new to the area and hadn't met the locals yet, but there was something in the air, a familiar bad vibe. *I sense something; a presence I've not felt since . . . the last time I got shot at! Which was . . . yesterday?*

We rounded a corner and the ANA saw something and took off at a dead sprint.

"*Goom-lie* [runner]! Ginge, stay right behind me," I said as we took off after them. "Omer, if anything happens, go low and hide against a wall, okay?"

"Okay, Captain Rob," he said as he pulled his *shemag* up so it would cover his face better. He had told me the night before he had relatives in the area, but they thought he was working in Kabul. He didn't want them to get murdered because of his chosen career. Or to get murdered *by* them.

We ran for about a hundred metres and then the ANA fanned out; they lost their *goom-lie* and were heading into the fields to find him. *They're surprisingly good*, I thought as they professionally moved into chase and block positions without having to be told.

The ANA shouted at CSM Shamsallah and together we entered a tall grape-drying hut. I looked for IEDs at the entrance, but Shamsallah just stormed in (*Geeewwww!*) and began rooting around. I told Ginge to stay outside while I went in, just in case Shamsallah grabbed something attached to a string, which was attached to a detonator, which was attached to a mahoosive IED. It was eerily reminiscent of the Taliban farmer's compound we had raided with the Brits outside of Salavat. *Was that two months ago now?*

A tall ladder was balanced against a wall with a viewport hacked out of the mud bricks at the top. The tall grape-field walls between the COP and the grape-drying hut were negated by the fact that the ladder reached almost two storeys up in the air. They could observe us at the COP from *inside* the two-storey hut and we'd never even know it. *Clever.*

Shamsallah found a Quran and a large map of southern Afghanistan in the corner. I was about to ask why they would need that, but then it became obvious: *They're not from here, they're probably from Pakistan. So they would need a map to get back.* We found some old PKM ammo and a few grenades, but no IEDs or parts thereof. I took a ten-figure grid and spoke directly with Major Obermann over the battle group net, letting him know what we'd found. He said, "Good job, continue with your patrol, over."

"Seven Two Charlie, roger, out." *Hmm, 72C—that didn't sound so bad after all.* Maybe the Wizard had found something in his book of spells to remove the curse of call sign "Anthem for Doomed Youth." Shamsallah tasked some ANA to muckle onto the Taliban kit and we continued heading south. We patrolled for another twenty minutes when, suddenly, we heard mortars start to fall in the vicinity of Zangabad. Knowing the Canadians were coming under mortar attack motivated the ANA to pick up the pace, and we marched quickly farther to the southwest.

We had been following a different footpath, with two shoulder-high walls on either side of the path, when the ANA stopped for an orientation moment. Shamsallah walked over and motioned with his arms to borrow my C8. The Afghans would often ask to look down our scopes to get a better view. I handed it over, and told Omer to let him know it was loaded, made ready, and on safe.

"I know 'loaded' and 'safe,' but what is 'made ready?'" he asked.

"There is a bullet locked inside the chamber, ready to fire. If he puts the weapon on 'fire' and pulls the trigger, it will go *bang*," I patiently replied. He told Shamsallah my weapon state and Shamsallah just shrugged, which was his way of saying, "Yeah, whatever." I walked over to one of the shoulder-high walls, facing east, and got out my map and GPS. I thought the mortars had stopped in the last few minutes; I couldn't hear any more explosions coming from the COP.

I was just about to send up a locstat when I saw three figures all dressed in black scurrying down a grape-field trench toward us. Time began to slow down as I realized one of them was carrying a long-barrelled weapon. It looked like a Chinese-made SKS rifle. *Timothy!* I couldn't believe my eyes. I had never seen him like this, out in the open, not surrounded by dust or haze like a shadow, but right in front of me! They were only a hundred metres away and coming closer.

As I watched them, duckwalking down the trench toward us, they kept looking to the north (the direction of the COP), where they thought the infidels were hiding.

"Down, everyone get down!" I hissed, ducking behind the wall. They were perpendicular to us, in a perfect ninety-degree angle to the ANA at the wall, coming right at us. *We've got them in perfect enfilade! We just have to wait until they get closer, then we'll gun them down!*

Where's Shamsallah? He's got my rifle! He had moved up to the wall and was glancing over at Timothy, through *my* scope!

"Stay down, everyone stay down!" I whispered as I crouch-walked over to him.

"Hey," I whispered, "give it back." I reached over and gently started tugging on its front cover. He snarled something and tugged back. "Hey, I'm not kidding . . . give it *back!*" I snapped, and began reaching over his arms to take my weapon back. *Really? Am I really having a freaking tug-of-war, over my own damn rifle, as we're about to ambush Timothy?* I could just see the headlines: CANADIAN OFFICER FIGHTS OVER PERSONAL WEAPON WITH AFGHAN SOLDIER, GETS SHOT IN HEAD!

"Give it back, damn it. Give. It. Back." We were both standing up now, fighting like two kids over a hockey stick signed by Gretzky.

Then I heard the swan song, the proverbial fat lady singing, to announce the sudden and violent death of my dream of getting the drop on Timothy. Some moron ANA soldier had stood up so the sneaking Taliban could see him in plain view. He had begun to whistle shrilly at them, as though he was trying to call a taxi in downtown traffic!

I let go of my rifle and shouted, "No! *Nooooo!* What are you doing?" I ran to the edge of the wall and looked over to see the three Taliban fighters stopping dead in their tracks, quickly pulling a one-eighty, and sprinting back the way they'd come. Shamsallah was already up and beside me, and began to fire round after round out of *my* rifle, trying to hit the fleeing Taliban. The rest of the ANA joined him and began pouring fire down at the fleeing insurgents. *Oh no no no no.* I was shaking my head, completely downtrodden.

Ginge shouted out, "Sir, can I fire?" He looked at me pleadingly.

I sighed deeply and said, "As long as you've got a legitimate target, go ahead." I looked back over the wall at nothing but an empty ditch. They were long gone.

I already had my map and GPS in my hands from before, so I radioed in the contact report and said we had engaged three times FAMs, who were now currently running for their lives to the south.

An unexpected thought ran through my head. I remembered a scene at the end of the movie *Jarhead*, where the sniper team was wigging out because an officer wasn't going to let them take their dream-shot and engage the target. I had laughed at the time, but I wasn't laughing now. I figured I knew *exactly* how they felt.

Shamsallah, realizing only now what he had done, slowly walked over and handed me back my rifle. He quietly said, "*Man mutasef astaam,*" meaning *I'm sorry.* I looked him in the eyes; he was genuinely upset about our little pre-ambush tug-of-war. I put my hand on his shoulder and said, "*Khob-as, beraader,*" which meant *It's okay, brother.* He smiled when he heard *beraader* and then quickly marched over to the whistle-blower, the smile draining off his face with every step. Soon it was replaced with a feral sneer.

He grabbed the mad whistler by the neck and banged him up against the wall and started shouting in his face. I nodded at Omer, meaning I wanted him to come over and translate the epic "jacking" this ass-clown was receiving.

Omer began to translate Shamsallah's shouting: "You are Taliban, why else would you be whistling at them, if not to warn them?" The whistler tried to respond. As I looked away to see what Ginge was up to, I heard Shamsallah deftly open-hand slap him across the face. "If the Canadians were not here, I would kill you myself and leave you in the ditch! You will never patrol with us again, and when we get back to Masum, you are finished. I will be watching you!" The CSM stormed off to the front of the patrol and got his men moving again to the south.

The Canadian FOO/FAC, the artillery observer, spoke over the net and said his guns were good to go—I only had to give him a target. I looked over the grape field and saw signs of life returning: some men, women, and children had begun picking grapes again and moving through the trenches. I looked farther south, on what I guessed was Timothy's E&E (escape and evasion) route, and saw a dozen large birds fly up and out of the trees, startled by something moving quickly underneath them.

"Negative," I said over the radio to the FOO/FAC. "The enemy has fled to the south, I have no viable target, I have no eyes on." *He's certainly keen.* But the FOO/FAC wasn't satisfied; he acted as though he hadn't heard me, and repeated his offer/demand to shoot his guns at something.

Okay, I don't have time for this. "Seven Two Charlie, the enemy has fled to the south. They are gone. I have *no* grid for their position to give you! There are now women and children working in the fields. This TIC is over. I am closing the book on this one. Thanks for the offer, but no thanks. Seven Two Charlie, out."

I had seen this before: it was probably the FOO/FAC's first time outside the wire, and possibly his last, so he desperately wanted to be able to say he'd done the job he'd trained for years for and shot his guns. He probably thought I was some thick idiot who couldn't take the hint, but I wasn't going to risk the lives of civilians just so he could say he called in artillery. Besides, we were way too close, danger close, to where the guns would've been dropping their high-explosive rounds; and if they were so much as a tiny bit off in their calculations, we'd all be turned into a red, gooey paste!

Shamsallah took point on the patrol and continued south for another twenty minutes, before he took us down a different path that headed west. We took a break in the shade, and I sipped down lots of water. I looked at my watch: it was getting close to 1100 hours and the sun was beginning to burn our faces. I forgot to put on my usual SPF-forty sunscreen, and I knew my combat shades would leave me looking like a fried raccoon by the time the day was over. I asked Ginge how he was doing and he said fine. He was in his element, having the time of his life, just like on the patrols I'd managed to get him on back in Sper. It was fun for me to have somebody who was keen along for the ride.

We continued marching west for about ten minutes. We would glance over walls and speak to the farmers and villagers if they could be bothered to stick around. I didn't blame them for hiding—I think I would have as well. Every now and then we would see kids and I would act like I was a monster and give chase. I had found that children all over the world loved to be chased, and these little village kids were no different. If I thought it wouldn't get them killed in a riot, I would hand over some gum, but only if they were out of view of the rest of the kids.

We had passed out of a village and continued to follow an elevated, narrow road when we heard a THUMP to our south. *Mortars firing!* The sound was unmistakable. *That means they're close, probably within a couple hundred metres.* I walked over to Shamsallah, but he didn't *need* to be mentored. So far, he was easily the most aggressive ANA soldier I had ever seen. *Finally, somebody who wants to do the job!*

He spoke on his radio to his sergeants and our column began to wind south toward the Taliban mortar team. I listened as the Canadians back at Zangabad began to talk in the usual clipped tones and laconic language of radio chatter. The mortars were getting closer to the engineers. *Not if we can help it....*

We patrolled for a hundred metres until we lost track of the mortars. The loud thumping had gone silent. *They must have spotted us and gone dark.* I told Ginge to scan around for dickers, somebody watching us.

I saw a two-storey building with a narrow staircase leading from the ground floor to the top, so I told Ginge to follow me as I quickly scaled the steps. They were incredibly narrow, and my armour and tac vest had a tendency to make me look fat, so I tried not to fall over the edge as we rapidly climbed the stairs. I watched the top of the stairs and not my feet, in case Timothy was waiting for us.

We reached the flat-top roof of the compound and scanned all around. It was empty, so I led us to the southern edge to try and get eyes on the mortar team. Just then we heard the thumping coming from behind a high wall, maybe one hundred metres away. I looked through my scope, but the wall was covering the shooters from view. I shot a bearing on my compass, and then oriented my map to north and placed my compass down on the map. I did some mental math (a challenge for me even at the best of times) and came up with an approximate grid for the enemy.

The battle group radio chatter was cutting in and out; we were too far away with too many high walls and compounds between us and COP Zangabad. I wasn't getting their signal, but thankfully Sean was up a roof near the COP acting as the RRB, so I sent him our locstat and told him we had an approximate best-guess position for the enemy. He acknowledged and said he'd pass it up to "higher."

I looked down and saw that some ANA had followed us up the stairs but had gotten off at the first floor rooftop. They were talking and pointing to the south, right at the position I had put Timothy at. *Always nice to have an independent second-party verification of Timothy's position.*

I turned and spoke to Ginge, saying, "Right, me ol' China-plate mate, let's head down the stairs and try to mentor the ANA over to that long wall." I walked over to the edge of the roof and glanced down to see Shamsallah and Omer with several ANA discussing the next phase of our kill/capture mission.

Suddenly Sean's voice was talking over my radio. I couldn't hear what the other party was saying, but Sean was definitely pissed as he said, "Negative, negative, you're not listening to me! I have just received a locstat for call sign 72C. They are danger close to the enemy, I say again, *danger close*! If you fire, you'll kill all of them!"

When Sean said we were danger close, he meant we were within four hundred metres of the enemy, so if the Canadians fired, they would certainly kill us too—because when those artillery shells landed, they could easily cover a four-hundred-metre spread. And if they were even a tiny bit off when calculating their firing solution . . .

Holy crap! The FOO/FAC was doing his thing again! My tired brain began to slowly piece together what was happening, based only on Sean's side of the conversation, and I didn't like the scenario I was coming up with.

The Canadians had an amazing piece of kit called the lightweight counter-mortar radar (LCMR), which (when a certain number of prerequisites came together on the battlefield) could give a fairly accurate location for the enemy's mortar position. And judging by Sean's heated conversation with the FOO/FAC, the LCMR had given the artillerymen the exact location for Timothy's mortar team.

But according to Sean, who could hear both me and the battle group, call sign 72C, a.k.a. "The Best and The Last," were *too* close to Timothy for our guns to fire. Well, they could fire, but we'd be turned into a reddish-brown, mucky paste along with Timothy.

However, this apparently wasn't a big concern for the FOO/FAC. I could only hear scattered bits of *his* side of the conversation, but there was no mistaking his intent when I heard him callously reply, "Good, they can call the fall of shot."

Garrhaaaa! We're danger close, you asshole! Danger close!

By his comment he meant it was good that my call sign and ANA were close to the enemy, because we would be in a great position to adjust and correct his artillery fire, and make sure he was on target. *He's going to kill us all. We've gotta make a break for it, before it's too late! Don't just stand around like an idiot, Rob! Do something!*

I looked at Ginge and shouted, "Move, Ginge! Get off the roof!" He just stared at me as I ran past him. I stopped, turned around and grabbed him by the shoulder, and dragged him roughly behind me. He didn't have my commander's radio, so he didn't have a Scooby-Doo clue what was about to happen.

"Our guns are about to fire and they don't care that we're danger close. We gotta get the Afghans and run for it!" I stood on the rooftop, pointed back toward the road, and shouted down at the ANA, "Move move move! Omer, tell the ANA to run back to the road!" I ran down the stairs two at a time. *Shit! We're not gonna make it!*

I had just come even with the first floor rooftop when time . . . slowed . . . down. An ANA soldier had his RPG up to his shoulder and looked ready to fire his warhead at the far wall. Unfortunately for Ginge and me, we were directly in line with his lethal backblast.

"Backblast, backblast!" I screamed as I threw my body backwards to stop Ginge and throw us back up the stairs. I smacked into him with a thud as we managed to get slightly around the corner wall of the first floor when I heard a massive WHOOSH and everything in my world turned red and black. It felt like someone had just hit me square in the nose with a baseball bat at full swing. I heard something pop in my right temple as shooting pain flooded my head and stars swarmed my vision, blacking it out.

I'd been concussed before, but this was ten times worse.

"Aaaggghhh," I moaned loudly, and while some distant part of my brain registered shame at crying out, I was unable to control my response as sickening waves of pain shot through my head and face and down the back of my neck. A mixture of snot and blood began to drip out of my nose as tears flooded my eyes. (I was to find out five months later that the *pop* I had felt was a blood vessel bursting in my brain from the blast. An MRI test showed I had a brand-new five-millimetre cyst in my right temple, what the doctor called minor brain damage.)

My brain, bruised as it was, for some reason thought it was incredibly important that I register where the ANA soldier's RPG warhead had gone, so through a veil of tears and stars I managed to make out the vapour trail from his rocket and saw it explode harmlessly into a tall tree, about a hundred metres *off* target. *Atta boy!*

That action took all of my energy, and I began to teeter uncontrollably over the edge of the stairwell, but Ginge grabbed me roughly by the shoulders and pulled me back. He was shouting something to me, but my ears were ringing so badly his voice sounded like it was underwater. I coughed as I swallowed dirt kicked up from the backblast and, with each cough, violent jolts shot through my head. I tried to wipe away the red mixture running out of my nose as I sat down hard on the stairwell and tried to get a grip. *Too many stars … I can't see … What …*

After what felt like ten minutes but was probably closer to thirty seconds, Ginge's voice finally started to get through to me. "Sir, sir! Holy shit! Are you okay?" He was looking over my shoulder to see if my face was still where it should be. We had all seen videos of soldiers accidentally walking behind a backblast, and most of the time (if they were close like we were), they were simply turned into a red mist.

"I'm okay, Ginge, I'm okay," I heard a voice say. "Are *you* okay?"

"I'm good, sir. Just take a minute, don't move." I registered concern in his voice. *Maybe he can see blood coming out of my ears.* I raised my hand to my right ear but besides the terrible ringing, there was nothing coming out of it. *I … what happened …?*

I heard the disembodied voice of Sergeant MacVitty from 2 Para swearing at me and telling me to *"Move, move! Get on your damn feet and move!"* and suddenly I remembered why we had been running down the stairs in the first place.

"We gotta move, Ginge! Incoming artillery … we gotta get off the stairs and away from here, now!" I teetered to my feet and almost passed out as the pain exploded again into red stars. I struggled down the stairs and jogged over to Shamsallah, every step sending jolts up and down my body. "We gotta move. The Canadians are going to fire artillery—we gotta get outta here, right now!" Omer's face dropped and he quickly translated for Shamsallah, whose face turned white as he realized a grisly death was only seconds away. He shouted in Dari and the sound made me cringe like I had the world's worst hangover, but there was no time for a pity party, so I started grabbing ANA soldiers around me and flinging them in the direction of the road.

"Herd them toward the road, Ginge. Get 'em moving!" I shouted. Ginge wasn't a small guy, and when he began manhandling the ANA and launching them toward the road, they finally got the hint and started jogging. I sprinted up to the lead guy and grabbed him by the arm and dragged him after me.

I looked back to see Shamsallah literally kicking his men in the ass in order to get them moving.

Finally the message sunk in and everyone started running for their lives, pell-mell toward the road, all dignity abandoned. I looked back for Ginge, who was trying to pass me as I sprinted. He was laughing and had turned our flight for survival into a church-picnic foot race! I dug deep and picked up the pace just enough to stay barely ahead of him. I wasn't going to have him taunting me for the rest of our potentially short lives!

After sprinting for close to three hundred metres we were almost back to the main road. I looked behind me; there were about fifteen ANA still behind us, trying desperately to catch up. The ringing in my ears had let up enough for me to hear Sean still arguing with the FOO/FAC. *In ten seconds, we'll be clear, behind good cover, and hopefully far enough away, maybe four hundred metres max.* The last stragglers were about to come into our hiding spot behind the high wall when Sean asked me for an update. I told him we were clear, and he quickly passed it up to the FOO/FAC, who immediately sent up his fire mission to the guns at Sperwhan. I ran back and grabbed the last couple of stragglers and dragged them into cover behind our wall.

Everyone was panting and wheezing. I heard static radio traffic from the battle group followed by "Shot out," a radio message that meant rounds were incoming.

"Take cover, take cover, everyone get down!" I shouted as Omer took up the shout in Dari, and soon everyone was ducking safely behind the wall.

BOOM! BOOM! BOOM! BOOM!

My head pounded every time the deafening explosions detonated over Timothy's position. It was like being at a rock concert, with the bass thudding in your chest. Shrapnel began to whistle through the air over our heads as I hugged the wall tighter. *Sucks to be you, Timmy!*

I didn't want to, but as the closest Canadian with a radio it fell on me to correct the fall of shot for the artillery. So I slowly peeked over the edge of the wall as the next explosions detonated in quick succession. My eyes took in a terrible sight as high-explosive rounds air-burst over Timothy's position— BOOM! BOOM! BOOM! BOOM!—raining down shrapnel in a 360-degree arc. I could see a sharp flash in the air as the rounds exploded about a hundred metres over the ground, followed by black bits of steel raining down in a deadly cone overtop of the enemy. Anyone caught in the open and not under hard cover would've been shredded alive. I radioed Sean and made one correction:

to swing the artillery more to the west, where I thought the Taliban mortar pit had been hiding. It was a moot point, however, because the air-burst rounds had covered so much area they'd probably shredded that zone anyway.

I looked back at the compound where I got to taste RPG backblast for the first (and hopefully last) time. If we'd stayed there, I was certain we would've been killed too. We were well within the deadly radius of the air-burst cone. *I can't wait to meet you, Mr. FOO/FAC! I hope you like the taste of raw fist, 'cause you're gonna eat it!*

I leaned against the wall and slumped down into the dirt, kicking up a pile of moon dust. I looked around at the ANA. Everyone except Shamsallah seemed badly shaken up by recent events. *Make sure and tell them* the Taliban don't wave, *when we get back. Although that wouldn't have saved us today.*

After the FOO/FAC's little demonstration of peace through overwhelming fire superiority, I didn't think I would have a hard time convincing the ANA that sometimes, *juste pour s'amuser*, the coalition would try and kill them.

But I'm sure they never would've fired until we said we were clear. I don't think...they would've fired. I hope...

I looked at Ginge and smiled. This was all terribly new to him, but he seemed to be handling the fact that his own side had almost wiped him off the map pretty well, all things considered. I thought of something and then angrily asked myself, *Was that on your war to-do list? You dickhead! Not laughing now, are ya?*

So much for the curse of 72C being lifted by the Wizard's magic! Evidently call sign "I Have a Rendezvous with Death" was alive and well, headache notwithstanding. But you've gotta still be alive to feel a headache!

I waited until I was sure the incoming artillery was finished before I peeked over the edge of the wall again. Everything was silent. I stood up and dusted off my butt, and took a long drag from my CamelBak. I'd gone through a lot of water so far and didn't have much left. *Raw fear will do that to a guy.*

I looked over the field and did some math. About three hundred metres to the compound; one hundred metres to the tall wall separating us from Timothy's mortar. *If we head back there now, to recover the mortar and search through the red pulp that used to be human bodies for any int, we can still be back in time for lunch.* Luckily I had some latex surgical gloves as part of my TCCC (tactical combat casualty care) bag, for rifling through the bodies. I was just about to ask Omer to translate, when Shamsallah barked an order and everyone started heading north up the road, back toward COP Zangabad.

I walked over and got Omer to find out what was going on.

"They want to go back for lunch," he calmly said.

"Right, but what about the mortar, what about their weapons? We should go and collect them, so the Taliban doesn't recycle them and use them against us later."

Omer translated and Shamsallah said, "No. We will head back now."

Suddenly we all heard the THUMP of mortars being fired again, and even though my ears were still ringing, it sounded like the sound was coming from exactly the same spot as before. I sadly realized the whole gong show we'd just been put through had probably been for nothing. I looked at Shamsallah, who looked right back at me.

I was about to say, *"Well, we've gotta go back and finish the job,"* when he sussed out what I was thinking and quietly turned and began walking toward Zangabad. *I guess getting air-burst artillery shot over your head was an only-once-a-day sort of thing for the Afghans.*

I radioed Sean and told him to let the Canadians know my ANA had had enough. We were coming back in, and nothing I could say or do was going to change their minds. As an OMLT mentor I had already found the fine balance between advising them and telling them what I wanted them to do. And since I was going to be with these guys for the next two months, I didn't think it would be smart to get them angry with me after our first and only patrol together. Besides, they'd made up their minds. *That was that.*

We walked on the road as the enemy continued lobbing mortar rounds at Zangabad. That was one of the longest walks of my life. I had felt like I'd failed the Canadians—horribly, utterly failed them. They were still getting mortared, and the ANA and I were just casually strolling away from where we knew the enemy had their mortar tube. I felt terribly low.

I heard Major Obermann begin to talk over the radio. He was never one to sit still and just take it like that, so he began putting together a plan to get some LAVs out there to kill/capture Timothy. I was ashamed that I couldn't get my guys to finish the job, but at least I could brief the major on our contact point, the lay of the land, and where I thought the mortar pit was hiding. I told Ginge to follow me and took off running back toward the COP. It was maybe a klick away and we had to cover the ground, *rapido!*

I ran into the compound where Sean and Stamps were up on the rooftop. I took a breath and asked Sean about the LAVs. He pointed toward the bottom of the COP, so I took off again. I realized Ginge, like a good fire-team partner, was matching me stride for stride, but I didn't want to risk getting him hurt since the mortars were still falling around the southern perimeter.

"Thanks Ginge," I panted, "good work today. Go back now and stay with Stamps and Captain Sean; get them off the roof, now that we're back. Grab some water, scrounge me some Aspirin, and get into hard cover. I'll be back in a minute."

"Okay, roger that, sir," he said. "Good luck." I turned to start running again when I heard him say "Sir . . ."

"What is it, Ginge?" I spun back around. "Quickly, I've got to brief the major."

"Are you okay?! I mean . . ." He looked very concerned for me.

"Ginge," I started off seriously, but then broke into a wide grin, "though I was raised by humans, my heart is Klingon. My *blood* hears the warrior's song!"

"Okay," he laughed. "Um . . . *ka'plah?*" He said the Klingon word for *success.*

"*Ka'plah!*" I shouted back and started running again.

I heard the chorus of Iron Maiden's "The Loneliness of the Long Distance Runner" play in my head as I rounded the corner, and right where Sean said the LAVs would be there was nothing but a completely empty field. *Awww, sonofabitch! Where the hell . . . ?*

I looked to the south and there they were, moving to the road I'd just left, about to push on without the OMLT's timely, highly accurate, and hard-won int! *Dig deep Rob, dig deep!* I shouted to myself and started running again. I looked to my left as mortar rounds continued to fall near the perimeter, but they were a good hundred metres away, so I'd be fine.

I overheard Major Obermann call his commanders over to his LAV for a final Frag-O (quick set of orders) before they pushed on. As the commanders dismounted and began to slowly jog over to the major, I ran past them at full sprint shouting, "Imperial walkers spotted on the north ridge!" They just shook their heads, probably thinking, "There goes that crazy OMLT bastard!" I found the major's LAV and quickly climbed up onto it. And that was no small feat since I was packing close to a hundred pounds of kit. I groaned and struggled but finally, after some good exertion, managed to pull my bulk up onto his LAV and smiled triumphantly. *I made it!*

The major popped out the back hatch of his LAV, looked up at me, and said, "Hey, Rob. We're going to do it down here. C'mon down."

I shot him a terrible stinkeye. Did he have any idea how hard it had been to climb up the damn thing? *Awww, motherfu*—I trudged back over to the side and grabbing a hand guard, lowered myself down onto the wheel, and then thudded onto the dusty ground. The major looked me over as I jogged up to him; I think my nose had started bleeding again.

I took a knee by his map and grabbed a dry blade of grass to act as my pointer. I showed him on the map where we'd heard the mortar tube, and I apologized for not being able to mentor my ANA effectively to neutralize the threat. He was about to say something, but I asked him his planned route; he quickly showed me, and then I warned him that the road became dangerously narrow at certain spots.

Then I warned him to watch his six as he travelled down that road in particular, because that was where we had fired on the three Taliban. I finished up by showing him the direction in which they'd fled and then asked him if he would like me to come along as the local area expert. I'd said the last part with a smile, although I didn't feel like smiling. As far as I was concerned, our patrol had been a top-to-bottom failure.

Major Obermann thanked me for the ground briefing and heads-up, and then kindly told me I had done my part, I could stand down now. I imagined I looked like I'd swum over the river Styx to get back in time to brief him. He clasped me on the shoulder and told me to go and find cover; I wished him luck and turned to leave. The incoming mortars were landing a couple of hundred metres away and I felt pretty done in, so I took off at a light jog back to the rooftop where I'd last seen Sean, Stamps, and Ginge.

I walked through the gate and was agitated to see them still up on the roof. *I thought I'd told Ginge to get them down—hadn't I?*

I shouted up to them, "Hey! Is there any reason you guys are still up on a rooftop during a mortar attack?"

They looked at each other and Sean finally said, "No."

"Then come on down," I said. Sean climbed down and walked over to me.

"Why are you so pissy?" he asked.

"I took an RPG backblast square in the fizzog, and it's left me a bit prickish. But that's no excuse," I said. "Sorry about that. I owe you *my life*, Sean. So does Ginge. That mental FOO/FAC would've killed us all if it wasn't for you!"

"Hey," he said. "Who would I make fun of, if you weren't around?"

"Fair one. But seriously, thanks. So I guess Major Obermann's off to clean house and we just hang out, eh?"

"Sounds about right. You look like hell. I'll call the doc."

"Do you have any Aspirin?" I asked.

"I don't personally, but Laddah might." Sean walked off to find our OMLT medic. I looked at Stamps, who'd just come down off the rooftop.

"Howdy, sir," he said. "Am I ever glad I'm not your fire-team partner!"

"Well, Ginge isn't staying with us in Mushan, so the position will soon be vacant. If you send me your CV, I'll have a look at it. Put it on top of the pile and whatnot, but I can't make any promises," I said.

"Yeah, I think I left my fire-team partner CV at home, sorry."

We found some shade and hunkered down. Laddah walked over to me and handed me some Aspirin. He took out his flashlight and shined it in my eyes, which immediately started my head pounding all over again. He told me I was lucky, and walked back to his RG. *Thank you, Captain Obvious!*

One of the major's LAVs had gotten stuck in the narrow roadway and the boys had to spend some time extracting it. Timothy could easily hear the rumbling LAVs as they came down the road, so they quickly hightailed it to safer climes, but the major got him to stop shooting at the COP, so mission accomplished.

The OMLT boys walked back to the RG and our LAV and made some lunch. No one had eaten yet because Sean didn't want to miss any critical comms relaying while he was stuffing his face. I was glad he didn't. His self-discipline had saved all of us a gruesome death. *Team first—gotta love it!*

Sean could tell I was still fuming over what the FOO/FAC had done. *Nobody gets away with trying to kill me and my men. I demand satisfaction!*

Sean patiently told me I was too ugly, too angry, and too well-armed to go over and have a little heart-to-heart with my new best friend.

"Cool down. Have a poisonous coffee. Chillax for a while," he said. I asked myself, *WWDCD? Indeed...what would Don Cheadle do?* I decided Sean was right so I dumped my kit and hung out with the boys, getting caught up in the banter. But there would be a reckoning....

Thanks to Major Obermann, the engineers could now work in peace, and in short order, they had completely ripped down COP Zangabad. Nobody around me was really quite sure why it was being torn down. Rumour control had it someone in higher headquarters had finally decided the experiment of putting up COPs Hajikan, Zangabad, and Talikan between Mushan and Sperwhan had failed. But instead of closing down the westernmost COP (at Mushan) and keeping the nearest COP (at Hajikan) open, they had done the opposite. Which, to me, didn't make a whole lot of sense. If Hajikan was in trouble, they were only three klicks away from Sper. Help could get to them quickly. Now if FOB Mushan was in trouble, Sperwhan was over twelve klicks away, through heavily contested ground.

Once at Mushan, we would be completely surrounded, and during Captain John's stint as OC of Mushan, they had been in contact with Timothy almost daily. They got shot at so many times that Zangabad, the next COP in line to the east of Mushan (before it was closed down) would radio Sperwhan on their behalf and say, "We think Mushan is in contact." Then the command post at Sperwhan would radio Mushan and ask if they *were* in contact, and John would say, "Mmm, not really. Well, maybe . . ."

Major Obermann's 2 I/C would then lose his nut and say, "Well, are you or *aren't* you? Make up your mind!" I heard those conversations a number of times myself, and they were always hilarious. John explained to me later that sometimes they were being engaged from so far away, they weren't sure it was *their* FOB being shot at. So he wouldn't even bother reporting it as a contact. But on other occasions, they'd been shot at from up close. *Too* close.

What was decidedly not funny was the fact that FOB Mushan had been mortared every day in a row for the last five days. The rounds had started falling four hundred metres out, but every day they were getting walked-in by a spotter, closer and closer, until yesterday they were only about fifty metres away from the FOB's big protective Hesco walls. Fifty metres was getting scary. You could hear shrapnel whistle over your head, and it was still lethal at that range. *How close will they be when I get there?*

John had been trying to mentor the ANA captain to hunt down Timothy, but the Afghan had developed a searing case of the heebie-jeebies, and had decided there was really no point in going after them. Although everyone knew that, for their mortar to remain accurate, they would have to fire from pretty much the same spot every day so one of our patrols should be able to find the spot and set up an ambush, especially since Timothy was mortaring us at the same time of day, every day.

But nuttin' doing! The ANA captain's only concern was in diverting all of his troops to keeping the local bazaar open. He wasn't overly concerned about his men getting mortared. I understood the necessity (in a hearts-and-minds war) of putting troops in the market to keep the Taliban away so it could stay open, but you couldn't really help the people if you were *dead*. And because Timothy knew every day the ANA would set up on the market roofs, he started trying to pick them off there. No, in a counter-insurgency war, you had to be unpredictable, pop up out of nowhere—make it so the enemy never had a clue as to where or when you would turn up. *Keep him on edge, all of the time.*

We spent that night at Zangabad, and the next morning we kitted up and hatted out. The long convoy began to make a new road back to the dry Arghandab riverbed, and we started all over again. As we pulled away we all looked back to see the massive pile of munitions and *matériel,* which couldn't be brought with us, blown up in place. The standard mushroom cloud began to form over the smoldering pile of abandoned kit. It was another information operations victory for the Taliban, who would now tell the locals how they had chased the Canadians out of COP Hajikan, then Talikan, and now Zangabad. Of course, that only left FOB Mushan. Timothy knew that attacking Sperwhan was a suicide op, so he would naturally shadow us to the west, to Forward Operating Base Mushan, all on its own.

I was pretty sure he'd be waiting on us there, and we'd meet him again shortly. . . .

Chapter 16

Our convoy entered the riverbed and made its way west for another seven klicks before turning south to Mushan (or "Moosh," as we called it). Again, the tail-end Charlies in our convoy were in shooting contact with Timothy the entire time. Thankfully there were no more IEDs, and our massive convoy slowly passed to the east of Mushan, drove underneath it on a small road, and then began to form a huge leaguer in the middle of a large, open plain just to the west of the FOB. Sean, Ginge, Stamps, and I dropped off our LAV and RG and walked over to Mushan as the long line of vehicles made its way in. The ANA had abandoned the convoy once the FOB was in sight, and began to form up in a small compound only fifty metres away to the northeast of Moosh.

We entered the FOB and greeted Warrant Duceppe, or "Big Joe," as he was affectionately known. In Captain John's absence, he was the acting OC of FOB Mushan. I had worked with him at 3 RCR, and like me, he had come across to help out 1 RCR man its OMLT positions. We shook hands like old cowboys and I felt his iron grip crushing my tiny little hand. He was a colossus. He was a jolly green giant, walking the earth, and although he was an all around great guy and enjoyed a good laugh, you didn't want to make him angry. Once aroused to the weaker passions he was like a cave troll out of *The Hobbit*. I had once seen him pick up a grown man off the ground using only one arm. I always told him I didn't want him angry at me because I was scared he would eat me.

We ran into Warrant Smith, my new 2 I/C, who quickly gave us a tour. We had a CF .50-calibre heavy machine gun in the watchtower (or sangar) in the northwest corner. From that emplacement we had really good eyes-on, almost 360 degrees around the FOB. We had a LAV in a run-up position against the high protective Hesco wall facing due west. The wall then ran twenty metres south and then turned due east, forming a square. There was a gap to let vehicles in, and then the Hesco continued another ten metres, until it turned north, continuing the square. In the bottom southeast corner we had an ANA PKM 7.62mm machine gun in another sangar. From there, they had eyes-on from one o'clock to eight o'clock.

South of that wall, about twenty metres away, was a smaller Hesco wall that ran from one o'clock, forming a half moon down to eight o'clock, with a dozen ANA bunkers and their kitchen between the two walls, which were connected with concertina razor wire. On the outer Hesco wall, the ANA had set up some machine gun bunkers that were manned 24/7. From the southeast sangar the main inner wall continued twenty metres north, where it turned due west and continued on until it completed the square.

Inside the compound we had two ISO living containers (long, rectangular boxes with steel sides and a thin layer of sandbags on top to try and protect us from incoming rockets or mortars) for the Canucks, and two locked ISO containers to hold equipment, food, and water. Next to those containers, in the extreme northwest corner, was our CP, a low-ceilinged building about fifteen feet wide by thirty feet long, its roof covered in protective sandbags. We had all of our radio equipment and maps against the south wall, along with some picnic tables, a deep freezer and fridge, a coffee corner with a toaster and microwave, and a flat-screen TV with an Xbox and a DVD player. Outside our CP against the eastern Hesco wall we had our large diesel generator, which provided electricity within the FOB. Of course, the ANA had spliced into it and were stealing from our electrical grid at an alarming rate.

South of our CP and the ISO containers, the ANA had built a small mosque, a storage container, and a makeshift workshop, and they'd erected a few tents and a mortar pit in the middle. In the extreme southeast corner was their CP, a small two-man room surrounded by a few bunkers for the ANA leadership to sleep in. Above their CP was the southeast ANA-manned watchtower. *All in all, not a bad little set-up. It would do.*

Between the inner wall and outer wall to the east, a dozen Royal Marines mortar men had set up shop to support a joint Royal Marines/Canadian/ANA operation to the north of the Arghandab River. They'd been firing mortars in support of the op for the last couple of days.

I found out later that Rich, the Wizard, and some ANA from Sperwhan had done a helicopter assault into that op. And it seemed Rich's curse of the mummy had followed him, because they were in the shit right from the start. Rich said on one particularly nasty day, they'd had a three-hour-long TIC and were getting hit with mortars, RPGs, and rockets. Then Rich became uncharacteristically serious. He put his hand on his heart and swore that the Wizard had literally dodged an incoming RPG warhead by inches. It was coming straight for his head and, like Neo in *The Matrix*, he used bullet-time technology to make time slow down, and at the last possible second shifted his head and body out of the way as the incoming warhead singed his eyebrows. Only his magic and ninja-like reflexes had protected him. I laughed and then asked Rich what it had been like doing a helo-assault into an enemy stronghold with the ANA.

He didn't smile—at all—and merely replied, "What do *you* think?"

Back in Moosh, Sean and I climbed up into the ANA sangar in the southeast corner. We wanted to see how the ANA had positioned themselves in the low-walled compound to the FOB's northeast. They were about fifty metres away and getting their kit offloaded and set up. They would be staying there until Captain John's outgoing ANA stole the proverbial kitchen sink and fled into the night, sometime in the next few days.

Sean, always the switched-on cat (although I would never say that to his face), had been walking around with a PRR so he could communicate with the Canadian OMLT command post. He didn't have comms with the battle group convoy, but the CP could relay messages to them if necessary.

POP POP POP POP POP!

Suddenly we heard a long blast of incoming machine-gun fire. Sean and I ran to the edge of the watchtower and looked to the north, where it seemed to have originated from. I looked down at the ANA, who had taken cover behind a long wall in their compound that ran east-west. *If they were taking cover, the rounds must've smacked close to them.* It wasn't like the ANA to take cover if not absolutely necessary. *Unmanly, don't you know.*

Some of the ANA popped up and began returning fire toward a two-storey compound surrounded by high walls, about a hundred metres to their north.

"That's official," I said to Sean jokingly. "It's a two-way range." Sean just looked back at me. "Well don't just stand there, numpty," I chided. "Call it in: *contact*. The ANA are in contact. Honestly Sean, I'm not going to be around forever to hold your hand." Sean may have had his PRR like a good storm-trooper, but I had my map and compass, so I laid them down on the sandbags to find a grid on the map for the ANA, and my best-guess grid for the Taliban.

"Sean," I said to get his attention. "I put the enemy at grid 1785 8380; sounds like one times PKM currently engaging our ANA forces, which are located at—"

Sean interrupted, "We don't tell them where *our* ANA are located!"

"We do if we *don't* want the Canadians to engage our ANA and kill them because they think they're Taliban!"

"Right, right . . . okay." Sean clicked his PRR and began to pass up the contact report to the CP.

BOOM BOOM BOOM BOOM BOOM!

Sean and I both jumped as our eyes were drawn to the southeast corner of the FOB, where on the southside of the outer Hesco wall, a long line of explosions had just strung out in the sand. They were only small explosions, about ten feet high. My brain began to race. *What the hell was that? It wasn't RPGs—they couldn't fire five of them that accurately and make a grouping that tight! Besides, there's no contour trails from the warheads. What could've . . .* My eyes slowly tracked from the settling explosions back to the ANA position. I saw an ANA soldier desperately waving to the northeast. *Why the hell would he . . . Oh crap!* My eyes rapidly tracked over the ANA as they cowered behind their wall, to the northeast, where I could just see a Canadian LAV breaking cover from behind a treeline, its turret pointed toward the ANA! *The Taliban don't wave! I'd just taught them that yesterday! Shit, they're being engaged by that LAV!*

"Stop!" I shouted. "Sean, get the Canadians to *stop* shooting!"

"What do you mean? They're not shooting, they're coming down the—"

"*Don't argue!* Get the CP to order all the Canadian call signs to stop shooting! Tell them to stop shooting at whatever they're shooting at! They're engaging our ANA in the compound!" I felt like a role reversal had just occurred. Sean had just become me and I had become Rich in Helmand, when Rich was trying to get me to stop everyone from shooting and I was arguing with him!

"The Taliban don't wave! The ANA are waving at that LAV, trying to get him to stop shooting at them!" I shouted.

Sean followed my pointing finger to the ANA soldier who was waving to save his life as his friends hunkered down lower than rattlesnakes under a top hat, hoping the Canadian LAV gunner's aim wasn't about to dramatically improve. His first rounds had fired over the wall, and exploded just outside our FOB. Their luck wasn't going to hold forever.

Sean twigged and immediately began ordering the CP to get the Canadians to stop shooting. I looked back at the LAV. Its turret was moving, tracking the wall. *I'm too late; they're all going to be killed.* I began waving like a lunatic, thinking maybe the LAV gunner would see me in the background up in the sangar, trying to get his attention. But the radio message must've been passed at record-breaking speed because the LAV came to a full stop, and then quickly swung its turret back in line with its hull. Sean and I each let out a long sigh as we began to grasp how close our ANA had come to being made full believers (*holy, full of holes*). The ANA were dusting themselves off and it didn't seem like any of them were hurt.

I take a lot of responsibility for that one, though. No doubt about it, I should've radioed the battle group to let them know the ANA were setting up in a compound, off the reservation. The LAV gunners were on edge from being shot at repeatedly over the last few days, so it was a "blue-on-green" friendly fire incident waiting to happen, and I should've seen it coming.

Sean looked at me incredulously. "Is this what it's always like, working with your ANA?" he asked.

"This?" I began folding up my map. "This was nothing. This was so minor it doesn't even register. But you know what they say: 'Never a dull moment!' But since this is your first time outside the wire, allow a seasoned veteran to explain, to the great unwashed and uneducated, what just happened."

"Fuck you," Sean snapped.

I continued with my play-by-play. "You see, my young fellow, the Taliban knew they had a great opportunity, so they took it. They set up in that compound to the north of our FOB, knowing full well the ANA were to the south, and the Canadians in the convoy were to the east, at right angles to each other. So the Taliban fired on the ANA, knowing they don't take kindly to that sort of thing and would fire back. Timothy then turned ninety degrees to his left, now facing east for the directionally challenged amongst us, and began firing on the LAVs, knowing damn well that wouldn't do any harm against those metal monsters. But that wasn't his goal."

"And just what exactly was his goal, Mr. Holmes?" Sean asked with his arms crossed, unimpressed with my battlefield synopsis.

"Hey, if you don't mind, I'm trying to explain modern Taliban deception tactics to the small children present in the sangar. Now, if I may . . . where was I? Ah, yes, they knew that once the Canucks cleared the wood line, all they would see were the muzzle flashes of the ANA engaging Timothy to their north, and the crazy Canucks would assume, incorrectly as most assumptions are, that they were being engaged by Taliban from behind their long wall. So they began to fire at our ANA. Only their poor marksmanship, the waving ANA, and your timely radio intervention saved the day. So, well done to you, good sir. I'm putting you in for a nice gong right after we take tea."

Sean was shaking his head, smiling. "You are easily one of the most idiotic, piss-poor excuses for an officer that I have ever had the *dishonour* of meeting."

I countered with, "First off, the sooner you freely admit that it just kills you that a two-month captain figured all of that out so much faster than say, oh, I don't know, the twenty-six *year* captain standing next to him, the better off we're going to be. You've created a poisonous work environment, and one day, Sean, your misery and hate will kill us all. But there's still hope for you, because it's like *The Simpsons'* Jebediah Springfield always said . . ." I trailed off.

Sean was grinning like a chimp. "Do tell."

"'A noble spirit embiggens the smallest man.' Now, if you're finished showing off, let's go make sure our ANA are okay. *After* you re-send their locstat to the battle group, that is. It doesn't *do* to be fired on, by one's *own* side, twice in the same day, what what! It's just not *cricket*."

Sean walked into the CP and made sure the map grids had been successfully passed, and then we jogged over to the ANA. They looked like they were in a mild state of shock. Omer translated as an ANA soldier pointed out a gap in the wall to us.

"He says he was standing here when the rounds passed in front of his face, *through* the hole in the wall, and out the other side." The ANA was shaking his head in disbelief.

I looked at the soldier and smiled. "*El hamdoo la'lah.* Allah must love you very much." He nodded in agreement, so we left him to find Company Sergeant Major Shamsallah, who didn't look overly impressed. *Can't say I blame him. Almost lit up by Canadians twice in the last two days; not a good omen for future ops!* But when I explained to him what had happened (minus the bragging tone and insults I treated Sean to), he understood completely and just said, "*El hamdoo la'lah.*" *Thanks be to God.*

A real litmus test for his bravery would be whether or not, after the last few days, he would be willing to go out to clear the compound and find the Taliban firing point. I breathed in deeply and got Omer to ask him for me. Shamsallah just smiled and said, "Why not?" I laughed and slapped him on the back and told him I would go myself to the CP and show the Canadians where we were going. I promised we would be back in twenty minutes. I asked Sean if he wanted to come with us, *juste pour la fun?*

"I have to start the handover. Some of us are here to work, and not just go out on adventures!" he mockingly replied.

"Heh, adventure, excitement; a Jedi craves not these things! It's best if you stay, though," I sneered. "I'm sure you'd just get us all killed. You go back to your air-conditioned office, son—it's what you're best at!" I punched him on the arm as we walked back to the CP. I asked Sean to radio Ginge, who was hanging out at the RG in the leaguer, to have him come on over for a patrol. I walked over and got Warrant Joe's and the radio operator's full attention as I showed them our projected patrol route and the suspect compound. They assured me everyone in the battle group knew the ANA's current location, and Big Joe said he would personally ensure they knew our patrol trace.

I grabbed Ginge, Shamsallah, and some ANA and we went to "knock" on the compound door. We bomb-bursted into the compound but the Taliban had long since fled. We found two firing points with expended PKM brass by the walls facing to the south and east.

* * *

Later that afternoon, Major Obermann asked if the ANA were ready to crack on with the original plan to go search the large village to our west. I immediately replied, "The roughnecks are always ready, sir!"

An hour later, the Canadians from the battle group stood to the side while Ginge, Shamsallah, and I kicked down dozens of doors and front gates as we cleared the compounds just to the west of Mushan. It was one of the funniest moments of my entire life, and it turned absolutely farcical as we got into the groove of things.

One of us would take a turn to kick down the door, then all three of us with some ANA would run in, clear the compound of Taliban, and then run down the street to do it all over again as the Canadians entered the recently liberated compound to conduct a proper search. We were having fun kicking down the doors—the Canadians were having fun letting us go in first, so it was win-win.

We did this all afternoon, oftentimes arguing about whose turn it was to kick in the gate, until after about four hours the ANA had enough and called it quits. Thankfully a Canadian civil military co-operation officer was following behind the Canadian platoons, handing out money to the homeowners for smashed-in gates and booted front doors. *Well, you can't exactly knock....*

As far as Shamsallah was concerned, everyone west of Mushan was either a Taliban insurgent, a blood relative to one, or a suspected sympathizer or collaborator, so they were all suspect and the word needed to be put out on the street. I soon found out Shamsallah was a firm believer in street cred. *Maybe he had a point.*

Later that evening I joined Sean for some handover points and we helped the warrants get some things squared away. I went to bed in an ISO container. It was filled with bunk beds and I didn't think there was any room left in the inn, but I managed to shift a guy's kit under his snoring bed space and made a little home for myself. I put on my welding ear-defenders and fell right asleep.

That night, I dreamed of small children playing on a haystack, having fun and laughing in the bright sun under a pale blue, cloudless sky. I was in uniform, but with no gear or weapons on me. I was watching them from a ditch when suddenly a massive explosion from inside the haystack ripped them apart and launched their shredded bodies high into the air. I stared as their little body parts started to fall all around me like rain . . . and then I fell to my knees and started screaming.

Chapter 17

The next morning I broke up a few fights between the incoming and outgoing ANA. I found Warrant Duceppe (who made for a very intimidating bouncer) and asked him to come with me. One look at him, and the ANA parted for him like the Red Sea for Moses and quickly went about their business. Sean and Warrant Smith walked over and said we were on schedule; the engineers would finish up around noon, and the battle group convoy would probably head out no later than 1500 hours. I saw some engineers working on the LCMR on the roof of our CP.

"What're they up to? Servicing it?" I asked, somewhat naively.

"Removing it," Sean said.

I felt like I'd been punched in the gut. "Removing it?" I stammered. "I thought this place was getting whacked by mortars every day for the last six days?" *Why in God's name would they be removing it?*

"I was told the battle group colonel in KAF has decided it should go to Gundy Ghar, in the north."

"I know where Gundy Ghar is. Why are they removing it, when we need it? Has Gundy Ghar even been hit by mortars?"

"No, I don't think so. But that was his decision, so TS [tough shit]!"

"Yeah, TS for *us*, not for you! You get to go back to your nice, safe little Batcave, but we get to be mortared on a daily basis! That's the only early-warning system we have. Warrant Smith said the operator pokes his head out of his hut, shouts, "Incoming!" and everyone runs for cover! What're we supposed to do now?" I couldn't believe it.

"Adapt and overcome. I'll put a word in when I get back, see if I can't get you a new one or get the old one back."

"Can't you ask now, while we still have it, before the bastards take it away?!"

"Rob, grow up. You know it doesn't work like that. He's made up his mind. But I promise, I'll see what I can do once I'm back. I'll talk to our OMLT colonel, and maybe they can duke it out."

"Okay, but I just can't believe it. Why would he do that? Take it away, especially since we're getting hit all the time?"

"Ours is not to reason why . . ." Sean said and went back to his paperwork.

We grabbed a quick lunch and then Big Joe and I walked over to the out-going ANA captain's command post, right underneath the southeast sangar. The warrant introduced us, and over the next half-hour we hammered out some of the stickier issues, like: "The incoming ANA are going to need all of the electrical cables and extensions and jacks you've been taking."

The outgoing ANA were taking everything not bolted down or arc-welded in place. They were stripping FOB Mushan clean as Warrant Smith desperately tried to stop them. He'd had some success, but already some big-ticket ANA items were going missing. I wondered if I told him the incoming guys—

KRAANG!

I flinched at the sound of a very loud, very close explosion; it had sounded strange, though, like two metal rebars banging into each other. I looked at the warrant. "Incoming mortars," he calmly said.

"Yeah, but that was super close," I said as I jumped up and made my way to the sangar ladder. I heard shouting in Dari and English as soldiers tried to make sense of what had just happened. I climbed up to the top and looked to the south, where the other mortar rounds had been falling the last few days. *Nothing.* I looked to the east and saw the Brit Royal Marines running into their mortar pits to ready their mortars for counter-battery fire.

I shouted down to them, "You guys okay?"

"We're good, mate!" their sergeant shouted up to me. *Well, where the hell…*

I looked to my left and into the compound, where I saw a large cloud of dust swirling into the sky. The incoming mortar round had landed about fifteen feet away from my meeting with the ANA, and had blasted the windows out of a Ford Ranger and popped its tires. Dust was floating between the truck and a nearby tent, and I couldn't see if anyone had been hit. Soldiers on the ground were yelling back and forth.

I raced down the ladder and ran up to the truck. I began coughing as the dust flooded into my lungs. I tried to swish it away and slowly it lifted enough for me to make out a wounded soldier, propped up against the truck's back wheel. Warrant Duceppe was running over to me, shouting something as he ran, but I couldn't understand him. Too many people were yelling in the dust and confusion.

I ran over to the soldier and bent down next to him, trying to see his face and figure out what had happened to him. As I squatted down I could see blood shooting ten feet out the right side of his neck in powerful streams with every heartbeat. *Artery! Crap, I've got to stop it before—*

Over all of the noise and confusion, everyone in the compound could hear the LCMR operator scream at the top of his powerful lungs, "INCOMING! INCOMING!" *Crap, where can I run to, where can I go?* If it wasn't so serious, it would've been funny as my feet and legs started running in two different directions while my torso went firm, fighting my legs' desire to panic until my head could find the best spot to hide.

I reached down for the Afghan. *We have to get him into cover before—*

Warrant Duceppe thundered into me, picked me up off my feet, and half-pulled, half-dragged me into cover behind a bunker as—

KRAANG!

Shit, that was close! But the incoming round hadn't made a whistling sound, like in the movies. *THIS ISN'T A MOVIE, ASSHOLE! Get your head out of your ass!*

Dust swirled again all over us as we began choking and wheezing. I got up and tried to find the terribly wounded Afghan through all the dust. I thought I saw a silhouette when two huge hands clamped down on my shoulders. It was Warrant Duceppe, who spun me around to look him in his eye. He was wearing his helmet and body armour. I had completely forgotten about coward hour, the time when we could expect the mortars to start incoming, and as I had been running around to make sure everything had gotten taken care of with the outgoing ANA, I'd also completely forgotten my PPE, my personal protective equipment, back at the sleeping container.

The warrant shouted full-bore in my face, "Go get your PPE on, sir, before you become a fucking casualty!" Then he spun me back around to face the

ISO container and shoved me so hard I had to run ten steps just to get my feet back under me. Once I'd regained my balance I sprinted for all I was worth back to the ISO container where I'd slept the night before. I opened up the door and saw it was packed full of Canadians. It was good cover, but there was no way I'd be able to snake my way past everyone to get my TCCC bag from my day sack.

"You!" I shouted, pointing at a guy I'd never met. "Reach into that day sack in front of you and get out my TCCC kit. Do it now!" I slammed the door shut and ran over to get my helmet and body armour from where it was hanging and began putting it on. . . .

"INCOMING! INCOMING!" the LCMR operator screamed again.

Crap, crap, crap . . . I spun around and cranked open the door to the little medic container and slammed the door shut behind me.

KRAANG!

The door muted the noise of the incoming round, but it was unmistakable. *That round sounded a bit farther away.* I looked around and met the nervous gaze of about ten guys, all crammed into the one container. *Med centre!* I saw what I was looking for and started stuffing as many Israeli and Oales bandages and plastic tourniquets as I could cram into my pant side-pockets. As I put on some latex gloves I went to the door and listened. No one was shouting "Incoming!" so I made a break for it. I ran across the wooden walkway and ripped open the other container's door and leaped inside.

"TCCC kit!" I shouted, as hands began to pass it forward to me. I didn't want to make eye contact with anyone as I said in a loud voice, "I won't order you guys to come with me, but I want you to know there are wounded soldiers out there who need our help!" With that, I turned and ran out the door, slamming it behind me. I covered the ground back to the truck and started searching for the wounded Afghan. Ginge rounded the corner of the tent and accidentally ran into the back of me—he had left the safety of the ISO container to come and help.

I told Ginge to look for a wounded Afghan as we peered under the truck to see if he had crawled underneath. *No, not there. Is there a blood trail, has he crawled into a bunker?* I started scanning the ground for a drag mark in the dust, but . . .

"INCOMING!" The LCMR operator yelled from behind us.

"Move move move!" I shouted at Ginge as we scrambled back around the other side of the truck and into some cover behind the bunker.

KRAANG!

Dust and bits of shrapnel flew in all directions as the round landed just where we had been standing. My ears began ringing and my head started pounding again. We coughed violently but got up and fought our way through the dust into the ANA CP. I almost ran into Sergeant Park, another one of our OMLT medics, who had all of his weight behind his hands as he pressed down on the Afghan's spraying neck wound. The ANA captain was in the corner, physically restraining an Afghan soldier who looked ready to kill Park. *He probably thinks the doc's hurting his friend.*

"Ginge, help the captain restrain that man!" I said, pointing at the soldier. I looked at Sergeant Park. "Doc, what can I do? I've got my TCCC kit, do you . . ."

"As I ran out here, sir," the medic said between clenched lips, as he strained to fight the artery's pressure, "I saw some more wounded . . ." he was fighting to keep his hands in place as the Afghan spasmed violently ". . . on the other side of that tent. I don't think anyone's gone to help *them* yet. Can you . . . ?"

"Done," I said, and then looked at Ginge. "You stay here and help the doc."

"Sir, I want—" he started.

"Do as you're told!" I shouted and turned to go back outside. I felt bad for shouting at him, but I didn't want Ginge to follow me. I knew he was brave to a fault, but today that virtue could get him killed. I sprinted out the door and ran to the far side of the tent where I ran face-first into Omer.

"Sir, sir," he cried as tears streamed down his dirty face, "Hassan is hurt. He is dying, he has blood all over his face and . . ." Hassan was another OMLT terp and Omer's best friend.

I grabbed Omer by both shoulders and looked him in the eyes. "I'll help him, Omer, but where is he?" Omer looked away, a vacant expression passing over his face.

I gave him a hard shake. "*Omer!* Listen to me! Where is Hassan? You said he was hurt. Where is he?"

"Come with me, sir, I will show you." Omer began to run around the tent over to the gap between the Hesco, leading us to the ANA bunkers. As we were running two Canadians ran up to me, a reservist sergeant from the OMLT and a young guy I'd never met.

"Sir, can we help?" the sergeant asked.

"Yeah, come with me!" I turned to follow Omer and half-tripped over an Afghan soldier who was moaning and twitching in the dirt. I looked down and realized he was in a terrible way. His legs had been ripped apart, both his shin bones jutted out from his trousers, and he had pink bubbles frothing from his mouth. *Lung wound!* His face was a terrible mess of blood and ripped flesh.

I started to help him when Omer shouted, "Sir! Hassan!" and pointed at the other side of the Hesco. My mind raced as soldiers yelled in the background. *This guy's in a bad way, but if I lose Hassan, I'm screwed—we can't speak Dari.* Then it hit me—I had to decide whom to save: Hassan, or the bleeding and twitching soldier at my feet.

"We'll come back for this guy. C'mon!" I yelled at the two Canadians who turned and followed me as I ran through the gap in the Hesco wall.

"INCOMING!" the LCMR operator screamed again.

Crap, where can we . . . I saw a large flatbed truck with gear strapped down on it, blocking the road to the bunkers.

I grabbed the sergeant and threw him underneath, then shoved the young guy right next to him. I dove onto my stomach and started crawling as fast as I could under the wheel well of the truck. I shoved my fingers into my ears and for the second time on my tour, I was truly terrified. I started praying in my head, *God, please don't let me die here! Not like this.*

KRAANG!

The incoming mortar had fallen on the other side of the Hesco, toward the west. I started to crawl out from underneath the flatbed. "Let's go guys, c'mon!" I yelled. I stood up, reached down to pull the guys out, and then told Omer to take us to Hassan, quickly.

We ran around the corner of the Hesco and saw ANA running back and forth, shouting in Dari at each other. One guy was waving at the others, pleading for help. *One with the doc, one over there, one back the way we came, and Hassan.* We chased after Omer as he ran to the first bunker and bounded down the stairs into the small room.

Just as we entered the bunker I heard a disembodied voice shouting "Incoming!"

I spun around to make sure we were all accounted for and then began searching the bunker for Hassan, but it was too dark to make anything out. There was only a small kerosene lamp, barely lighting up the back corner of the bunker. I found Hassan next to the stairs, moaning softly and holding his head as blood ran down his face between his fingers.

KRAANG!

Other side of the Hesco, more shouting.

I reached into my trouser pocket and ripped out an Oales bandage. "Hassan, it's Rob, can you hear me?" I asked as I squatted down next to him.

Omer started pleading, "Please help him, sir—"

"Be quiet Omer, please. Hassan, it's Rob, are you okay? We're going to move over by the lamp and I'm going to move your hand . . ." I gently peeled back his hand and parted his hairline to see his scalp. He had only a small cut on his head, but because the skull was so vascular, any wound on it bled like crazy. *Aw, man! Why are we wasting our time here, when I just tripped over a guy ten times worse than Hassan!*

"Omer," I said as I quickly began wrapping the bandage tightly around the top of Hassan's wound and the back of his neck. "You're going to stay here with Hassan, okay?" I ordered Omer, "Keep talking to him, keep asking him questions, and don't let him fall asleep, okay? Can you do that?" *We have to get going; there's no time for this!*

"Yes, sir."

"Whatever happens, don't leave this bunker until you're told it's safe, okay? Don't poke your head out—wait until someone comes to you. Stay here!" I shouted. I started running up the stairs as I told the two Canadians "Let's go, on me!" I ran out of the bunker and took off around the corner at a dead sprint, hoping we'd get to the ripped-apart soldier before he bled out.

He was right where I had abandoned him, his body horribly twisted as he coughed up pink froth and started to spasm.

"Sergeant, grab his legs. You, grab his middle. I've got his feet." We all squatted down around him.

"One, two, three, lift!" We hoisted him up as gently as we could. I felt his legs twitching and my hands quickly became soaked with blood.

"Around the corner, go go go!" Even though he probably weighed only one hundred and thirty pounds, in his near-unconscious state he was incredibly hard to carry. His body was completely limp and no matter how hard we tried, he kept slipping out of our arms. I had to keep my TCCC bag scrunched under my armpit as I carried the Afghan, but I was struggling to do both.

I suddenly heard myself shout, "Medic!" but then realized, *The doc's busy; I'm TCCC qualified—I just became the medic!*

"Careful, careful," I said as I walked backwards to the nearest ANA bunker, next to the destroyed truck. Shamsallah ran over to us, carrying extra bandages.

"Open the tarp, move the tarp out of the way," I said and motioned with my head, pointing at the bunker entrance. He ran down the steps and pulled the tarp back so we could enter. I went down the steps as carefully as I could, but only got a few feet into the bunker when my legs rammed into something. It was dark and my eyes were having a hard time adjusting from the brilliant sunlight to the pitch-black bunker. I strained to see what had stopped me and realized it was an American cot in the way.

"Shamsallah, please move that, quickly," I said and again motioned with my head at the cot. He took a few seconds to figure out what I meant, and then—

"Holy fuck, get in there! WE'RE STILL EXPOSED OUT HERE!" the sergeant roared down at me.

I wanted to shout back, "I'm fucking *trying!*" but knew that wouldn't be helpful, so I took a quick breath and said in a calm voice, "Sergeant, there's a cot in the way. Shamsallah's moving it. He's shifting the cots as fast as he can. Please don't shout at me, okay? That's not what we need right now."

"I . . . I'm sorry, sir," he said, shame resonating in his voice as he realized panic had made him shout.

"Don't be sorry, it's okay. You're not the only one . . . I'm scared shitless right now! But we've got to get a grip so we can help this guy, because fuck me, he's in a bad way." Shamsallah had finally gotten the last of the cots out of the way and I was able to walk backwards all the way into the bunker. We entered the bunker and slowly lowered the wounded man to the ground. I started pulling out the bandages from my pockets and ripped open my TCCC bag to get at my scissors.

I looked at the sergeant, who was gently holding the Afghan's bleeding head in his hands. "Sergeant, you take care of the wounds on his head. You," I said to the young Canadian, "what's your name?"

"Pastel, sir." He looked a helluva lot calmer than I felt.

"You're gonna take care of the wounds on his torso. After you've done your anterior primary, let us know and together we'll roll him so you can check posterior, okay?"

"Yep," he said, and began unbuttoning the Afghan's shirt to get at his chest.

"I've got his legs," I said, and swallowed nervously. They were bleeding heavily and obviously shattered. As I took in the scope of his injuries, my mind started to unravel. *Ah . . . I can't see, there's no light. Why doesn't someone get us a light? Where's the doc? Why can't they just open the tarp? I don't have my flashlight, this isn't fair. THIS ISN'T FAIR!*

Sergeant MacVitty's cruel, hard voice took command and shouted over top of my smaller, panicking voice. *"Oi! Cunty!"* he raged. *"Stop whinging and moaning about what's fair and what ain't, and git to fuckin' work! Shut up and do the job!"*

I took a few deep breaths, and then once I'd regained some calm, I took my scissors and began cutting the injured man's trousers from the ankle, all the way to his hips on both legs. I looked at his shins. The blast had broken his lower legs and thrust both his tibia bones out through the skin to the front. I quickly made two donut bandages and placed them over the protruding bones.

As I was prepping the bandages, I looked at the Afghan's torso. Pastel opened up his shirt to find two small holes above his left lung. *Entry wounds.*

I looked at the Afghan's face, where the sergeant had begun applying bandages. The sergeant had to pull back a long, loose flap of skin and then bandage it back in place. I went back to his legs and started applying bandage after bandage to his numerous wounds. Some entry wounds were the size of a quarter, others the size of a penny, but he literally had about thirty holes peppered all over his legs. I looked at his upper thigh and there was a fist-sized chunk of flesh missing, right over the femoral artery. *Why wasn't that squirting blood? Must've just missed the artery.* I knew shrapnel could migrate, and I was afraid any second he would start shooting blood across the room, so I got out a tourniquet and began to apply it to his leg, going a few inches above the wound. I started cranking it and cranking it until I couldn't anymore, then locked it off in place. I looked for a pen to mark a "T" for tourniquet on his forehead, along with the exact time I put it on him, but I didn't have one. *I'll just have to remember and tell the doc.*

As we worked feverishly to stop his countless wounds from bleeding him to death, his friend was right up close to his face, talking to him the entire time. At the start, the wounded soldier was muttering things back, but now he was becoming less responsive. *He's fading. What've we missed?*

I feared he would soon become fully unconscious so I got out the pharyngeal airway from my TCCC bag. I applied the lubricating agent just like I'd been taught, and then put the long, rubber airway hose into his nose and down his throat. It would keep his airway open if he passed out.

I looked at Shamsallah and pointed to the bandages. "We need more bandages. Please, go and get more bandages." He quickly grasped what I meant and ran out the door with no thought for his own safety. I hadn't heard any more shouts of "Incoming." *Maybe the Brits had killed the enemy mortar team with their counter-fire. I hope they killed all those bastards, for what they've done!*

Pastel said he was ready so we tilted the Afghan gently onto his side and saw two small holes on his back, over his other lung. *Entry or exit wounds? Damn it!* I got out the clear Asherman chest seal bandages and quickly sealed the wounds off so no air could get in. If he had a sucking chest wound, and it certainly seemed like he did, the bandage was designed so the air that was building up inside his chest cavity could escape through the plastic valve on the bandage.

Sergeant Park, the doc, poked his head into the bunker and asked what we were dealing with. I spoke for the group and said, "One ANA, multiple shrapnel wounds to his legs, two protruding tibias, and two entry wounds over his right lung anterior, two entry wounds left lung posterior." *Did I say those backwards or was that right?* "Multiple cuts to the face and neck, we put a pharyngeal airway down his nose. Was semi-conscious five minutes ago, but now seems fully unconscious." *Did I forget something? Oh yeah*—"And I put a tourniquet on his upper thigh."

"Okay, good work guys," the doc said, "but what about his eyes—are his eyes gone?" *Good question.* We all looked at each other. The doc waited.

"Have you checked his eyes?!" he asked, more agitated now.

"We don't know, we haven't checked," I said. It was obvious none of us wanted to do it. The thought of peeling back his eyelids to find nothing but empty holes filled with muck was a little too much to bear.

"Oh, for God's sake," the doc said and came down the steps. He gently nudged the soldier's friend out of the way and then deftly peeled back his eyelids. "No, they're still there."

"Doc, with those four entry wounds, should we do a needle decompression?" He looked at me and then leaned closely to the soldier's mouth, listening carefully.

"No, he's got a good airway. Best to leave it, for now. Good work, I'll be back."

Before he left I asked, "How many wounded have you got?"

He turned back to face me and used the nine-liner code. "So far, one VSA or Echo, two Bravo, five Charlie, one Delta." That meant one guy was vital signs absent (dead), two guys were in need of urgent surgery, five guys were priority cases, and the last guy was considered routine. *Probably Hassan with his head wound.*

The nine-liner was the medical evacuation request form we used over the radio. Obviously, it was made up of nine separate lines that would have to be filled out accurately and sent up properly if we wanted the medical evacuation choppers to arrive on time, in the right spot, and carrying the right gear.

I couldn't help myself; I had to know. "Any Canadians?" Pastel and the sergeant both looked up at the doc.

"Negative, all Afghans. I gotta go." He turned and pulled back the Hessian flap and walked back into the bright sunlight. Shamsallah came running back in and handed me more bandages. I was sweating like a madman, racing against the clock. I worked feverishly to seal off the soldier's leg wounds, and by the time I thought I'd gotten them all, I had applied twenty-seven bandages to his legs. Shamsallah had made three bandage resupply runs, just for us.

Ginge poked his head into our bunker and said, "Doc wants all the wounded outside, where he can see 'em." *Fine, but where are the damn choppers?*

We looked at each other and then on my three-count we gently lifted our patient up into our arms. Shamsallah and the wounded soldier's friend helped us, and together we carried him outside and laid him down on one of several cots that someone had placed in a row. I looked around to take in the damage.

The Ranger was still smoking from under its hood, and the tent next to us was pockmarked with hundreds of tiny holes where the shrapnel had perforated it. Someone was shouting in the distance as Canadians and Afghans began to walk around the corner and come out of the nearest bunkers, carrying the wounded. Some of them were crying out in pain; some were unconscious. One Afghan had sat down by a tent and was crying into his hands.

The wounded were gently laid on the cots as the doc walked up and down, looking at them and making notes in his FMP.

He approached the soldier we'd been trying to save and told me to put him on his side, with his good side up, and place a sandbag under him to keep him in that position. I motioned to Shamsallah, who grabbed a sandbag, and together we put the soldier in the position that would help him the most. Canadians were running around and I could hear the THUMP from the other side of the wall as the Brits continued firing their mortars at the Taliban.

Sean walked over to me and asked if I was okay. He had looked at my uniform and saw that it was completely soaked in blood from my ankle up to my ribs from where I had been leaning over the bleeding soldier and pressed up against him. I told him I was fine, and asked if he needed help. I realized

I'd been more of a labourer and less of a foreman, but he said there were more than enough chefs.

"Keep doing TCCC," he said. "I'll let you know if I need you."

"Fine. What's the ETA on the choppers?" It had seemed like a long time had passed since the call for a chopper would've gone up the chain. *Where were they? Why was it taking so long?*

Sean shook his head in disgust. "They won't launch until we've given them the MIST!"

"Who gives a shit about the freaking MIST? We need those choppers, now!"

"I know, the warrant's giving them hell for it, we're trying to get them here . . ."

The doc was doing the best he could, but he was only one guy, so I ran over to help him collect the all-important MIST [method of injury, injury, signs, treatment given]. I started going from wounded to wounded to see if I could help, or if the guys needed bandages or tourniquets. I saw Stamps and my heart filled with pride—I knew he'd been working hard all afternoon, running around to help out where he could. All of the Canadians had been going above and beyond. Some of the OMLT guys had been out at the vehicle leaguer, and when they'd heard the FOB was being mortared, they'd put on their PPE and ran over to help, dodging incoming mortar rounds as they sprinted into the FOB.

A young soldier I'd never seen before ran up to us, holding a pen and paper, and asked about the MIST. *Again with the damn MIST!*

"Hey!" I shouted at him. "Every single guy here got wounded by mortar rounds, that's all they need to know! We can send them the MIST when the birds are in the air! Get back in there, and tell them to launch, *now*! Stop waiting for the fucking MIST!" Everyone looked at me and then went back to work. *I shouldn't have snapped like that; that's not helping anyone.* I made a mental note to find the guy and apologize later.

He was just doing what he had been told to do. It wasn't his fault the choppers weren't taking off until they had every single tiny piece of information. *What happened to "As long as you send up lines one, three, six, and nine of the nine-liner, they'll launch, and you can give them the rest while they're en route?" Where the hell are they? My guy's fading, he's slipping away—and we're just standing here, helpless to stop it!*

After what seemed like an eternity, but I found out later was actually one hour and forty-seven minutes, we were told the evac choppers would be landing any minute. We had placed the wounded on stretchers and carried them over to the north end of the FOB in anticipation. I had thought of it a little too late, but told Ginge to run and get some thermal blankets. He came back from the medical container and handed them out. The OMLT soldiers began to gently wrap the wounded ANA in the blankets to keep them warm for the flight.

We carried the ANA to the helicopter landing site on the other side of the Hesco wall. Warrant Smith popped smoke and the American Black Hawks (out of KAF) began to set down, one at a time. An American medic would disembark, run over to Sergeant Park, have a quick "transfer patient care" meeting regarding the Afghans, and then help us load the wounded on board.

We would fill up a Black Hawk and then another would land. We filled them up with injured ANA until we had only the dead Afghan left. His entire body had been covered with a thermal blanket. I grabbed one end of the stretcher, but a crying Afghan soldier nudged me out of the way. I guessed it was his friend, and as a final gesture, he wanted to be the one to help get his friend's body on the chopper. I stood to the side and let him take my spot.

At the last minute I realized that both Hassan, who was actually wounded, and Omer, who wasn't, were getting on the last chopper. I shouted at Omer but he ignored me and hopped on board next to Hassan. I would never see Hassan again—he had been wounded and treated and that was enough for him; he went AWOL (absent without leave)—but Omer came back about two weeks later. *So that's that. Now I have no terps.*

After the last chopper had left, we slowly walked back to the inner compound. Ginge came over and I told him thanks for his hard work, but I had one more job for him. I knew it could prove to be very traumatic for the ANA to see dozens of bloody bandages littering the ground where their friends had been bleeding to death, so I politely asked him if he would put on some latex gloves and go police up the garbage and used bandages. He said he would square it away and jogged off around the corner.

One of the Brits saw me and said, "Oi, mate, I think you're hit."

I looked down at my body and said, "No, it's someone else's blood." I walked back toward the inner FOB with a warrant I hadn't met before. *Maybe he'll know,* I thought to myself. I looked at him and asked, "What the hell took the choppers so long? I mean, what happened to the golden hour?"

The general belief was that if the choppers could collect you and get you back to KAF in under an hour—the so-called golden hour—you stood a better-than-average chance of living through your ordeal. It had taken the choppers *over* an hour and forty-five minutes to finally appear.

"I hate to say it," the warrant said, "but I think it was because they were brown."

"No. Bullshit," I snapped. "I don't buy that for a second." I wasn't having it. I knew those choppers would go to hell and back to get the wounded out. *Any* wounded—Afghan or coalition. The only reason I could come up with was that they knew the enemy was still present, near the helicopter landing site, and they couldn't risk the choppers and their crews getting hit. *They weren't allowed to land, but the Brits had taken care of the enemy mortar team, hadn't they?*

"Do you think they would've taken so long if it was coalition troops that had been wounded?" he asked, not willing to drop it.

"Yes, if the choppers were already tasked out, or in a different part of the country. Yeah, they have a lot of choppers, but they're not limitless, ya know? There's still only so many in the country and they can't be everywhere at once."

The warrant dropped it and we parted ways as I walked over to the ANA command post. I found the ANA captain and said, "*Man mutasef aastam.*" *I'm sorry.*

He shook my hand as tears brimmed up in his eyes, then he turned and walked back into his CP. I saw Ginge and thanked him for cleaning the place up. He had been everywhere at once, all day. We wandered back over to the OMLT CP, where the boys were sitting outside, sipping coffee out of Styrofoam, their blood-red hands stark against the bright white of their cups.

I found the OMLT sergeant who had worked on the wounded Afghan with me and plopped down next to him. I looked at him out of the corner of my eye, but he hadn't even registered that someone was next to him. He had the proverbial thousand-yard stare. *Not a good sign.*

"Sergeant," I said. *Nothing.* "Sergeant. Hey, Sergeant!" He finally snapped from his trance and looked over at me.

There was no life in his voice as he quietly said, "Oh, hey sir."

"Hey, Sergeant. That was a pretty messed-up day, eh? I'm glad I didn't have a full bladder!" I tried to get him to smile but he seemed to be getting that vacant look back.

I kept going, hoping he'd listen. "I just wanted to come and find you. You did an awesome job today. I think the guy we worked on is going to make it. We got him to the chopper in decent shape, and that was thanks to you and Pastel."

The sergeant suddenly became animated and turned on me, saying, "You don't gotta blow smoke up my ass, sir!" He stared at me through angry, tired eyes.

"And what do you mean by that, exactly?" I asked, staring right back.

"I didn't know what to . . . we didn't . . ." he droned off.

Oh, I get it. "Sergeant, if you're feeling bad because we didn't do all the right things, or you felt like you weren't sure what to do, well, I got news for ya! Look at me! You don't have a Red Cross badge on your shoulder. And guess what? Neither do I! We've got TCCC training, and what's that? An extra two weeks of combat first aid? Those medics spend years getting to that level, and they still make mistakes! Don't get comparing yourself to them, okay? OKAY?"

"Okay, sir, I hear ya. Thanks."

"We did the best we could, with what we had, and that's all anyone can ask of us. Think about this. Nobody forced you to run outside during a freaking mortar attack to come and save ANA soldiers! Those weren't Canadians in the line of fire, but Afghans. Look at me!" His eyes slowly tracked up my face to meet my gaze. "I ran into that ISO container, and you know what? It was chock full of Canadians. And no one can fault them for taking cover during a mortar attack—that's what you're supposed to do! But *you*, and all the rest of the OMLT guys, all of you put the lives of the dying ANA soldiers ahead of your own. And no officer could ever be more proud of his men! As far as I'm concerned that was heroic, what you did today. Absolutely *heroic!*"

I put my hand on his shoulder. "But what happened today, we're going to be carrying that around with us for a long time. So don't feel like you gotta figure it all out today, okay?"

I got up slowly to find the others. My body ached all over, and my head was killing me. But I knew I had to make the rounds. I found Ginge, still running around and helping out, and stopped him long enough to tell him how proud I was of him. I told him he had singlehandedly saved lives—he'd been everywhere at once. I told him that when he was done he should find the newly installed shower and wash all the blood off.

I found the doc and told him I'd never seen anyone act so calmly and professionally. He was everything the CF had hoped he could be, in that terrible moment. I told him I was incredibly proud of him, and I knew Sean would be putting him in for official recognition, because holy crap, did he ever deserve it!

I ran into Sean and asked him if I needed to fill out any reports or other officer paperwork. He looked at me and grinned. "As always, numbnuts, I've done all of your work for you. Go get cleaned up."

I tried to think of a witty retort but drew a complete blank, so I just half-smiled back, said thanks, and went to find Big Joe. He was over by the damaged truck. I walked up to him and just gave him a moment alone. He was looking at the shattered Ranger and the tent with a thousand holes in it.

I got his attention and we shook hands. His large hand was still covered in blood. I kept his hand in my grip and thanked him for saving my life. I told him that if he hadn't picked me up and dragged me behind the bunker, the next round probably would've ended me. I said, "I thought I had whiplash from when you shoved me to go and get my PPE, and at the time I was going to have words, but I thought better of it." The warrant laughed and slapped me roughly on the back, shifting me a foot.

We looked at the damage: the blown-apart Ranger, with smoke seeping out from under the hood; the tent with hundreds of shrapnel holes in it. There were bloodstains all over our triage centre, but in some spots the ground was saturated with pools of dark red liquid. It was a haunting image.

"One of the guys was standing right next to that," I said, pointing at the tent with all the holes.

"It's a miracle they weren't all—"

"Hey guys," a voice cut in from behind us.

The warrant and I turned to see a Canadian captain I'd never met before.

"Hey, what's going on?" I asked.

He coughed nervously and said, "I just came by to see how you guys are doing, and to talk about something." *Really? To "talk about something"? Okay, here we go. . . .*

"And what exactly would you like to 'talk about'?" I enquired, looking at Big Joe, who seemed equally unimpressed.

"Well," he began, "it's just that someone here gave the Royal Marines permission to fire their mortars, but it's not their AO."

"Yes," I said, immediately not liking where I thought the conversation was going. *Stay calm, Rob. Hey, wait a minute, let me guess, this is the mad FOO/FAC bastard from the Zangabad teardown!* I looked at his badges and crest. *Yep, FOO/ FAC!* The right side of my head began to throb painfully from where I'd been backblasted by the RPG.

"So you see what I mean," he continued with a lump in his throat. "The Royal Marines weren't supposed to fire, and . . ." I felt my blood pressure rising a little too quickly. Joe looked like he was about to pick the clown upside down and shake him until he got some common sense. *Breathe, Rob, breathe.*

"You mean, *the Royal Marines* whose counter-mortar fire probably saved all of our lives? You can't possibly mean *those* Royal Marines?" I asked sarcastically.

"Well, yeah—them." He looked back and forth between Joe and me, his eyes searching our faces for some sign of acknowledgement that we gave two fat shits about his firing-in-someone-else's-AO lecture. Of course, we couldn't care less, and worse, it was actually insulting. *That's it, I'm losing it—I'm losing it!* My vision began to turn dimly red and my head started to pound even more violently.

"I mean," he continued, "we can't just have *anybody* shooting off mortar rounds—"

Okay, that's it. But just don't shout. Do not shout.

"Right, that's enough!" I shouted, cutting him off mid-sentence. "*First off*, do you really think the Taliban give a fuck about who's trying to kill them, the Brits or the Canadians? Is that what's important? Or, maybe, *just maybe*, is it *more* important that somebody—on *our* fucking side—is actually trying to kill *them* when they're trying to kill *us*? And come to think of it, I didn't hear your guns from Sperwhan firing! And then you fucking march in here, you don't ask about our wounded, or what you can do to help—that doesn't even cross your mind. All you care about is finding the OC of FOB Mushan and giving him some piddly ass Sunday-school lecture on who can shoot in whose AO?" I was absolutely livid.

"Well, it's not that—" he stammered.

"Enough! Look at him!" I said, pointing at the warrant, all covered in blood. "LOOK AT ME!!" I wrung out my pant leg so hard that my hand became soaked in blood. I held it up to his face and shouted, "I'm fucking standing here *soaked* in another man's blood!" I flicked my bloody fist hard at his feet, spattering blood all over his boots. "Do you think I give a *fuck* about your stupid AO rules, right now, here, in this place? Didn't you see the pools of blood as you walked in?" The warrant had inched closer to me and now placed his big arm across my chest, holding me back. I put my bloody hand up to the idiot's face, where he could see it clearly. My mind began to race with thoughts of extreme violence.

"It's time for you to leave," Warrant Duceppe said with menace dripping from his ice-cold voice. The FOO/FAC didn't need to be told twice. He spun on his heel and jogged away through the gap in the Hesco wall.

"Easy, sir," the warrant said. "Stand down. He got the point. Shit, you really tore into him."

"Warrant, honestly, did that really just happen? Did my mind just make that up? Did he really come in here and try to lecture us on artillery rules in an AO? Am I losing my mind?" *I am losing it. There's no way that just happened.*

"Oh, you know some people, sir, common sense ain't that common!"

"Okay, but did he think if the Brit mortars fired at the same time as our guns fired, the rounds would meet in mid-air, smash into each other, and cancel each other out?! What the hell, man?" *Breathe, Rob, breathe.*

"C'mon," the big warrant said, "let's get some coffee. Hey, did you hear that those mocha sachets are actually supposed to be poisonous?"

"After today," I sighed, "who gives a shit?"

I grabbed a coffee and garnered stares everywhere I went. *Oh yeah—the blood.* But I wasn't going to get in the shower before any of the enlisted men. I walked from soldier to soldier and tried to encourage everyone. I could tell most of the guys felt like me—sort of hollow inside.

Some guys would keep busy with chores or the handover; other guys would sit and stare into space, their minds replaying the afternoon over and over again, on a crazy loop. The engineers got back to work on their teardown. They had Hesco walls to repair where the mortars had ripped into them. I wondered how many rounds had actually landed inside the FOB. *It sounded like five, maybe six.*

Major Obermann and his CSM had walked over to check in on us. I realized the FOO/FAC had undoubtedly told the major I was losing it. He walked slowly over to me and looked at my bloody side. "Are you okay?" he asked, looking me in the eyes.

"Yeah, I'm good, sir. Thanks. We had at least four rounds land directly in the FOB itself."

"Inner or outer FOB?" he asked.

"At least four inner, maybe one hit the outer part. We had one KIA, two Bravo, five Charlie, and one Delta. My terp was the Delta, and before anyone could stop his best friend, my other terp, he hopped on the last chopper with him. And my Dari isn't that good. I've been going around all night, talking to the boys, doing a sort of informal decompression, making sure everyone's holding up, but they're good. There's a few guys we'll have to watch, but that's normal. But I tell ya, sir, I've never seen anything like it."

"Like what?" he asked.

"You would've been proud of them, sir. They were courageous beyond belief, and I think everyone of 'em should be put in for recognition."

"Well, I'm glad you guys are all okay. Talk to Sean about the recognition part. I'm sorry you took KIA and wounded; it was a terrible day. When we found out you were getting hit, we mounted up and gave chase, and using the grid from the LCMR, we actually found the Taliban mortar tube. I'm not sure—"

"Yeah, thanks sir, the ANA will take it off of you. They like the idea of using Timothy's own weapons against him. Thanks for going out there."

"You don't have to thank me for that. You did your part, we did ours. Get cleaned up and try and get some sleep."

"All right, sir. Thanks again for coming by to check on us." He walked into the CP to find Sean.

I asked around and everyone had had a chance to shower and get cleaned up, so I walked over to my sleeping container and grabbed a towel, soap and, knowing I would need it, a scrub brush. I reached into my rucksack and pulled out my spare pair of pants and a clean brown shirt.

I walked into the small little shower module that had been installed just that afternoon. *Probably right around the time of the mortar attack.* The shower unit was surrounded by thin wooden sheets serving as walls.

I looked into the mirror and sighed at a face I could hardly recognize. My eyes seemed to have shrunk back into my head; my hair was matted with sweat and blood. Salt stains had formed crow's feet around the corners of my eyes. I felt like crying, and suddenly I became very angry. I was angry at the Taliban, angry about the choppers not arriving soon enough, angry that no matter what we did to save him, we couldn't stop that soldier from fading away, right in front of us. I became angry at the FOO/FAC, and then incredibly angry with myself.

I remembered overhearing Hetsa at the end of the Helmand op, bragging to his friends, saying, "So far, we haven't been in a *real* firefight." This made me mad, so I had taken him to an empty briefing tent and we had a little talk about "How *real* does it have to be before it's real enough for ya?" and "When it is *real*, we won't want to be there!"

I was mad at him and I got the point across, but afterwards, I was ashamed because I realized I wasn't as upset with Hetsa as I was with myself.

I looked at the haggard face in the mirror and my mind started to rage.

Was that on your war to-do list? Tears began to quickly well up in my eyes. *WAS "HOLD A MAN AS HE'S DYING" ON YOUR STUPID FUCKING LIST? WAS THAT SOMETHING YOU'VE ALWAYS WANTED TO DO?? WERE YOU "MAKING WAR FUN" NOW? WAS THIS AFTERNOON* REAL *ENOUGH FOR YOU?*

I wanted to punch the stupid face in the mirror, so I cocked my fist back next to my ear.

YOU STUPID FUCKING ASSHOLE! You had the balls to shout at Hetsa, but it's you! You, with your STUPID, childish lists and "make war real!" That was *war, this afternoon, that's what happens! People get ripped apart and they're bleeding to death in front of you, and there's nothing you can do to stop it!*

Tears spilled down my cheeks as my fist shook next to my ear, waiting for my inner voice to shut up long enough for me to punch the mirror as hard as I could. My head twitched involuntarily to my right and my eye caught something written on the wall. I glanced over at the wooden panel and saw handwriting on it. It said: SHOWER INSTALLED ON NOV. 17, 2008, DURING A MORTAR ATTACK. *The civilian engineer must've written that. He must've been putting the shower in when we got hit.* I slowly lowered my fist and began to breathe in, shallowly at first, but then more deeply.

I had found a marker pen that afternoon to put "T"s and "M"s on the foreheads of the wounded, so I reached into my pocket and pulled it out. With a quivering hand, I slowly added in block letters underneath his line, 1 X VSA, 2 X B, 5 X C, 1 X D.

My anger subsided and I felt more tired and empty than I had ever felt before in my life. I slowly got undressed and turned on the shower. I washed my body with soap, and panic began to rise up in my throat when I couldn't get the bloodstains off my leg.

I suddenly became afraid that I was going to have a major freak-out when a serene inner voice reminded me that I had brought along a scrub brush. I grabbed it and started roughly scraping off the dried, crusted blood.

I got dressed in clean clothes and walked back to the ISO container. I saw Warrant Smith on the way and asked him how things were going. He said fine and just sort of looked at me. I realized I was holding the bloody clothes from this afternoon; I didn't know what to do with the pants. No amount of scrubbing in the little tub we had was going to get the blood out.

He said that after a big incident like today, "You can put your pants into a black garbage bag, and then request fresh ones from the store back at KAF." He ran and found me a garbage bag, and handed it to me. I thanked him, put the pants and shirt into the bag and hid it out of sight, behind the container. I walked into the CP to see if I could help, but Sean had everything well in hand. I was grateful that he was there, because I was feeling pretty done in. After that day, I wasn't good for too much.

* * *

That night we talked about the next day's plans. The battle group was heading back, the engineers had done their work, and the necessary kit had been dropped off. I took a deep breath and asked Sean if they were still going to take away our LCMR, after we just took four mortar rounds in the middle of our FOB.

"That's the plan," Sean said, and tried to quickly change the subject.

"Even though the guy shouting, 'Incoming!' had saved our lives. And the only way he could possibly know we had incoming was because he had a fucking LCMR, to read its radar screen and then shout out his warning."

Sean looked at me patiently, "Rob, we've gone—"

Shut up, Rob, you're not helping. And besides, this isn't something to be argued about in front of the guys; morale already got the boots laid to it today. "Yeah, I know," I said. I wasn't angry anymore, just really tired, and contrary to my character, my GAFF (Give a Fuck Factor) was at an all-time low.

Sean continued on with the briefing, and once we were satisfied that all the points had been covered, we went our separate ways. I grabbed a coffee and headed outside.

I found the guys just hanging out, so I would join one group and then go over to another. Someone asked, as a joke, if I had been scared and I said, "Absolutely terrified. I was praying under the flatbed, praying because I didn't want to die." I looked at the group of guys and said, "There's nothing in our training that prepares us for a day like this. Oh sure, at the TCCC course they'll lay out a dummy and pour out cans of tomato juice around it so we can recognize how many litres of blood a guy's lost, but they can't make us ready for a day like this. There is no *ready*."

The guys were nodding their heads, but I didn't want to bash the CF; that wasn't the point of my speech. I wanted to get something through to them.

"That's why it's so important that you guys talk amongst yourselves. You've got to vent what you've seen here today. It was horrible and gross, and I don't know about you, but since it happened I've been angry, sad, mad, I've felt sick. But that's all normal. What happened today, that's *not* normal. What happened today is so far outside the width and breadth of normal experience that there's never been anything in your life to prepare you for it. Maybe you've seen car accidents or been hurt, but you've never seen anything like today. But what you guys have to do is be there for each other when you need to talk. You need to tell yourself it's okay if you were afraid, okay if you were terrified, okay if you felt sick, or angry, or full of rage. That's all normal."

I realized I was blathering so I summed up. "You guys did great, today—every one of you. But like I told somebody earlier, don't feel like you've got to figure it all out today. Allow yourself some time to make peace with it. I'll see you later."

I walked away and went back to the CP to watch some TV. The boys were watching *Dexter*, and I'd never seen it before, but I found it quite good. In hindsight, I don't imagine a trauma therapy specialist would recommend watching a television show about a good-hearted serial killer after the day we'd just had.

Over the course of the night, my mind kept wandering back to the wounded soldiers. *Had I done everything right? Maybe I should've needle decompressed that guy anyway...* I caught my mind going onto a negative-loop feed and decided to take my own advice. I did my best to push the thoughts to the back shelf and give myself time to sort everything out. I told myself that *I did the best I could, with what I had at the time.*

I went to bed that night and was sound asleep when someone slammed the metal door to the container as they left to go on radio shift.

KRAANG!

Warrant Smith and I shot up in perfect unison and stared around blindly in the dark. *Were we being mortared again? What was...?*

"It was the door," he said, and went back to sleep.

My heart raced for a good ten seconds and then I lay back down and stared at the bunk above me. I wasn't sure if I could handle another day like today.

Chapter *18*

The next morning, Warrant Smith and I walked around the FOB and found that five rounds had actually landed inside FOB Mushan itself, with a sixth one just on the other side of the western Hesco wall.

I looked at the warrant. "That's really accurate for them, isn't it?"

Warrant Smith had been to the Stan five times before, so his experience and advice were not to be questioned when he said, "Yeah, not bad, but I suppose they had five good days of practice before they got it right."

I walked over to the leaguer to say goodbye to Major Obermann and my friends from Mike Company. They all wished me luck and then mounted up to head back to Sperwhan. I found Sean and the rest of the OMLT boys who would be going back and told them thanks for everything. I found Big Joe and thanked him again for saving my life. He told me to shut up.

Sean asked if I needed anything and I asked him again to pester the battle group lieutenant colonel to try and get the LCMR back. He said he'd try, but no promises. During the night, the engineers had created a dummy LCMR on the rooftop of Moosh, just where the old one had been. And to their credit, it looked just like the old one, except it was made out of wood, fibreglass, and Hessian sack. But for some reason, I didn't think it would work quite as well as the original.

The convoy began to head to the west before it would turn north to the dry riverbed. I jogged back to the FOB and said good morning to the guys. I was the new OC, Warrant Smith was the 2 I/C, and also there were Stamps, Iropolous, and a bunch of guys I'd never worked with before: Carns, O.B., Simmons, and Pastel. *Pastel?* He'd worked with me in the bunker on that Afghan. I looked at his shoulder—*now* he had his medic patches on.

I apologized for ordering him around in the bunker. If I'd known he was a medic, I would've deferred all of the decisions to him as the expert. He laughed and said, "No problem, sir, you were making good calls, so I didn't feel the need to step in."

It was just a small comment, but it got me square in the chest. Up until he said that, I didn't know if I was making the right calls or not, and I was trying hard to quash the self-doubt that comes after a terrible day like that. But when he said that, I felt ten times better—about a lot of things—and even though he was just making conversation, it meant a lot to me.

I talked for a few minutes with our new interpreter, a young guy called Max (no relation to the Max(s) from Masum Ghar). It seemed that the anglophone in charge of giving Afghans English names—being too lazy to pronounce their real ones—had decided that every other interpreter should be called "Max."

This Max was scheduled to leave on the convoy today, but he got roped into sticking around when his boss called him from Masum and told him he couldn't leave because we'd lost Omer and Hussan yesterday in the mortar attack. So if he still wanted a job, he had to stick around. And he was *none* too happy about it.

He asked if he could speak with me privately, so we walked over by the generator. He leaned forward conspiratorially, and looked over his shoulder before he spoke.

"Captain Rob, I do not wish to stay here. I want to leave. I have worked hard and I was told I would be done here yesterday, and now I want to go."

"Yes, you were told you could leave, but that was *before* both of my other interpreters got hurt in yesterday's mortar attack. So you understand how that changes things, just a little bit, right?"

"Yes, but I do not care. I want to leave."

"Okay, but you understand they'll fire you, and you won't have a job with the Canadians anymore, right?"

"Yes, I do not care. I want to leave."

He'd obviously made up his mind, but I had to have at least one interpreter. As good as Warrant Smith was (and he was certainly very good), he wasn't fluent in Dari or Pashto, and I had to have someone who could speak both. *Okay . . . I hate to use Dark Jedi mind tricks, but he's left me no choice.*

I looked Max straight in the eye and said, "Did you know the other OMLT guys found an interpreter hanging from the lamppost, here in the local bazaar?" I wasn't lying; that was completely true—he was a terp working for the CF who'd been murdered and strung up by the Taliban.

"No, I did not know that." The grotesque image was now firmly planted in his brain.

"You can leave, Max. I can't stop you. Nor would I even try. But how were you planning on getting back home to Kandahar city? By *taxi?*"

"Yes, I was going to take a taxi."

"Did you know that most terrorists around the world use taxis to supply them with information? Taxi drivers quite often work for the terrorists."

"I . . . I did not know that." *Good, good. Let* The Fear *flow through you.*

"And Max, what do you think they will do to you, if they capture you?" *You're a bad man, Rob Semrau.*

"I . . . I do not . . ."

"I would really like it if you could stay, Max, at least for a little while. Omer will probably be coming back in a few weeks. Can you please stay just until he comes back?"

"I . . . yes. I will stay until he comes back."

"Thanks, Max. Let me know if you need anything."

Master Yoda's voice began to echo in the back of my mind: *If once you start down the dark path, forever will it dominate your destiny, consume you it will.*

But I also remembered the sage words of a dying Vulcan: "The needs of the many outweigh the needs of the few . . . or the one." And I don't speak Dari, Pashto, Farsi, or Uzbek! I only speak some Québécois—and Canadian Farmer!

That afternoon, Captain Ghias got a cellphone call from an NDS spy, who told him a famous Taliban mullah would be preaching at the local mosque in Mushan village and stirring up the good citizenry to acts of violence. *I didn't think spies were supposed to discuss things of that nature over a cellphone whose signal could easily be intercepted, but I suppose that's neither here nor there.*

Ghias and Max then approached me and said the captain wanted to do a major operation (involving his entire company) early the next morning:

an old-school "snatch and grab" on the mullah, who was stirring up trouble. I said the OMLT was always game, but how would we find him in that huge village? It was spread out all over the place, to our south and west. How could we find him in all of *that*?

Ghias looked at me like I was a pure idiot. "He is a mullah, is he not?"

"Yes, that's what you just told me," I replied.

"Well, tomorrow is Friday. He will be preaching in the biggest mosque in Mushan, the one in the south end. We will go while it is still dark, wait outside the mosque, and grab him when he comes to preach. Simple," he said with a big grin. Granted, the plan was a stroke of genius for its simplicity, but things had a nasty way of going south in an awful hurry when you worked with the ANA.

Yeah, right—simple! Nothing could ever go wrong with that plan! His followers wouldn't try to kill us when we kidnapped him. The ANA couldn't possibly get lost on their way there. The Taliban would never plant false information and then set us up in a four-sided ambush. Like the captain said: simple.

I discussed the ANA plan with Warrant Smith, who said, "I'm glad tomorrow's your turn to go on patrol." *Thanks.* But then he suggested we stick Stamps up in the northwest sangar with an amazing piece of kit called the "Coral Sea." Why was it called that? No idea. But the etymology of the name wasn't the important thing. What did matter is that it could pick out a heat source the size of a kitten from about a kilometre away. If anyone was setting up in the pre-dawn mist to brew us up, Stamps would spot them miles away.

The Coral Sea machine was a big boxy thing that weighed around fifteen pounds. You were meant to look through it like binoculars, but it was so heavy and ungainly that you had to prop up your elbows on something before you could hold it up to your face. And from the heat waves it put off, you could rest assured you were getting a healthy dose of cancer-inducing radiation. But we were willing to trade off a brain tumour for a modern-day crystal ball that could keep us alive in the here and now.

I radioed Sperwhan to tell them the plan and to request UAV support. To actually have an unmanned drone flying high above us, giving us real-time int on what was happening on the ground, would be an incredibly valuable asset. And if we were really lucky, it might even be armed with Hellfire missiles, to rain down the pain on Timothy. *Do I dare to dream a dream?*

But I had no illusions. It was highly unlikely we'd ever get the UAV. We'd never gotten one before, ever. That is to say, our OMLT team had never gotten one. Not at Sper, not here in Moosh. I don't think any of the other OMLT commanders had ever gotten one either. UAVs were a battle group asset, and apparently, the battle group needed them more than we did. But I'd put up the request almost twenty-four hours in advance, so who knew. *Hope in Afghanistan springs eternal.*

I returned to Captain Ghias in his CP, where I opened up my map to discuss the plan. And after some good mentoring, we had the line of departure established, the routes we'd take into the objective, the cut off/blocking positions for his different platoons, and his best platoon under Shamsallah designated as the grab team. Timings were agreed upon, we covered the pertinent actions-on ("What to do if . . ." scenarios), and after we were both happy with the plan, I went back to my command post to send it up the chain.

It was Simmons's turn to go on patrol, so he would be my fire-team partner for the big mission. That night we checked our batteries, cleaned our weapons, and put infrared (IR) glow sticks on the backs of our helmets, so anyone wearing a set of night-vision goggles could see us. We then handed out IR glow sticks to all the ANA sergeants, CSM Shamsallah, and Captain Ghias, who finally decided this mission was important enough for him to come and join us.

I was concerned with the ANA's ability, or more accurately, their *inability*, to see well at night. I'd heard back in Canada that the ANA couldn't see at night, and I thought it was twenty-first-century racism. *They can't see at night? Why, because they have brown skin? Get real!* But we'd tried a night patrol earlier in Mushan, and I'd seen the First Company ANA in action during low-light and night conditions back at Sperwhan, and I found out to my surprise that it was very much the truth. If there was no moon or it was obscured, then they really *couldn't* see, at all.

To a man, I believed they had a vitamin A deficiency, which was something easily attributable to their diet of rice, some onions and tomatoes, and naan bread. Every blue moon they would eat mutton or beef. But the whole time I was in the Stan, I'd never once seen a carrot. So the thought of sixty ANA soldiers stumbling around behind me in complete darkness, with their fingers undoubtedly on their triggers, as we possibly strolled into a Taliban ambush, was somewhat disconcerting. *Yeah, but what're ya gonna do?*

We woke up at 0300 hours the morning of the op and went about our work in total silence. Well, Simmons and I did. The ANA were stumbling, turning on flashlights, speaking too loudly, giggling. Shamsallah, who knew the score, was running around and delivering vicious kicks to his soldiers' butts, trying to get them to shut off their flashlights to save their already trammelled night vision, and to stop shouting so loudly everyone in the nearby village could hear us. As an added bonus, Captain Ghias would be leading the patrol—for the first and only time.

Simmons and I cracked all of the IR glow sticks, handed them back to the Afghans, and made sure ours were squared away tightly on the back of our helmets. We had our night-vision goggles (NVGs) attached to our helmets and, once lowered, they covered our non-dominant eye (the eye we didn't use to shoot with). The IR glow sticks, although invisible to the naked eye, brightly lit up the back of our heads when viewed through NVGs.

I met again with the warrant, who told me that the battle group had finally come through for us: we'd finally be getting a dedicated UAV for a mission. My friend Nick back at Sperwhan put the word up to KAF, and someone there deemed our snatch and grab important enough to justify sending us the UAV asset. We could expect it in half an hour, which was right around the time we'd be needing it. The warrant wished me luck and then went in to man the radio and be the critical link between me, Sperwhan, and the UAV operator in KAF. We were good to go. *All right, thumbs up, let's do this!*

Everyone had their magic IR glow stick, the ANA were in the proper order of march, and we even set out on time, but as one could reasonably expect, things started to quickly go wrong.

The ANA patrol column quickly became dangerously spread out (their guys were talking and smoking until Shamsallah caught them and hoofed them in their shins), and Ghias got lost about fifty metres outside our FOB's main gate. I had looked for a reference point the day before, and knew we needed to march toward a high wall off to the southwest. So I had put that bearing in my compass, and when Ghias covertly approached me to ask for directions, I checked my compass and quietly (so he wouldn't lose face) pointed him in the right direction. I radioed Stamps, who was on the PRR, and asked if he saw anything through the Coral Sea. He had no visible heat signatures on his scope, anywhere, so we were good to go. In the sangar, Stamps was also standing right next to a .50-cal heavy machine gun, ready to bring the hurt to Timothy if need be.

We continued on, with Ghias, me, Simmons, Max, and Shamsallah up at the front of the column, acting as the combined recce/HQ element, when we came up to the wall I was using to steer us in. I lowered my NVG and peeked around the corner. *Nothing.* No one was stirring in the village, no DEWS brayed, no village dogs barked to give away our position. Everything was on the up and up. *Huh. Imagine that!*

I whispered to Max, who whispered my recommendation to Ghias, who thought about something for a moment, and then called his sergeants in for a quick last word. They followed the plan and knew where they had to take their platoons. One platoon was going south to act as a cut-off force (blocking platoon) to stop anyone trying to flee, another platoon would go southwest to carry out the same role, and then Shamsallah would lead his platoon into the village to set up and hide around the mosque itself.

The night before, I had suggested to Ghias that we might want to join Shamsallah as part of the grab team, or be near them at least, since the commander always wanted to be in the best position to influence the battle the most, but nothing doing. Ghias told me we *would* be in the best position—four hundred metres away, safely hidden behind a large wall. His plan called for his HQ element to stay safely in the rear with the gear. So once Shamsallah sprung the trap, the southwest platoon would march north and act as the western cut-off group. Everything was set. Ghias gave the word, and the platoons marched silently off into the early-morning darkness.

I looked at Simmons. We were both really cold. In the dark hours the desert got bitterly cold, and since we'd stopped marching, our sweat was putting off vapour fumes into the cold morning air. I looked toward the east. We'd had to get up early and start marching long before the sun came up, because the mosque would be open an hour before sun-up for the first prayer of the day. Shamsallah and his men had to be hidden around the mosque long before then.

Over the next twenty minutes, Ghias's platoon commanders and Shamsallah radioed in to say they were in position. *The trap's set. Excellent!*

Simmons and I joked quietly and waited for the sun to make its first appearance of the day. And slowly, ever so slowly, it began to rise in the east. We felt its warming rays heating us up and it was glorious; we'd been shivering for the last hour.

POK POK POK POK POK POK POK POK POK!

Suddenly we heard AK fire, which sounded like ANA outgoing, from the area of the southern cut-off force. At first I thought it was the usual warning shots, but when I heard ten AKs all firing at the same time, and a couple of rounds snap over our heads, then it officially became a contact. I got on the

radio and sent up the initial contact report, but I told Smith to wait before
sending it up. I needed Captain Ghias to reach his men on the radio and find
out what was happening. He was trying to get a hold of them, but no one
was responding. *Did we get set up? Was their spy fooled by a double agent, and now
we've walked into a trap?*

Soon the southwest platoon was also in contact. His sergeants had finally
radioed in and Ghias was able to give me a grid for his platoon's positions.
His southernmost platoon was in contact with about five or six Taliban, just
a couple hundred metres beneath us, and his other platoon was going to help
them out. I radioed Warrant Smith and filled in the missing data from my
contact report. I gave him my location and said the HQ element was going
firm at my grid. I asked about the UAV and he said, "Wait, out." Smith would
find out soon after he sent up my contact report.

Suddenly my combat antenna started to go off. When the shooting
started to our south, we all pressed up against the nearest wall for cover.
But now I felt like someone was watching us. I scanned around, and five
metres to our west was another wall. Twenty metres behind that one, with
a small road in between them, was a tall wall, behind which I had just seen
a couple of heads duck down. *Is it Timothy or curious civvies?* I answered my
own question: *It's too early for it to be civilians, and besides, civvies wouldn't hide,
for fear of getting shot at.*

I grabbed Simmons, Ghias and his signaller, and Max, and we jogged over
to the west wall, five metres away. *Wait a minute: Simmons, Ghias, signaller, and
Max…that's it? Where the hell did Ghias's close-protection group go? A TIC is raging
a couple hundred metres to our south, I just caught somebody taking a little too much
interest in us, and all we've got for force protection is one, two, three guys, and a terp?*

When the platoons had taken off to get set up earlier, we'd had about
ten ANA stick with us to watch our backs. Sometime in the last five minutes
they'd lit out. I went over and asked Captain Ghias where they'd gone, and
he said he'd just launched them as a reserve. But *we* needed the reserve! *Why
hadn't he sent Shamsallah as his reserve? Surely the mission was a complete washout
by now!* If those heads twenty-five metres away started shooting at us, we'd
be in serious trouble.

I pointed the wall out to Simmons, told him what had just happened,
and ordered him to keep eyes on. Just then, Warrant Smith spoke over the
net and said the UAV was finally en route. *It's late, but who cares?* It could
use its high-powered optics to tell me who was peeking at us on the other

side of that wall. I got out my map and GPS and reconfirmed my grid, then sent it to the warrant and told him to get the UAV over my grid, ASAP.

"Mushan, roger. Wait, out," he replied.

I peeked over the wall. Nothing. Dead quiet, in that direction anyway. To our south the war was still raging on. But it sounded like the ANA had the best of it. The odd angry shot continued to whang over our heads, but the gunfire had lessened considerably. Just then Simmons and I turned to the sound of a high-powered skidoo shooting through the sky, coming closer to us, about four hundred metres up.

WEEEEEEEEEEEE!

We called it the UAV "skidoo," for the obvious resemblance its low-powered propeller motor had to that of an actual SkiDoo. But as far as it being a *highly covert observation platform*, the only people who couldn't hear it as it flew "covertly" overtop were the deaf. The Americans had a twenty-million-dollar UAV that flew silently through the ionosphere and could shoot laser-guided Hellfire missiles from space, while we had a kid's remote-controlled plane with a camcorder taped to the bottom of it. We looked up into the cloudless sky and could actually see it coming toward us. I started to chide myself: *Don't be an ingrate, Rob; just be happy you've finally got one!*

Then, for reasons completely unknown to the boots on the ground, the UAV turned sharply, about three hundred metres shy of us, and started to fly south on a new heading. *An entirely useless heading!* After a minute, we couldn't hear its little motor straining any longer. It was gone, into the sprawling Registan Desert. *Huh. Not exactly where I needed it to be....*

I got on the net and asked the warrant to confirm the grid he had sent up for my location, the spot I wanted the UAV to hover over us. He sent me the ten-figure grid back and it was correct. Then I asked the warrant to please retransmit it to Sperwhan, so they could resend it to the UAV operator, because I didn't need the UAV to commence patrolling the Registan Desert on counter-narcotics operations, I freaking needed it over *me*, at the grid we just gave the operator!

"Mushan, roger. Wait, out," he replied.

"I got movement," Simmons whispered next to me. I peeked over the wall and could see it too, a couple of heads moving suspiciously behind the far wall. *Damn it, where's that UAV?*

"Mushan, 72C. Still waiting for that UAV to come to *my* grid, over."

"Mushan, roger. Wait, out."

"Stay frosty Simmons, and maybe put your earplugs in." Simmons glanced over at me. I'd already put mine in, but kept the right one partially out, so I could still hear a bit.

"Seven Two Charlie, Mushan. They say the UAV is currently over your position now, over."

"Charlie, no; it is most certainly *not* over my position! You can hear it a mile away, and we could hear it *and* see it as it stopped short of us, turned south, and flew into the desert! Tell them to pull their heads out, and get it sent back to me, now, over!"

"Mushan, roger. Wait, out."

Aw, what the hell? Seriously, is it that hard? Doesn't the operator just punch the grid into his computer, send it to the UAV's GPS, and the UAV flies itself right to the grid?

Wait a minute—is that it? Simmons and I looked up as we heard the skidoo coming out of the desert and back on-mission. *Okay, accidents happen, it's not too late. We're not dead—yet! It can still use its optics to see what's going on over at the other wall. C'mon, skidoo!* It was perfectly in line with us, travelling slowly through the air, but in a few seconds, it would be right where I needed it.

WEEEE-OOOOOOO-ooooooooooo....

Simmons and I stared in sheer disbelief as the UAV flew right over us— and then kept right on flying, far away into the north, the Doppler Effect from its little motor fading into the distance. It just kept right on flying as it crossed the Arghandab River, making its way to Uzbekistan.

I pounded my fist impotently into the mud wall, "Aw, damn it, damn it, damn it!" It took all of my self-discipline to *not* rip off my helmet, throw it against the wall, and start screaming complete gibberish as I jumped up and down like a tantrum-throwing toddler.

Warrant Smith spoke calmly on the net. "Seven Two Charlie, Mushan. They say the UAV is currently over your position now, over."

GAAHAAAA!

Rage...rage...RAGE! My eyes involuntarily clenched shut as my head began throbbing mercilessly. All of the frustrations and anger I'd been carrying around with me since I'd first gotten to this effing hellhole threatened to consume me in one massive ball of hate. I could hear the evil Emperor from the *Star Wars* movies, giggling with delight in my head, *"Good—use your aggressive feelings, boy! Let the HATE flow through you!"*

"Seven Two Charlie, Mushan. Confirm the UAV is over your position, over."

Breathe, Rob, breathe. Don't give way to the anger, to the hate!

I felt myself gain some internal composure as I breathed in deeply and said, "Mushan, 72C. Prepare to copy, over."

"Mushan, send over."

"Charlie, please tell Sperwhan that the UAV is not, I say again, is *not* currently over my position. It flew up to us and is now about seven klicks away, north of the Arghandab, over."

"Mushan, um, did you just say 'north of the Arghandab'? Over."

"Charlie, that's a big rog. UAV currently north of the Arghandab, over."

"Mushan, roger. Wait, out," he replied.

"Simmons, me ol' scrote," I said to my fire-team partner. "I'm not making that up, am I? The UAV really flew over us, didn't it?"

"Hell yeah, sir, it flew up to us and then kept right on going! It's *way* north of the Arghandab now!" He pointed to the north, helping me in case I wasn't sure which direction north was.

The firing had completely died down and then stopped. We continued to watch the wall, but no one made a move. Slowly, the ANA platoons started to rejoin us behind our wall. I scanned around but couldn't see anything suspicious. *I guess the UAV scared off whoever was hiding behind the other wall. Good for something, I guess.*

Every now and then I got whispers of conversation from Sperwhan. My MBITR would pick up parts of what they were saying to the warrant. Smith was arguing back and forth with them, graciously, mercifully saving me from their inane efforts at persuasion.

Something caught my eye off to the southeast. It looked like . . . *oh crap* . . . about a klick and a half away a Taliban recoilless rifle team was manoeuvring a Spig 9 rocket launcher on a rooftop, pointing it toward Mushan.

"Break break break!" I shouted into the radio, cutting off the warrant and Sperwhan in mid-argument. "Mushan Mushan, take cover take cover, you've got incoming you've got incoming!" The Taliban rocket team was too far away, out of rifle range, so I had been watching helplessly at the Spig 9 on the rooftop when suddenly a huge plume of smoke billowed out its end as it fired. A second later I could hear the KERBAAMMM! echo across the empty fields between us. Something wasn't right, though; the rocket seemed to be flying high into the sky. *Their barrel, it's pointed too high, it's at too high of an angle.* Like the stoned Afghan border cop in Helmand, they had just launched their rocket harmlessly into space. *Well, it's going to come down somewhere, but nowhere near Mushan.*

I looked at the Taliban, who were quickly packing up their recoilless and vamoosing off the roof. I didn't have too much hope, but I thought I'd ask Captain Ghias if he wanted to go after the shooters.

"No, we are good," he replied. *Yep, figured you'd say that. But I gotta ask.*

We collected the ANA platoons and patrolled back to Mushan without further incident. When we got in I thanked Stamps for covering us with the Coral Sea and the .50-cal. I entered the CP where the warrant told me that when he received my warning message on the net, he involuntarily turned sideways, as though he would present a thinner profile for the rocket. We had a good laugh and I told him about the time I slowly slunk down into cover at Sperwhan, when rounds were cracking right next to my head. Sometimes your body just does strange things. When you get shot at, the *normal* human reaction is to duck involuntarily, not slowly slink down. And when a rocket's fired at your base, turning sideways isn't *really* going to help. . . .

* * *

The next day we went about our normal routine, and after I'd written a bunch of reports, I found time to wash my clothes in a washbasin with a bar of soap and a washboard. The following day I came in from a patrol to find everyone very serious and quiet. I approached the warrant, who told me we'd just been told a comms lockdown was in effect. My heart dropped into my stomach and I felt sick. Later that night, we found out that Warrant Wilson, Corporal McLaren, and Private Diplaros from the OMLT had been killed by an IED strike on their vehicle.

I had worked with the three soldiers before, in Texas and on a few other exercises, but all three of our fallen brothers were very well known to everyone at Mushan, so their deaths came particularly hard to the guys. After supper, everyone was sitting in a circle on the picnic benches in our CP, so I told the guys I was really sorry, because I knew they had been good friends with the fallen soldiers. I told them I wasn't going to force them to all say something, because even though that's what the manual advised, I didn't believe in that. But if they wanted to talk to me, about this or anything else, I was there for them—any time, day or night. They thanked me and I got up to leave. The officer isn't always wanted or needed to be standing around, making guys feel like they're constantly being watched, so I went to my bed space and told Smith the same thing when I saw him: I was sorry, and if he wanted to talk, I was there for him.

The guys were really upset, and no one could blame them. They'd just lost their best friends. We were too far away to get choppered in for the ramp ceremony, so we honoured their memory the best way we could—by patrolling the next morning.

* * *

The warrant and I continued to take turns on patrols, and thankfully things remained calm in our neck of the woods. Smith gave the guys lessons on how to fire a mortar (using the mortar tube Major Obermann had taken from the Taliban), and I gave map and radio lessons, and had the boys act as the CP radio operator when the warrant was on the ground and I could watch over them and give them pointers. Our base hadn't been fired on once since that first mortar attack (unless of course you counted the recent Taliban "surface-to-space" rocket from the previous week), and we had some good hearts-and-minds victories, like the time we paid back a villager right away (out of my Commander's Contingency Fund money) for accidentally smashing his well. As a rule, we needed to stay on good terms with the farmers whose land was within grenade-throwing range. Besides, I always believed a key component in winning the hearts-and-minds campaign in counter-insurgency warfare was to find the farmer and pay for the damages you caused before he even found out you had caused them.

Hearts and minds, boys, that's what it's all about—hearts and minds.

Chapter *19*

On December the thirteenth we had another comms lockdown, and everyone had the same stunned look on their faces again. So many things go through a soldier's mind when he hears that. He quickly tries to think which of his friends are on leave, which ones are still in theatre, and which ones were out on an op. Everyone holds his breath and feels sick to his stomach, waiting to find out who had been killed.

We were sent the news over the encrypted e-mail. Private Jones, Corporal Hamilton, and Private Curwin, all from 2 RCR, were killed by an IED as they worked with the PRTs, the Provincial Reconstruction Teams. I thought of my friend Mike—he was an officer in 2 RCR, and he was with the PRTs. *They were probably his men.*

I looked at the guys sitting on the picnic benches, and I started to feel really angry. *Are you going to tell them you feel sorry, again? Are you going to tell them you're "there for them if they want to talk," again?* I didn't know what to say, so I got up from the computer and left the command post.

I wandered over to the northwest sangar and climbed up. I said hi to the ANA soldier on duty, and stared over the fields and into the village. *When this is all done, and those of us still alive get to go home, will any of this have mattered?* I asked myself. I remembered something Shamsallah had told me, after a few weeks of patrolling with him. He came up to me and said, very seriously, "Thank you for being here. Thanks to all Canadians. If Afghanistan was rich, like Canada, and if *you* were in trouble, we would come to help, like you have come to help us." No one had ever told me thanks before that moment. An old man in Kabul once thanked me, but no one on this tour had ever done that. "Thanks to *all* Canadians," Shamsallah had said.

When he'd told me that, I quickly said, "You're welcome," and we moved on to something else. But thinking about it now, after three more Canadian deaths . . .

Although I valued peace very highly, I also knew that at some point, as soldiers, we could be called to stand and act as a shield and a spear, to protect those who couldn't protect themselves. I firmly believed that the men who died had died acting as a shield, trying to protect the Afghans and to make their lives better at the same time. *And there was honour in that.*

I thought of the little kids who were playing on the IED haystack in Sperwhan, and how Hetsa and Longview had run to save their lives. *The parents of those children would say their kids' lives were worth it.*

* * *

A few days later, I helped Stamps put up a Christmas tree he had cobbled together out of pieces of wood and decorated. He placed it in a little area next to a large sign he'd labelled "Talibucks Coffee Shop." He was a surprisingly good artist for a grunt, because he'd also drawn a caricature of Osama bin Laden on the sign, and it looked great. Everyone was getting into a festive mood. The Canadians had all received gift parcels from home, as well as tons of small boxes and letters from Canadian civilians wishing us well.

In the current war, Canada had decided to contract out some of its chopper resupply and mail-run missions to a bunch of Russian chopper pilots out of KAF. The way they flew their Mi-8 Hip chopper (erratically), the way they staggered as they walked and slurred their words, and their bloodshot eyes all pointed to severe inebriation. But we were just happy to be getting our mail, so their sins were forgivable. Every time they turned up and dropped off our supplies, we'd have at least forty letters from people back home whom we'd never even met before. It was a great feeling, and we had lots of fun with it. A school in Newfoundland sent us T-shirts from their academy, so we all wore those around when not on duty, although we looked like a bunch of escaped convicts posing as students, because we had been growing out our beards. The beards were just for morale's sake. The Afghans loved it, because a beard to them was a symbol of manliness and honour. We had fun with it because some of our guys weren't even old enough to vote, so their beards would come in wispy and freakish.

We celebrated the Royal Canadian Regiment's birthday on December twenty-first with a shot each of medicinal brandy sent to us from our HQ. We had a fun night and celebrated with steaks on the barby and some episodes of *Dexter*. Before we ate, the warrant read from the regimental catechism. We took a moment to remember our honoured dead, and then raised our Styrofoam cups and toasted the regiment.

* * *

I was scheduled to go on one of the last patrols before Christmas Day. So I grabbed Carns and Stamps, we got kitted up, and we went to join the ANA under Shamsallah.

We patrolled out the front gate, headed north, and cut across a few fields. Shamsallah stopped to talk to the farmers and everything seemed fine. The locals had stopped hiding whenever we'd patrol through their neck of the woods, and I had fun acting like a monster as I chased the little kids. Only once did a little guy break out in tears because I scared him, and I felt terrible. Shamsallah had some candy, though, and he cheered the boy right up.

After a few minutes Shamsallah walked over to Max and spoke in a hushed tone. I waited for the translation and wondered what was so secret.

Max walked back over to me and said, "He wants to know if those wrestling fights are real—the ones on TV."

"You mean where they're always shouting and dressed funny and hitting each other with chairs? Stuff like that?" Max walked back over to Shamsallah to ask him.

Max walked up to me and said, "Yes."

"Tell him we would all like to *believe* it's real, but—in my secret heart—I am afraid it is not. . . ." Max walked over and told Shamsallah the bad news.

We patrolled to a field just north of the bazaar. The bazaar had been shut down ever since my ANA had refused to keep a constant presence there, and since we'd almost stepped on three IEDs in the middle of it just a few days before, we hadn't been back. A young boy had run out to warn us that we'd just walked over two IEDs and were about to step on a third. On that occasion, we'd all come a little bit too close to shedding mortality's yoke, so we'd given the bazaar a fairly wide berth. But if we never again patrolled the bazaar, then the Taliban had achieved their aim. So we were going back.

Shamsallah split up his patrol, with some ANA going around a long wall by a compound, while some stayed with us. I was talking to Carns and Stamps, who were in a ditch, when I turned to look back at the long compound to our south. I thought I'd heard— .

POK POK POK POK POK POK POK!

Someone had just cut loose with a burst from an AK-47, maybe thirty metres away, but is sounded like it had come from the other side of the wall. *But was it incoming or outgoing?*

When I heard the rounds go off, I didn't even budge. I had become so inoculated to gunfire that my first reaction was just to look at the compound and try and figure out where it came from. I should have been down in the ditch in some cover, and scanning from there. I had become complacent—and that will get you killed. *That sounded like it came from around the corner, where the ANA had just gone.* Shamsallah had started walking slowly toward the corner where his ANA had disappeared from view.

Maybe they saw someone who turned and burned, so they fired warning shots.

CRACK CRACK CRACK!

Three AK rounds screamed mere inches over my head! "Okay, everyone take cover," I sheepishly stated the obvious, as I ran back to join Carns and Stamps in the ditch.

I glanced at Stamps. "Well," I said, "that makes it official. We got ourselves a *contact.*"

Stamps looked back and smiled.

Carns shouted angrily, "Ya fucking think?" *Oh yeah, that's right. Not everyone's been shot at—yet.*

I pressed my radio button, "Mushan, 72C, contact, wait, out."

Shooting continued on the other side of the wall, incoming and outgoing, and Shamsallah took off at a dead sprint across the open field to get to the corner of the wall.

"We gotta go boys, Shamsallah's off and running." I got up to take off after him and Stamps was right behind me.

I could hear Carns say to Stamps behind my back, "Is he serious?" I guessed he was content to stay in the ditch, but that wasn't our job. You can't mentor someone from four hundred metres away. Sure, if Shamsallah was getting shot at, with dust kicking up all around him, then we would've stayed put, but the firefight had shifted and we had to go and figure out what was happening.

"Right, let's go," I said as I took off across the field. My feet were churning up the freshly turned earth in the farmer's field and I had that old "I'm not moving fast enough and I'm getting stuck and any second I'm going to get shot" feeling. It felt like the anxiety dreams where your feet are made of cement, but this was worse, because it was a nightmare feeling *and* you were fully awake for it.

We finally made it to the wall, with no more incoming our way, and I snuck a peek around the corner. Against the far wall the ANA were spraying rounds into a compound behind it, but I couldn't see any targets to shoot at. After a few more seconds the ANA stopped firing, so I led my two guys down a low ditch to get to Shamsallah. Some incoming rounds snapped over our heads as we tried to duck and sprint down the ditch at the same time. By the time I got to the end of it, I was huffing like a chain-smoker after taking ten flights of stairs. Sweat was pouring off of my face, and I didn't recall if Shamsallah had ever seen me in full sweat before. It was a disgusting sight, and could turn the stomach of the strongest man, even a combat vet like him.

It had suddenly grown very quiet. Then Smith spoke over the net and said that the guys in Sperwhan wanted us to go firm, right where we were. I asked why. He came back with, "They're trying to get you a UAV!"

"After what happened the last time?" I thought for a second and asked, "What's the ETA on it?"

Smith replied, "Forty-five minutes." *Holy crap, are they for real?*

"Wait a minute—they want us to go firm for forty-five minutes, to wait for a UAV they won't be able to get? And if, *if*, they get it, it'll fly right over us and into Iran?"

"Yep, that's about the size of it."

"Tell 'em it's nice of them to think of us, but I'm way too scarred from my last experience, so they can poke it! We're moving. Out."

We followed the wall and joined Shamsallah and some ANA at the other wall where Timothy had been shooting. This wall was really high, at least eight feet up, so we'd have to buddy up to get over it. I jumped and reached the top, and then pulled myself up as Stamps, Carns, and even Max pushed on my feet to help me with my girth.

"You . . . fat . . . bastard . . . sir," Stamps groaned as he pushed on my feet.

I got my chest on the wall and draped one leg down the friendly side, the other leg down the enemy side. I scanned the alley. *Nothing.* I had a look into the other compound. *Where did you go, Timothy? Why would—*

GAAHAAAA!!

The last thing I remembered was that someone on the friendly side had grabbed my leg and shoved me over, and now I was falling through the air, eight feet to the ground, until I landed with a sickening THUD into the hard dirt in the alleyway.

"Aaaggghhh . . ." I groaned.

Damage control: Report! Assessing . . . assessing . . .

I had landed almost squarely on my head, but at the last second was able to swing it out of the way and take the fall on my right shoulder. But I felt pretty messed up; my entire right arm was tingling from my wrist through my shoulder. It felt like my right arm was one big funny bone, and the nerves were firing and screaming like crazy.

Sergeant MacVitty's cruel voice started shouting at me: *You're a sitting duck, you colonial fuckwit! You've gotta get up, you gotta move!*

I managed to prop myself up a bit and then spit out a mouthful of gross dust. Stamps was propped up on the wall, shouting down at me, asking if I was okay. *You've gotta warn him!* I tried to shout but I was winded from the fall; I tried to stand up and—

"Motherfuck—aaaggghhh!" Stamps was screaming like Icarus falling from the sky.

WHAM!

Dust kicked up all around him as he crumpled into the dirt on his side. I heard all the air shoot out of his lungs as he was winded like never before. Someone had apparently given him a healthy shove over the wall as well, and he'd landed just as hard as I did.

"Who in the *hell* is pushing people over there?" I shouted.

"Max gave you guys a shove, sir. He thought you needed—" Carns started to answer.

I cut him off. "Max didn't give us a shove, he freaking *launched us!* Max, you lunatic, stop pushing people over! No one needs your help!"

Stamps is moving, that's a good sign. Max had apparently seen both Stamps and me with one leg on each side of the wall, and good Samaritan that he was, he thought we were stuck so he gave us a push to help us over. It was a miracle both of us hadn't been paralyzed. I ran over and asked Stamps how he was doing as I scanned down the alleyway and high walls for Timothy.

"Pretty terrible. How about you?"

"You've gotta be *alive* to feel terrible," I said with a big grin. "Don't worry, we'll jump Max on his way to evening prayer and kick the snot out of him! C'mon, we gotta get up and catch Carns. He's only five feet tall; Max will throw him over like it's a midget-tossing contest!" Carns had gotten propped up on the wall with Max's help, and just as I said that, he shrieked violently as Max went for a three-peat and tried to push him to his death. But this time Stamps and I were underneath Carns just enough to catch him and break his fall.

"Max, you son of a bitch!" I cursed. "What did I say about shoving people?"

I could hear a disembodied voice from the other side of the high wall reply questioningly, "Stop...doing...it?"

"Ding ding ding! Now find a way around the wall and get over here!" Stamps and I started to brush the dust off of ourselves, and when we looked at each other we started laughing.

"What is it with this place?" I asked them.

"Whaddya mean, sir?" Carns asked.

"Why in the hell is *everyone* trying to kill us? The coalition, the ANA, hell, *even* the Taliban! I mean, we're nice guys, we're easy to get along with. Why can't they just invite us into their homes for tea and crumpets and get to know us a bit? Then they'd realize 'Hey, these guys are all right! Why *have* I been trying so hard to kill them?'"

"Can't we all just get along?" Stamps asked.

"That's what I'm talking about!" The fall on my head made me wax philosophical. "I've looked into the heart of darkness, boys, and do you know what was there?"

"A mirror," Stamps said with heartfelt conviction.

"Exactly!"

"Are you guys okay?" Carns asked, certain that we'd completely lost the plot.

"Never better," I said. "C'mon, let's go find the ANA." Stamps and I faced the front while Carns walked backwards to cover our six as we walked toward the suspect compound. The ANA had just started to clear it and we could hear some shouting. We arrived and watched as they collared some civilians and put them into the middle of the compound.

I asked Shamsallah what had happened and he said his men had been shot at from this compound. So the ANA did a surprisingly good search of it, but came up empty-handed. Shamsallah shouted back at the civilians, not too worried if they were upset or not, and then started to collect his men to leave.

We walked outside of the compound and I noticed an Afghan male (in the fighting age bracket) about thirty feet away, just watching us. Something seemed very odd about him. He was slowly walking toward us, and I immediately began to fear he might be a suicide bomber, waiting for enough of us to leave the compound before he charged us.

I was just about to say something when a couple of ANA walked out of the compound. One of them spotted the civvy at the end of the alley, brought his AK to bear on him, and started shouting at him. Stamps, Carns, and I took up firing positions and we all took a bead on him. *Was I right?* The ANA soldier shouted at the man, who started walking toward us. He was bringing a potential suicide bomber in danger close to us! *GEEEWWWW!*

"Stop! Stop! Max, tell him to stop!" I shouted, pointing my rifle at the civilian. Max relayed my orders, and the ANA and civilian just stared at me.

"Max, get him to lift up his shirt. Tell him to show us his chest and his back." Max translated, the civvy lifted up his shirt to show us a bare chest and back, and then lowered his shirt. *False alarm, but there's no harm in being cautious, not after today.*

He continued to slowly walk over to us, then the ANA soldier nearest to him ran over and roughly shoved him against the wall.

"Max, what's going on?" Stamps asked.

"This ANA soldier is saying this is the man who was shooting at him, he recognizes him!" Then the soldier looked at the suspect's feet and added, "Besides, he is wearing Taliban shoes." *Right, Taliban shoes, okay. They're sponsored, or what?*

But we'd heard of insurgents checking out their handiwork before. At the Panjway bazaar, an IED maker planted his bomb and detonated it at the first patrol he saw. As the patrol was collecting its wounded soldiers, the bomb maker strolled right in to the middle of the incident scene and started taking pictures of his handiwork with his cellphone! Maybe this guy here was doing the same thing, getting a battle damage assessment. *I sure as hell thought he looked guilty of something when I first saw him.*

Shamsallah came out and shouted at him, then took some zap straps off of his tac vest, spun the suspect around, and strapped his hands together behind his back. The man was protesting the entire time, but his cries fell on deaf ears.

Suddenly a door across the alley from the suspect compound opened up, and seven boys and girls, from ages five to fifteen, bomb-bursted out the front gate and swarmed on the fighting age male, who was obviously their father.

A hellacious cacophony of tears and wailing ensued, as the children obviously thought this would be the last time they'd ever see their father on this earth. A woman wearing a burka ran out and latched onto the father, but Shamsallah roughly shoved her aside as he led her husband away to the FOB. But you could tell by the sound of their wailing they thought he was going to be summarily put up against a wall and shot.

But I knew what would happen. We'd take him back to Mushan where Captain Ghias would ask him questions, I would hover in the background to make sure he had water and wasn't roughed up or put in stress positions (the ANA never did that anyway), and then after four hours of letting him sweat bullets, the ANA would send him back home with a *And don't do it again!* speech. We had no evidence (except the ANA soldier's eyewitness testimony), but there were no courts to hear the case, no prisons to hold him, no means of transporting him. There was no system whatsoever for dealing with terrorists or criminal suspects. So he'd walk. *In about, oh, four hours.*

I called Max over and said, "When we've walked away a bit, tell the family that he will be returned to them, unharmed, in four hours. They are not to worry—he'll be fine and he'll come back to all of them in four hours. Please go and tell them that."

As we walked away I saw Max approach the distraught family and pass on my message. They calmed down a bit, but not much. *Well, they'll see.*

As we walked down the road back to the FOB, Warrant Smith's voice came over the PRR net. "Seven Two Charlie, Mushan, be advised, we have a VIP in Mushan, waiting for you to get back from patrol, over."

Crap, seriously? I didn't hear a chopper come in. What if it's a general and I haven't shaved? I've got a full beard . . . I saw a flash of red from around the corner of the FOB, right where we'd be entering the base. *Red? Why the . . . ? Wait a minute, Warrant Smith just got a parcel from home, I bet. . . .*

"Warrant, this VIP—does he by any chance say, 'Ho, ho, ho!' and give out presents to all the good boys and girls?"

There was hesitation before he responded. "Maybe . . ."

I started to laugh. As we rounded the corner into the FOB, bringing in our person of interest, all of the Canucks were covered in dirt after getting pushed off an eight-foot-high wall, we'd run like idiots through a ditch as bullets whanged all over the place, I had taken three rounds right over my head, women and children wailing—and now this!

My weird-shit-o-meter just spiked into the red. To say the moment had become surreal didn't do it justice.

Santa Claus jumped out from behind the corner of the Hesco wall and was shouting, "Ho, ho, ho! Merry Christmas! Merry Christmas, children. Here, take a water!"

Warrant Smith was dressed up magnificently as Santa: black leggings covered his brown desert boots, he wore bright red pants and a red shirt stuffed with a pillow (covered by his body armour and tac vest because—technically—Santa *was* outside the wire), and he sported a bushy white beard and flowing red pointed cap as he handed out water bottles.

We all burst out laughing at the sight of him; everyone, that is, except the person of interest, who probably thought this was the way we started all of our interrogations. I could just hear his thoughts: *The infidels and green Christians are trying to break me mentally by having this . . . thing . . . with a white beard offer me water!*

We thanked Santa for his gift of water as he escorted us back into the FOB, a crate of water in one hand, an RPG rocket launcher in the other. His wife had sent him the Santa outfit and he thought he'd surprise us and get us into the Christmas spirit of things. The person of interest hadn't taken his eyes off of Santa. He was probably afraid if he lost visual contact with the creature in red, then the dark magic spells that it was surely casting would begin to take effect.

We walked into the FOB as Shamsallah escorted the FAM to the outer perimeter. He wasn't allowed to come into our base to see the layout or assess our security measures. *Give him a little time to sweat. To fear the creature with the long white beard! I'll take him some water in a minute.*

We dumped our kit and sat in the shade of the Talibucks Coffee Shop and laughed about the patrol. *Most definitely one for the OMLT yearbook!*

Warrant Smith went back into the CP and came out again, carrying his red sack full of goodies. He approached Shamsallah and, speaking through Max, he explained who-knows-what for ten minutes, and then Smith went to the northwest sangar and climbed the ladder up into the tower.

Shamsallah started bellowing in Dari to his men, and after a few minutes, they were all lined up in three neat rows, standing at attention. The CSM went to the front of the parade and started speaking in a loud voice. I called over Max and got him to translate what was being said in real time.

"He says someone is going to come and explain the Christmas to them. This is a Christian holiday and it is very important to all Christians. We have Eid—Christians have the Christmas—*so pay attention!*" For some reason he kept calling it "the" Christmas. Then Shamsallah took a few steps back, as if signalling something to happen.

Perfectly on cue, Santa Claus started bellowing, "Ho, ho, ho!" from the top of the sangar as eighty pair of Afghan eyes shot up toward the strange sounds coming from it (not everyone was on that patrol, so they hadn't been greeted by Smith all dressed up). Santa, having a hard time because of his girth, struggled to pass between the sangar sandbags, but finally squeezed through and started to climb down off the CP roof. He hopped onto the Hesco wall, then onto a small sandbag wall, then landed with a THUD in the dust. He walked confidently between the rows of ANA and began handing out candy canes from his sack. The ANA clearly didn't know whether to crap their pants or go blind. This was really putting their weird-shit-o-meter into the red.

After Santa had passed in front of every single Afghan and made sure they all had a candy cane, he stood at the front and began to explain what Santa was and how he operated. The warrant gave a very tight, accurate synopsis, and waited while Max translated.

Santa was still up at the front, explaining some last-minute details about chimneys and cookies, when two ANA soldiers in the back started giggling to themselves. Our other terp, Omer, had actually come back to us (another Christmas miracle!) on one of the drunken Russian subcontractor chopper drop-offs, so he was translating for me as Shamsallah marched over to deal with the snickering troops at the back.

Shamsallah walked up to the two soldiers and started delivering vicious kicks to their rear ends, hoofing them over and over again, shouting in Dari. Santa tried not to notice, since he was still talking about Yuletide cheer in front of the good little children, but the shouting of Shamsallah and the screams of his men were hard to ignore.

Omer asked if I would like to know what Shamsallah was shouting about, and I would've been a liar if I'd said I wasn't a *little* bit interested, so I said, "Sure, what's he saying?"

Omer began to translate but had to pause as Shamsallah continued to lay into them with roundhouse kicks to their asses. "He is saying: 'You two . . . idiots . . . How dare you . . . speak . . . while Santa Claus is talking . . . When Santa talks, you will listen!'" *Awesome! They were being ass-kicked for disrespecting Santa Claus!*

Santa finished his speech and the ANA were dismissed. As they were leaving, Smith put his company sergeant major–mentor hat back on and said, "And don't forget, put your candy cane wrappers in the garbage when you're done!" *Fantastic!*

We had a lot of fun that day. It turned out to be a good day for the person of interest as well. I went out with Captain Ghias as he asked his questions, and after ten minutes, he was convinced his soldier had fingered the wrong guy in the line-up. So he let him go, after only a thirty-minute stay on the outer perimeter of FOB Mushan. *New record. Woo-hoo! Truly, Santa's Christmas spirit was infectious!*

Later that afternoon, two ANA soldiers approached me with Max in tow behind them. Max listened to them while they spoke, and then turned to me.

"Captain Rob, they would like to know why would Christians celebrate the return of a red demon once a year that comes down stovepipes to steal cookies and milk from small children?"

What? I started choking on my coffee. I sputtered for a few seconds and said, "I'm sorry, a red demon who comes down to . . . ?"

"Steal cookies and milk from small children."

"Oh," I said, smiling mischievously. "It's because the children were bad."

Max translated and the ANA said, "Oh, that makes sense, okay," and went back to their duties. Something critical had definitely been lost in translation as the warrant explained Santa's modus operandi to the ANA. *It's okay though, I've set 'em straight.*

We celebrated Christmas with a fresh turkey cooked on the BBQ and a shot each from the leftover bottle of brandy that was sent to us to celebrate the regimental birthday. We exchanged some gifts with the ANA, who, bless them one and all, knew it was better to *receive* than to give.

My parents had sent some gifts neatly wrapped up in Christmas finery for the ANA officers, and when I presented them, they didn't want to open their gifts. I got Max to ask them why not, and they were embarrassed because they thought the gift-wrapped box *was* the actual gift, because they'd never seen such pretty paper and bows before.

My wife had sent an Ottawa Senators toque for Shamsallah and a Montreal Canadiens toque for Captain Ghias, and when I presented them their gifts, they got choked up. And even though it had been dropping to zero degrees at night, and was only ten above during the day, neither of them *ever* wore their toques. Not once. They didn't want to wreck them or get them dirty. The gifts were too precious.

Then we were stunned on Boxing Day when we were told "comms lockdown." Our hearts sank as we waited to find out who had been killed. Late that night we were finally told it had been a 3 RCR battle group soldier named Private Freeman, who had been killed by an IED. Three other soldiers had been wounded in the same attack.

I was beginning to feel very numb again. Our morale was doing a lot better and now, after this, everyone seemed to feel numb and hollow all over again. Then the very next day we were shocked when we got put on another comms lockdown.

Everyone felt devastated. No one talked and everyone sort of kept to themselves until we were sent the names: Warrant Officer Roberge from the Royal 22nd Regiment and Sergeant Kruse from 2 Combat Engineer Regiment were hit in an IED strike and killed in action.

We had a punching bag set up in our tent of a thousand mortar holes, so I went and beat the hell out of it to try and get some anger out. It had seemed like every other day (or back-to-back days, like had just happened) we were being told a fellow soldier had been killed. And always by the fucking IEDs! It was maddening.

We took the next few days off for Christmas and then started patrolling again. The guys, always very mentally tough, were on the up and up, but the constant death notifications had taken a toll. Some of the guys had taken me up on my offer to talk, so I'd spoken with a few of them privately and together we'd tried to make some sense of it all.

One of them asked me if I thought all of the soldiers' deaths had been worth it. I said I didn't know. I told him I would never try and tell a fallen soldier's parents, or spouse, or children that it was worth it, but I *hoped* it was. The people living in Afghanistan just wanted peace. Their country had been wracked by so many wars, back to back, that a whole generation of children didn't know what the word *peace* meant. We were trying to help the Afghan government establish the necessary security to finally bring peace to their war-torn country, and that was an honourable thing.

Over the next few days, more guys approached me, and we had some good talks. I was honoured that the guys trusted me enough to talk openly with me. One of them, Pastel the medic, got my attention when he looked me straight in the eye and said, "Sir, you're going to die here." *Holy crap, thanks a lot!*

He paused and then continued. "What I mean is, you can't always be the *first* guy over the wall. You can't always be the first guy to kick down the door or go running into the compound. Sooner or later, your number will come up; it's a game of odds, statistically speaking, and you're probably *well* past due."

I thought about what he had said for a bit and then replied, "I'll tell you something, Pesticular—I'm not a good officer. I know that, and I'll tell you why. A good officer has to be able to send his men to their deaths—from a distance—if the mission calls for it. And if any of you guys ever got hurt, well, that would destroy me. I don't think I'd be able to deal with it. So that's why I go first, because I would rather it was me, not you, who got hurt. Besides, you're just a pup—how old are you, fifteen? Where have you been, what have you really done? You don't even have any salt in your wispy beard! I'm an old man compared to you, and I've had a good go. And when it's my time, I'm a-goin'! It don't matter if I'm in the rear with the gear, or first man through the door. Sooner or later, God cuts us all down. And one place is just as good as the next."

Then Pastel said something that I've never forgotten. He said, "If you were ever hurt, sir, we would come to get you. All of us. Because we know *you* would do the same for us."

"Thanks, Pastel," I said, trying not to show how much his words had gotten to me. "Now go on, get outta' here, before you make an old man cry." That was one of the kindest things anyone had ever said to me. And because it was said in a war zone, where our friends and brothers were being hurt and killed, it was all the more powerful.

The weather turned foul and began to rain and rain, swamping our FOB in huge puddles. Mud was everywhere, and our legs constantly got stuck on patrols as our equipment made us sink in the muck up to our knees. The Canadians would struggle to pull each other out as the ANA laughed at us, but we didn't find it funny. It certainly wasn't helping our morale.

We did a few more patrols, and then out of nowhere, I was told by the warrant that Rich, my best friend, was inbound on a chopper. *What the hell? He's two weeks early?* Rich wasn't supposed to replace me until my leave came up in the middle of January. We had no idea he was even coming, so when we found out, the chopper was on final approach. Smith sprinted out to the helicopter landing site just in the nick of time to pop a smoke grenade in order to signal the chopper it was clear to land.

I got Shamsallah to pull up in a Ranger to help the "new guy" with his kit. The CF Chinook chopper landed and Rich and two soldiers I'd never seen before popped out of the back. I walked up to him and gave him a big smile, but he never smiled back. *Okay…what's wrong?*

I looked at the two soldiers. They were a bit older than average *(warrant officers?)* and had a lot of gear in big army boxes with them. They were off to the side, waiting for something. *Are they the LCMR operators and that's their gear?*

Rich took me by the arm and marched me off a ways as the Chinook took off, spitting up dust into the air. I looked at Rich's face; he was dead serious. No smiles, no banter, nothing. He didn't want to say anything until he was sure I could hear him—the chopper noise was too loud so he was waiting. *Oh no, has someone else died? Is someone in my family dead?*

My mind was screaming with the possibilities. I couldn't take it anymore. "Rich, why are you here?" I shouted over the noise of the departing chopper, "What is it, what's the matter?" Dust kicked up all around us, and clung to our faces.

"Rob," he shouted, and then paused as he looked at the two soldiers. "These guys are with the NIS, they're special military police. They're here to arrest you—for murder."

Epilogue

I was placed under arrest by the two National Investigation Service military police officers and was told to read the charge: "Under Section 130 of the NDA, An offence punishable under section 130 of the National Defence Act, that is to say, second degree murder, contrary to subsection 235(1) of the Criminal Code of Canada. Particulars: In that he, on or about the 19th of October, 2008, at or near Helmand Province, Afghanistan, shot, with intent to kill, an unnamed male person."

I couldn't possibly have imagined that after the four months I'd just spent in the Stan my life could have become any more bizarre, scary, or surreal—but I was wrong. The Afghanistan chapter came to an abrupt end, and then my life as an accused murderer began for me and my family.

I was rushed back home to Canada, under arrest, and I saw my wife and new baby girl again for the first time in four months in the CFB Petawawa military jail. It was a heartbreaking reunion. Of course we were grateful I was still alive, when so many of our soldiers had only come home from that place in coffins, but the reunion was tempered by the fear of me being ripped away from them and sent to a federal prison for the next twenty years of my life.

But Amélie remained unbelievably strong and brave throughout the entire ordeal. She was the rock that kept me grounded, and when I thought

I would lose my mind over the surreality of it all, or was close to collapsing in fear, she would pick me up again and tell me everything was going to be okay. Her strength was unheard of.

My brother and his wife, my parents and mother-in-law, and Amélie's brother and his family helped us in more ways than anyone could ever imagine, and we were grateful for their love and undying support.

Then I began to receive cards and letters and notes and telephone calls from men and women from all over Canada. They wanted to wish me well and to let me know they were behind me and supporting me all the way. I was incredibly moved and wrote back to everyone who had a return address on their envelope to tell them thank you. I started to get e-mails from serving members in the Canadian Forces from all over the world, telling me to keep my chin up and to let me know they were behind me; and under the leadership of our new CO, my unit became incredibly supportive of me. An old friend of mine teamed up with an officer I had served with, and together they created a Facebook page dedicated to "Captain Semrau." I was deeply moved by the continual outpouring of support.

I was given the job of acting operations officer of 3 RCR, my old unit, after I was conditionally released from jail, and immediately men who were having issues from the war came to talk to me in my office. I was startled to realize that many of our soldiers were deeply affected by their time in Afghanistan, and before, during, and after my trial, I made it my mission to try and get them the help they so desperately needed. But the CF's system for diagnosing and treating them was taxed to the limit, and many times they were forced to go to civilian hospitals to see someone who could help them.

The General Court Martial for Captain Robert Semrau began on January 24, 2010, with pretrial motions, and after they were heard and the judge excused himself from the proceedings for personal reasons, the trial began on March twenty-fourth. The prosecutors had added to the charge sheet attempted murder, conduct unbecoming an officer, and failure to perform a military duty. The panel that would decide my fate was made up of five officers, none of whom (as far as any of us knew anyway) had ever seen or faced anything even remotely close to the tour I'd just experienced. My lawyers submitted an application to have non-commissioned members (NCOs) as part of the panel, but that was a decision that would have to be made by another court system, and at a later time.

I tried to wrap my mind around the fact that I was being gainfully employed, investigated, prosecuted, *and* defended by the same organization—the Department of National Defence. I was assigned a Canadian Forces defence lawyer, and his boss soon joined our team. They were incredibly smart, switched-on, and, like master chess players, always ten moves ahead.

Amélie told us we had to carry on with our lives and try and keep them as normal as possible, for the sake of our daughter, but also for ourselves. And she was right. We decided to carry on with our original plan of trying to have another child, determined not to let circumstances, no matter how extreme, dictate what we could or couldn't do.

So as the court martial was nearing its end in Canada and we were about to go to Afghanistan to hold a portion of the trial there, I was allowed two days off to be with Amélie as she gave birth to our second daughter, Chloé. After I held our beautiful baby girl for a few minutes, I had to go and hide in the bathroom to cry tears of pure joy. And as always, I had to struggle with the unrelenting fear of being taken away from my family.

I had to push the fear into a dark corner in the back of my mind. So I became very good at compartmentalization, a trick I had learned in school, because without it, I would have surely lost my mind. I would think of going to jail for the next twenty years, acknowledge my fear, and then put it on the back burner. But I firmly believed if God could take care of me in the Stan, then God could take care of me during a murder trial. As I drove to my court martial, I would think about how I was once again in a surreal and seemingly chaotic situation, just like I'd been in the war. I was, however, grateful to be home with my family and I thanked God that I lived in a country where I didn't have to fear IEDs as I travelled the roads, or see extreme hardship, poverty, and suffering everywhere I went.

A week after my second daughter's birth, I had to go back to Afghanistan for the court martial. I had the dubious distinction of being the first CF officer charged with a battlefield murder and the subject of the first murder trial to be held in an active theatre of operations.

Once again, I was back in the Stan, but this time I was solely in KAF, and it was terrible. Again, the heat, the stink, the dust—it all came back to me the second the ramp lowered on the Herc. I'd been here twice before, but not like this, and my "third tour" was definitely the scariest. At least in combat, I could act and react, but in court, I couldn't jump to my feet and shout, "That's a damn lie!" I had to just sit there and not allow myself to become angry, or sad, or scared, or seem overly interested or disinterested by what someone on the stand was saying. For seven months of court, I had to just sit there and take it.

One day, we all took cover under the tables as KAF was rocketed, and although I doubted if anyone needed it, the rockets served as a very poignant reminder for everyone there. Thankfully, no one was hurt.

One night, the entire court martial attended the repatriation ramp ceremony for one of our fallen soldiers, and this was incredibly difficult and terribly sad for me. I broke ranks to help a poor sergeant who had collapsed in grief back to her feet.

Everyone waited to see if I was going to take the stand when the prosecution finished their case in Afghanistan, but my defence team and I decided against it. We returned to Canada, now with only four panel members because one had become ill, and the panel rendered its decision to the court martial on July twenty-sixth. The four-member panel found me not guilty of second-degree murder, not guilty of attempted murder, *guilty* of conduct unbecoming an officer, and not guilty of failure to perform a military duty. Three current serving members of the CF put their careers on the line and testified to my character, for which I remain very grateful. The judge then told me I would find out my fate on September ninth. That date was then moved to September eleventh, then September twenty-first, then October fifth. Two new lawyers joined the team and I was grateful for their hard work and professionalism. I know that they made a difference, as did everyone in the defence council services office who worked on my case at one point or another.

I lived under the shadow of getting taken away from my family for almost three months (the charge I was found guilty of could carry a five-year sentence in jail), from the time I was convicted to the day I was sentenced. But my wife and daughters, family, good friends (in and out of the military), and the lawyers appointed to me by the CF saw me through it, right until the end, when on October fifth the judge sentenced me to dismissal from the CF and demotion in rank to second lieutenant. Obviously I was hoping I could still continue to serve my country, but I was grateful to not be going to jail for the next twenty years, when that had been one of the options the panel members could've chosen.

Then the CF (being the big green machine that it is) took four months to put my discharge papers through, but I was happy to still be getting paid, all things considered. I used the remaining months to try my best to help the soldiers I knew were suffering from the effects of the war, and I'd like to think I was there for them, making phone calls and turning up in person to try and get them help faster. I did what I could, but it never felt like it was enough. Every other day it seemed that someone would walk up to me and tell me about their terrible experiences in the war. The system that was in place couldn't see them fast enough and there was only one psychologist for the whole base, so the soldiers, many of whom were really suffering, would have to wait for very long periods before they could even be seen by the psychologist.

Looking back on it all now, with hindsight and more clarity than I had at the time, I am amazed that I survived with any shred of sanity. Big Joe, the warrant from FOB Mushan who saved my life the day of the mortar attack, worked for me later on when we were both back at 3 RCR. He walked into my office one day and said, "Sir, I don't know how you do it. If I were you, I would've killed myself a long time ago or become an alcoholic." I think a lot of people shared his sentiment.

But self-pity and despair were never options for me, because my wife and daughters were counting on me, and I wasn't about to fail them.

January 7, 2011, was my last day in the Canadian Forces, and it broke my heart to be kicked out. I knew then, as I do now, that the CF is made up of the best men and women that Canada has to offer, and I am incredibly proud to say there was a time when I was in charge of its soldiers.